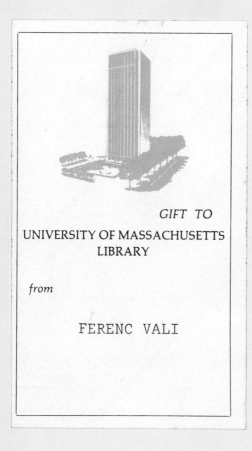

The
Soviet
Paradigm

Fp THE FREE PRESS *New York*
COLLIER-MACMILLAN LIMITED *LONDON*

Roy D. Laird

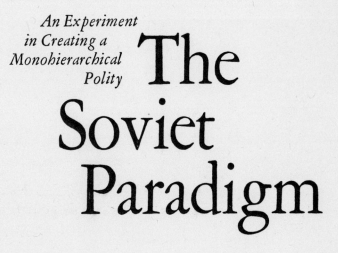

*An Experiment
in Creating a
Monohierarchical
Polity* The
Soviet
Paradigm

The Free Press
A Division of The Macmillan Company
866 Third Avenue, New York, New York 10022

Collier-Macmillan Canada Ltd., Toronto, Ontario

Library of Congress Catalog Card Number: 75-122278

printing number
1   2   3   4   5   6   7   8   9   10

To Mike and Ann
with many thanks
for many things

Preface

"THIS is the Soviet Union of twenty years ago!" A colleague who kindly read a portion of this work in draft meant his remark to be critical. Yet, this is much of the point of this book. An "in thing" among Western intellectuals is to argue that over time the trend in the USSR has been in a more liberal direction. Unfortunately, the evidence examined in the present look at the Soviet political scene will not support such a conclusion. Much change has occurred in the half century or more in which the Soviet political system has existed. Stalinist terror is gone. Indeed, the pace of change has stepped up considerably since the death of Stalin in 1953. Yet, at the beginning of the 1970s this student of Soviet affairs is impressed both by how fundamentally similar the present Soviet political system is compared to what it was under Stalin and how deeply its authoritarian roots are buried in long centuries of Tsarist authoritarianism. Indeed, with the exception of such temporary reversals as the creation of the Duma in 1905 and the

major acceleration of change at the time of the 1917 Bolshevik
Revolution, and again during the "revolution from above" (the
forced collectivization imposed upon the rural areas by Stalin in
the late 1920s and early 1930s), most political change within
Russia from early Tsarist times until now can be seen as a slow,
relatively linear evolution toward a special type of political model.
This model is particularly marked by its monohierarchical character, being primarily dependent upon a highly disciplined and bureaucratic apparatus.

In recent years, several excellent studies of the Soviet political
system have been published. Some books include more detail than
this work does. Some books stress the Party, some the historical
development, some the behavior of the leaders, and some, as in
the present case, present the Soviet system as a particular political
model. Entire volumes have been written on most of the subject
matter covered in the individual chapters presented here.

This book is primarily intended to be a text that will introduce upper-level college students to the study of Soviet political
affairs. However, the author hopes that some of the material used,
and some of the interpretations offered, will prove to be of value
to his colleagues who are established scholars in the field. Certainly,
the work should serve to continue the controversy among Western
specialists over the role of Marxist–Leninist thought, since the balance presented between belief ("an evolving Soviet nationalism"
as a new ideology) and practice is considered to be the necessary key to understanding Soviet politics. Defined broadly, Soviet
ideology is presented as a vital and evolving force inextricably
woven into and governing the politics of the USSR. The members
of Soviet society are seen, as in other systems, as believing beings
who share a web of common convictions that contribute to the
system's viability.

Although most studies of Soviet politics devote considerable
attention to the bureaucracy, this volume stresses perceptions, suggested by Max Weber, to emphasize that no other political system
can match the Soviet success in creating a bureaucracy that is "completely carried through." Even though the Party–state bureaucracy
encompasses virtually all activity in the USSR in a single hierarchy
of rule, the achievement does not satisfy the need for controls.
Institutions familiar in other societies (e.g., schools, communica-

tions media) have been exploited as part of the Soviet system of control, and other less familiar institutions (e.g., voluntary militia units, comrades' courts) have been created to aid in this process. In total, such adjuncts to the bureaucracy provide vital support functions for the monohierarchical paradigm.

The student of chemistry cannot begin to understand the subject without first learning its vocabulary. Similarly, the student of Soviet affairs must grasp a whole new lexicon, whether he is reading the Soviet press or analyses of Western specialists on Soviet affairs. Not only are there special Russian terms, such as *blat* (string-pulling), that must be understood, but of equal importance is the need to understand that although words often are borrowed from other languages, the meanings used by Soviet leaders and writers often are very different from those used in the original languages. For example, the word "freedom" for the Westerner carries with it strong elements of lack of restraint and maximum opportunity for individual initiative, whereas Soviet philosophers stress the "perception of necessity," arguing that the height of freedom is really a matter of restriction since the key is a matter of conforming one's actions to the demands of Marxist–Leninist science. Therefore, included at the end of this volume is a Soviet Lexicon that contains much more than just the terms covered in this book in the hope that it will be of further value in reading either the Soviet press or other Western analyses of the Soviet political process.

As always in any extensive writing effort, a full list of credits to all who in conversation or writing have contributed to the author's understanding would involve thanks to scores of individuals. Yet, special credit must be given to some, while emphasizing, of course, that they do not share in any of the faults in the work. As an instructor and interpreter of the Soviet political process, Professor Alfred G. Meyer probably is without equal. Similarly, in this author's early research and writing, Professor Alec Nove made a lasting impression upon his view of Soviet affairs. Over the years, the impact of discussions and papers presented by graduate students in the seminar on Soviet government and politics at the University of Kansas has been deep. Specific thanks to students need to go to Hans Brisch and Randall Oestreicher, who a number of years ago gathered together terms included in an earlier lexicon, which has been vastly expanded for this work. Few writers have the good fortune of having such an excellent secretary as Mrs. Darlene Haecock, who not only typed the manuscript many times but also assisted enormously in many of the petty details that are so necessary for the production of a book. Too, I should like to thank those readers and editors (anonymous) hired by the publisher to submit criticisms for final revisions in the work. Honest men and scholars disagree (particularly, in the field of Soviet studies), but I did find each of their suggestions judicious and I hope that when they see the volume in print, they will agree that it has improved where I have accepted their suggestions. Left to last only because her efforts were most important of all, Betty Laird has read and reread every line, offering many criticisms resulting in changes that have gone far beyond removing split infinitives. Admirably, most of the work involved in revising and expanding the lexicon was her labor of love.

Roy D. Laird

Contents

TABLES

FIGURES

Introduction

THE Union of Soviet Socialist Republics is a successful experiment
in the creation of a new and different system of rule. In 1967 the
USSR celebrated its fiftieth anniversary. In the history of mankind,
few if any, adventures in reorganizing the political, economic, and
social affairs of a people have achieved as many significant changes
in so short a time as has the rise of the Soviet Union. Indeed, one
of the special features of the Soviet experiment is the degree to
which its leaders have adhered in their decision-making to the
Marxist principle that the social, political, and economic aspects
of human affairs constitute an inseparable whole. In practice, there
is in no other modern state as much unity of these elements as there
is in the USSR. Even among the Communist states, the Soviet
system is unique.

The Model   The major thesis of this volume is that in a
and Forces   relative world bereft of perfection, the Soviet
for Change   political system stands out as a unique para-
        digm of a successful centralized monohier-
archical polity buttressed in many ways by attitudes, practices, and
institutions peculiar to a Soviet political culture but also growing
out of the Russian past. Nevertheless, forces for change are continually working in the Soviet political world, forces which have
appeared to many to indicate a trend toward "liberalization." Bor-
rowing from Sir John Maynard (*Russia in Flux*), during the decade
of the 1960s the rate of flux in the Soviet Union seemed to be
greater than at any period since the convulsions attending the
onset of Stalin's rule. Moreover, our judgment is that forces for
change will be accelerated even more during the 1970s.

  Whatever the pace of flux, however, change does not have to
be in a specific direction. In the USSR, future change could be
toward liberalization or it could be toward even greater social and
political conformity than in the past. Before making any judgment
as to the possible direction of change, however, a discussion of
what is meant by liberalization is in order. Since the primary focus
here is on the system of rule rather than on the economy, we are
most interested in the political factors that identify liberalism.
Approaching the question from a comparative view, what are the
key attributes of an "open society" which are lacking in the USSR,
characteristics which would need to be adopted if a liberalization
trend is, in fact, in the making? Modern political liberalism is a
Western invention, and central to the concept of a liberal regime
is a pluralistic political culture fostering more than one party, a
loyal opposition, interest groups, and open public debate of conflicting viewpoints. (The *sine qua non* for such a debate is a free,
uncensored press.) In short, the key question is whether or not the
USSR is evolving into a pluralistic political culture. A number of
Western observers seem to believe that it is. Basing their arguments
on new empirical techniques, they point to the existence of latent
(i.e., potential) political interest groups, especially among the
specialists and technicians, such as the educators who are credited
with having had an important impact on the outcome of Khrushchev's educational reform. These observers call attention to the
greater degree of independence enjoyed by a segment of Soviet

writers. Such groups are said to have influence upon Soviet decision-making. However, such conclusions tend to ignore the way in which most writers and artists are organized to serve the state's cause, and they fail to account for several questions: How were the specialists trained? How are they selected and promoted? What means does the system afford for independent influence? (The lack of such influence is a major theme of Dudintsev's *Not by Bread Alone*.) The evidence offered here indicates that unlike the situation in pluralistic systems—in which the experts can be found in the various parties, in and out of government, or allied with various competing interest groups—the Soviet model encompasses a bureaucratic hierarchy who use the opportunities (underscored by Weber) to capture the specialists' talents for the central leadership's ends. Indeed as recorded here, Western scholars who have demonstrated the potential for the development of opposition groups among the experts still conclude that in practice such specialists' views await the beck and call of the top Party leadership.

This author will attempt to show that when the possible forces for liberalization are set alongside the forces which tend to enhance controls, or at least to retain present levels of control that characterize the monohierarchical polity (see Chap. 15, The Balance Sheet), there is little evidence to support the liberalization theory.

The Essences of the Paradigm Soviet leadership does seem to have presided over the evolution of a viable political model with important characteristics peculiar to the system. These characteristics not only may be expected to mark the system for any foreseeable future but also since the USSR continues to serve as a model for other states, many of the features may be expected to be repeated in other Communist political systems. Key characteristics of the model discussed here may be summarized as follows:

1. The model's all-encompassing bureaucracy now has been "completely carried through."

2. All social, political, and economic activities are treated as part of an administrative unity, thereby rejecting any conception of separation of powers in government and rejecting the reservation

of any activity as private and beyond the primary concern of the state—activities that are regarded as private affairs in other societies are either directly subsumed under the hierarchy or securely plugged into the hierarchy as an activity under one of the adjuncts to the system.

3. Buttressed by traditional Russian nationalism and modified by the lessons of experience, the monohierarchy rests upon a single truth (i.e., the Marxist–Leninist "science of society") rejecting all other sources of belief as inevitably opposed to the truth. Moreover, it is incumbent upon the state to exploit fully every available means of indoctrinating members of society in the lessons of the science.

4. Political concerns, that are only faintly influenced by popular control, are preeminent over all else in administrative decision-making.

5. Power and authority are a tightly held monopoly of a single, highly disciplined political elite called the Party, but which is quite different from political parties as they have evolved in the West. Several important characteristics of the model are dependent primarily upon the Party:

(a) Since truth is one and absolute, the role of the Party demands that the Party serve as the depository of all truth—papal-like sovereignty is the right and duty of the top leaders.

(b) The highest official in the Party (i.e., the General Secretary of the CPSU) must serve as the final authority in all matters. As a result, many faults in the system are closely linked to the personal shortcomings of the top Party leadership.

(c) There is an enormous centripetal force to concentrate all important decision-making in the hands of the Kremlin party leaders.

(d) Active Party membership is essential if an ambitious individual is to strive for a top leadership position in any important area.

(e) Advancement of individuals in the Party hierarchy depends primarily upon cooptation from above, never from open political competition by various candidates for advancement.

(f) Not only can no organized non-Party political opposition be tolerated but also the Party must always guard against the tendency for internal Party factions or groups to develop.

6. Since the political leadership is clearly defined and the model is dedicated to creating a known future outlined by the doctrine, comprehensive long-range planning becomes an essential ingredient in most decision-making.

7. Although administrative patterns have remained remarkably similar to those first established by Lenin, an important source of flexibility in the system has stemmed from constant administrative tinkering reflected in never ending reforms rendering most governmental institutions highly artificial and relatively unstable.

Soviet Successes   Since this writer views the Soviet Union through critical Western eyes, he cannot avoid pointing out many of the system's imperfections, not least of which is the failure of Soviet reality to reflect the humanitarian ideals originally set forth by the founding fathers. However, does the disparity between the Soviet system in practice and Marx's vision of communism in *Das Kapital* or Russian communism in Lenin's *State and Revolution* prove that the USSR is a failure? Hardly! If such a test were applied to any state system, surely none could be judged a success. The United States, after nearly two hundred years, differs sharply from the original vision of a land of equal opportunity. Such an assertion of American inconsistency might not have been recognized even in the court of informed United States' opinion two decades ago, but in recent years, black Americans surely have reminded this country how far the American experiment in democracy is from the Declaration of Independence's statement of equal rights and opportunities for all. Yet, is the American dream wholly a fraud, the great experiment a total failure? No! In the flesh and blood world of imperfection, although America has much work yet to do, slavery no longer exists and the doctrine of separate-but-equal schools was finally struck down by *Brown* v. *The Board of Education*. Similarly, the USSR is far from being a workers' utopia. Yet, one can no more understand the Soviet system without knowledge of the visions of Marx and Lenin than he can understand the American political process without a knowledge of the European and American political theorists whose thoughts outlined the United States' experiment as a democratic republic.

Beyond passing the test of survival with flying colors, the

USSR experiment, weighed on a pragmatic scale, must be judged to be a resounding success. Some of the more obvious reasons are as follows:

1. Not only has the Soviet system survived more than a half century, in spite of civil war that raged the first several years and a massive Nazi invasion later, but also it appears stronger and more viable than ever before.

2. In the economic realm, in spite of serious shortcomings, the Soviet Union has transformed itself from one of the lesser developed areas of Eurasia into that area's largest industrial complex—one that in all the world is second only to the USA.

3. In international politics, the USSR started life as the inheritor of Tsarist Russia, which had been defeated by the Kaiser's army and had lost most of what influence on world affairs it had had. Today, the USSR is at least the second, and some would argue the first, most influential power in the world.

4. Although many serious problems persist (e.g., national antagonisms and literary censorship) in the Soviet social realm, a once predominantly illiterate society has become one of the most highly literate peoples in the world. Standards of living have improved. In short, the citizenry has reason to be positive toward the system, and as a result the society is relatively tranquil.

5. In the political realm, Westerners can rightly point to little, if any, increase in the political freedom of the citizens. Nevertheless, the system has now rather peacefully (since the horrors following Lenin's death) accommodated to several leadership transitions. Terror no longer is a major instrument of rule. Yet, the Party monopoly over political power continues to thrive.

6. Ideologically, a new, more viable corpus of beliefs seems to be evolving. The belief system of the USSR at the end of the 1960s is not the communism of Marx or Lenin, yet Marxism–Leninism is not dead. Like other successful belief systems, it has proved to be capable of change; thus a new Soviet nationalism seems to be evolving, one that incorporates Marxism–Leninism among its several elements.

7. The Soviet experiment has served as a model for other Communist states created since 1917 and, to a lesser extent, for some of the now-developing nations.

"The USSR incorporated" can be criticized for having failed to evolve into a political democracy, for shortsightedness in foreign policies that allowed a decision to rape Hungary in 1956 and attack Czechoslovakia in 1968, for economic policies that have failed to produce an adequate surface transport system and to meet citizens' reasonable consumer demands. However, many of the criticisms leveled against the USSR must be seen less as objective evaluation than as prejudiced measuring through the imposition of Western values on the Soviet system. Should not a system be judged first in light of its own beliefs and goals? Specifically, neither Marx nor Lenin promised the creation of Western parliamentary democracy; indeed, such a system was cursed as a sham, since they believed real democracy could come only after the economic environment had been set right, and then not until communism had captured the whole world rather than just Russia and a few other nations. Many Soviet foreign policies have been highly successful. Although Soviet practice has failed to achieve the promise of plenty, Lenin, and particularly Stalin, made it very clear that the achievement of the industrial construction goal would require long and serious sacrifice from the people. Soviet foreign policies have failed many times, but they also have achieved notable successes. Clearly, many of the important goals peculiar to the unique Soviet political model have been achieved.

Of course, the USSR is not all that unique. Indeed, social scientists, who have seen the changes which have occurred as evidence of the phenomenon of political modernization, are correct. Obviously, the USSR has become more urbanized, more industrialized, and, as we shall emphasize, much more bureaucratized. Moreover, political attitudes and alignments have changed. Thus, for example, where peasant youths once were destined to remain in their villages, the ambitious now know that advanced education and participation in Communist youth activities are major keys to success. Yet, if the growth in import of political parties and interest groups are vital aspects of the process, then the Soviet Union remains in the Dark Ages. Similarly, from the economic standpoint, although Soviet urban industrial activity has grown enormously, as we shall see, nearly half of her population, and the single largest economic activity, remains agricultural. Again, therefore, although the student of political modernization may well cite changes in the USSR as important examples of the process, the deviation from patterns found elsewhere are highly significant.[1]

The Four Component Parts of the System
In the attempt to delineate the key elements of the Soviet paradigm, the first part of this volume is an appraisal of the setting of Soviet politics, the physical and historical heritage of the society that provided the base upon which the new system was built. No adventure in government, however clever and dedicated its leaders may be, can escape from the past of the people or the given geographical features of the land and its climate. Therefore, a prime measure of the Soviet achievement in political creativity is the success the leaders have enjoyed in surmounting the shortcomings inherited from Tsarist Russia, while exploiting the opportunities offered by the nation's geographical environment. The USSR is what Tsarist Russia was plus whatever changes the new leadership has been able to impose on the base inherited from tsardom.

The second part of the study evaluates the beliefs of the leaders and the citizens which have provided both the motivations and the plan that the USSR has used to chart her path. True, successful leaders everywhere, at all times, have displayed a high degree of pragmatism in their decision-making, and Stalin was one of the most pragmatic of modern rulers. Yet, even he always had to justify his behavior in the name of Marxist–Leninst dogma. Regardless of how much Stalinism perverted the Marxism that Lenin himself had revised significantly, Marxist–Leninist–Stalinist doctrines have become an important part of the Soviet "myth-system." As Professor Robert MacIver has noted, these are the "value-impregnated beliefs and notions that men hold, that they live by or live for. Every society is held together by a myth-system, a complex of dominating thought-forms that determines and sustains all its activities. . . . Every civilization, every period, every nation has its characteristic myth-complex. In it lies the secret of social unities and social continuities, and its changes compose the inner history of every society."[2] As the second part of this book attempts to illustrate, a viable Soviet nationalism has been evolving, a "myth-complex" composed of traditional Russian nationalism, lessons derived from practice, and Communist doctrine. This evolving emotional cement holds the USSR together in a way that Stalinist terror never could. This new belief system is a significant ingredient of the Soviet experiment in Communist politics. Indeed, Soviet political behavior is the particular Soviet myth-system modified (often drastically) by the pragmatic demands of the moment.

As discussed in the third part of this study, the Soviet model is particularly unique in that the leadership has created the most all-encompassing bureaucratic apparatus in the history of mankind. A political system derives social cohesiveness from its beliefs, but practical success depends upon the organization of rewards and punishments in administering the pursuit of its goals. Western political scientists studying Western systems have found it meaningful to consider separately such components as political parties and governmental administration. Similarly, the interpretation of economic and production activities is left largely to economists and students of business. Even though there are separate party and state organizational hierarchies in the USSR, the unitary nature of the Soviet bureaucracy, in practice, is such that the political, governmental, and business functions are all part of a single administrative Leviathan. The unitary aspect of Soviet rule is the single most important element of the Soviet experiment in government. Compared to other state systems, the Soviet polity is the most monohierarchical of all modern advanced systems.

As discussed in the fourth part of the work, the central leadership's desire to capture the whole of Soviet man has meant that arranging for all workers to be employed by the same bureaucracy is not enough. Beyond the usual organizing of political and economic functions, the USSR, more than other states, indoctrinates her youth, organizes individual adult leisure time, and carefully guides local community affairs as well. In sum, much extragovernmental attention is devoted to creating "the new Soviet man," a human being who will be fully integrated into a total community. Perhaps even more than a further strengthening of the bureaucracy since Stalin, an advance in the penetration of the Soviet citizens' social and private lives by various adjuncts to the more familiar institutions of rule explains why the leaders have successfully been able to abandon terror as a mainstay of Soviet rule. Many Western observers of the USSR during Stalin's day implied that the Soviet system would collapse if terror were ever removed. Terror has been removed from its central position, and such relatively unique (in degree if not in kind) components of the Soviet political process as the indoctrinational assignment given the educational system, the management of information practiced by the communications media, and the engineering of social pressures through "voluntary" citizens' groups play an enormous part in the success of the post-Stalin Soviet experiment in integrated authoritarian control over all aspects of human affairs, *sans* terror.

Should the abandonment of terror as a mainstay of Soviet rule be seen as having diminished the value of the totalitarian model in analyzing the nature of the system? If, as argued in our previous writings, the essence of totalitarianism is a high degree of success in imposing a monolithic view of truth on a society, in creating a monopoly over decision-making and leadership by a unified political elite, and in focusing upon singular domestic and foreign policy goals since Stalin, then the USSR has evolved the first *mature* totalitarian system of rule. Yet, as many scholars have argued, employing other models (e.g., developmental, industrial, bureaucratic, and so forth) helps to provide important additional insights into the Soviet system. More than this, Professor Alfred Meyer probably is right in suggesting that an overly long bracketing of terror with totalitarianism has tainted the totalitarian model and branded it a creature of the cold war. Perhaps, therefore, a fresh start can be made by selecting a more neutral conceptualization to describe the unique system that has emerged in the post-Stalin era. Hopefully, our use of the term *monohierarchical* is a move in that direction.

In the real world no system is perfect, and the critic might protest the use of "monohierarchical" by asserting that there is no single hierarchy of rule in the USSR; there are two important hierarchies: the government agencies and the Party apparat. However, whereas Stalin deliberately kept the two hierarchies separate, one to check on the other (and he imposed yet a third, that of the secret police to watch over both the Party and the government organs), a major change in the system since the early 1950s has been an increase fusion of the two hierarchies' functions to a point where their separate existence seems to be less and less meaningful in practice. These two hierarchies have become inseparably fused as a single-purpose arm of the central leadership. Thus, for example, the movement of officials (at all levels of the polity and economy) from Party to state positions seems as easy as the transfer of a US government official from one branch to another of the Department of State, or some other federal agency. If this is the case, viewing the USSR as the paradigm of a monohierarchical polity would be of value. Surely, the Soviet Union is the first model of a highly industrialized, thoroughly bureaucratized system that has succeeded in bringing virtually all social, political, and economic activities under the tight constraints of a unified conception of truth buttressed by a highly disciplined, single political elite.

Samokritika   Having said that the USSR can be character-
ized as a monohierarchical system of rule does not mean that we believe it is perfect; thus, the concluding chapter of this work devotes particular attention to the forces that oppose the unitary thrust of the system. There are important flaws in the model we pose, for example, the attempt to achieve a fully integrated society. From Lenin's time to the present the Party has experienced the existence of important factions that would tend to become solidified into opposition parties or political pressure groups in more open societies. Still another example of this aspect of Soviet reality is in the campaign to create social sciences in the USSR which exhibit significant forces at work that could help to evolve a more pluralistic system. Indeed, the picture of the USSR presented here will suggest that at the end of another fifty years even more changes will have occurred than those that have accumulated since 1917. Moreover, the forces for change that are identified provide some basis to hope for genuine political liberalization. Be the future what it will, however, even if such a transformation should occur, would the evolution of a Soviet "open society" prove the failure of the Soviet experiment or would it be proof of resounding success?

Let us make abundantly clear in the beginning that this study is written with the inescapable prejudices of a Western political scientist who subscribes to the assertedly superior virtues of an "open society." The USSR is a "closed society" in which today's leadership vigorously promotes the superiority of a monolithic view of truth. The author's previous writings have been damned in the Soviet press as the views of a "bourgeois falsifier of the role of the Communist party." Hopefully, the charge is not true. Communism, either as theory or as practiced in the USSR, is not our cup of tea, but to say this does not contradict the conclusion noted earlier that in an imperfect world, the Soviet experiment must be regarded as having been highly successful, certainly successful in achieving an impressive number of the goals her political leaders have set for themselves. Nor have Soviet successes just been internal. The shot fired at Lexington in 1775 was heard around the world. The signal fired from the *Aurora* and the Peter and Paul Fortress in 1917 echoed far beyond the Russian borders. Today, the worldwide distribution and reading of the works of Lenin are second only to those of the Bible. For good or ill, therefore, those who would attempt to understand our world surely should be advised that the longstanding Western view of the Soviet experiment as a temporary phenomenon destined to pass quickly from the world scene must be cast aside in view of Soviet achievement. In short, an attempt to know our world as it is surely must include recognition that the Soviet system has evolved an enormously important, viable model of political behavior.

PART I The Soviet Environment

CHAPTER 1

The Land and the People

THERE are few, if any, hard and fast laws in the study of politics. Nevertheless, there are some observations that approach the absoluteness of law, and one of them is that in the modern, complex, industrial world, a nation cannot be a major power without being big both in territory and in population. The Union of Soviet Socialist Republics fits this qualification, for she encompasses some 8.5 million square miles, and she supports some 236 million people.

The USSR is nearly three times the size of the contiguous continental USA, i.e., the area that comprised the 48 states before the addition of Alaska and Hawaii. In other terms, this is about one-sixth of the total land surface of our globe. From north to south there is a distance of some 2,700 miles, and from east to west nearly 7,000 miles. In still other terms, when the clock says 12:00 noon in Leningrad, it is 9:00 A.M. on the Kamchatka Peninsula, as there are 11 time zones in the USSR. Physical size, however, is only one element in the compound, and without being a geographic determinist, one can conclude that other physical attributes also have had an enormous influence on the evolution of the Soviet Union's system and society.

The USSR has a number of navigable rivers, but unfortunately, most run north and south, whereas the traffic—the commerce and the movement of the people—is mainly east and west. Although the Soviet Union has made extensive use of her rivers, they have not provided nearly the degree of inexpensive transport for heavy goods that they might have, had they been laid out differently on the continent. Similarly, there are 28,000 miles of coastline, but for purposes of commerce with the rest of the world, much of it is useless. In the northern areas, the ports are frozen over for a good part of the year. There is the warmwater port of Odessa on the Black Sea, but the exit to the Black Sea is the Bosporus, and there has been a long history of antagonism with the Turks. Russian ships frequently have had to sail out under Turkish guns.

Thus, Russia under the tsars and the Soviet Union under the Communists have had enormous transport problems, problems that have been compounded by severe climatic conditions. For example, many of the rivers are frozen over for five or six months a year, and just to keep roads open in the wintertime would require an inordinate amount of snow removal equipment. To put the USSR into proper perspective, when considering location on the globe and the resulting influences, one should think of her as comparable with Canada. Indeed, Carl Zoerb, a specialist on the Soviet Union, compared agriculture in Saskatchewan with that in Khrushchev's new-lands area in Kazakhstan which is in the southern part of the USSR. In his comparison, Zoerb found that the climate and growing conditions of Kazakhstan are very similar to those in the grain-growing regions of Canadian Saskatchewan.[1] Thus, climate not only has been a problem for transportation but also, as we shall soon touch upon, it has created enormous difficulties for the nation's agriculture.

The USSR is blessed with abundant natural resources. In the late 1950s, it was estimated that she had 23% of the world's energy resources, topped only by some 6% by the United States. She is enormously rich in raw materials, yet there is a tendency for the raw materials to be where the people are not. That is to say that population-concentration maps reveal that the great bulk of people are in the western regions, whereas natural-resources maps show that most of the coal, iron, and other minerals are in the central regions and even beyond, i.e., Siberia. The cost is shown in an estimate that in 1937 some 30% of the coal that was being mined had to be burned just to transport the coal to the western regions where it was to be used. Similarly, it has been estimated that the Soviet Union may have as much as two-thirds of her water power resources in such isolated regions. She may have as much as one-half of the world's iron reserve, but this too tends to be isolated, and more than this, much of the richer ores have now been depleted and the bulk of what is left is of lesser quality. She has, of course, vast lumber reserves, but considering the rate at which modern society uses up such resources, one probably should not label them "limitless." The USSR in recent years has developed oil deposits that seem to be more than adequate for any predictable future uses that she may have.

As implied earlier, geographic determinants have had an enormous, largely negative, influence on agriculture. Tsarist Russia was known as a great grain exporter. Agricultural pursuits in Tsarist times were clearly the major occupation of the great bulk of Russia's population. More than this, obviously, agriculture was her major economic activity, and, in fact, it is still today the largest single economic activity in the Soviet Union, but she is no longer an exporter of grain. There is a tendency to see on a map the huge sweep of land and to conclude from such evidence that she is richly endowed in her agricultural potential. In fact, in relative terms, the USSR has a small proportion of fertile land as compared to that of the USA. The late Dr. Lazar Volin, one of the leading students of Soviet agriculture in the Western world, estimated that only about 25% of the land in the Soviet Union was tillable.[2] Contrast this to estimates for the USA of some 60%. True, Central European Russia is famous for its vast areas of *chernozem**—"rich black soil." However, in the first place these areas are not that vast, and in the second, there tends not to be a nice, neat identity of the richer soils with areas of adequate rainfall.

* This term, incidentally, along with the rest of the soil classification system, is of Russian origin. *Chernoy* is the Russian word for "black," and *zemlya* is the word for "earth" or "soil"; hence the combined term, *chernozem*.

A comparison with the United States can be helpful in understanding Soviet food production problems. In the United States, the corn belt begins in eastern Nebraska and Kansas and extends eastward to the Appalachians. This vast central plains area is where corn can be grown successfully without irrigation, where the corn/ hog economy has developed, and where a corn/beef economy is rapidly growing. This area, before the white man came with his axes and saws, was forested with hardwoods because there was the needed warmth, plus adequate moisture carried up from the Gulf of Mexico by the south winds in the summer. This moist, warm air moves over the central plains landmass where it clashes with the cold, prevailing northwest winds and produces rain. West of the corn-belt line the hot, south winds have to cross Mexico and Texas, and by the time they reach the central states, they are dry. When they hit the cold northwest winds, there may be some thunder and lightning (often called "dry lightning"), but that is about all. This, then, is wheat country. It cannot support corn, and formerly it grew grasses instead of trees. Much of the USSR is somewhat comparable to these arid western central plains, and there is no great area of high food productivity comparable to the United States' corn belt.

The prevailing winds in the USSR come also from the northwest, but there is no Gulf for south summer winds to blow across, only the Black Sea and the Caspian Sea. The south winds do pick up a little moisture from these two bodies of water, and in fact, there is a very small subtropical area on the northeast coast of the Black Sea, but there is nothing comparable with the moisture-producing Gulf of Mexico. True, in Poland and Germany, agriculture does very well in regard to moisture since these countries reap the benefits of the great body of water to the northwest of Europe, but at Soviet expense, for the clouds from that direction have rained onto Poland and Germany the great bulk of the moisture they picked up from the North Atlantic, and by the time they have reached the Soviet Union, the clouds too are dry. Therefore, vast areas of that nation have less than adequate rainfall for satisfactory agricultural pursuits. More than this, a great landmass of this sort, isolated from the moderating influences of the sea, tends to have a short growing season with very cold winters and

very hot summers. All of this adds up to a drought in about one
out of every five years.

In this author's opinion it was such a drought, rather than
foreign-policy problems, that precipitated the ouster of Nikita Ser-
geyevich Khrushchev from his post as leader of the Soviet Union.
He had built his reputation on the promise to solve agriculture's
problems. He made some progress, it is true, and, indeed, there
were those who thought he would succeed, but what he did was
not enough, and then the drought of 1963 forced the USSR to
accept the ignominy of buying grain abroad. She bought huge quantities of grain from the United States and Canada, and she continued to buy from the latter. Indeed, with her climatic and
geographic problems, Russia never should have gained a reputation
as a grain exporter. Had the tsars stored grain during the years of
plenty so that Russia could have fed her people during drought
years rather than periodically permitting hundreds of thousands
of them to go hungry and starve to death, she would have had no
excess grain to export. Such are some of the more important physical realities that have enormously influenced Soviet politics.

The USSR has been aptly described as the most developed of
the underdeveloped nations. Since development is measured primarily by the degree of industrialization, the USSR may seem to
be the second most developed nation in the world, following only
the USA. Yet, the USSR exhibits many traits of an underdeveloped
nation, as well. For example, her road system is grossly inadequate
by any Western measure. The lack of variety, quantity, and quality
of consumers' goods is extremely evident. But a more important
indicator of development is the proportion of a population that is
engaged in agricultural pursuits, and for the vast majority of the
Western developed nations, this is a very small percentage. In the
United States, less than 10% of the population is listed in agriculture. In the USSR, however, as revealed by Soviet population
figures, there are still some 45% of the people living in rural areas.

Official population figures of the Soviet Union (Table 1),[3]
beginning with 1913, well before the Soviet experiment, and then
skipping down through recent years to the present, reflect the history and the current situation in the USSR in interesting terms.
In 1913, the year before the outbreak of the First World War,

Table 1

MILLIONS OF PEOPLE

Year	Total	Urban	Rural	% Rural
1913	159.2	28.5	130.7	82
1940	194.1	63.1	131.0	67
1950	178.5	69.4	109.1	61
1959	208.8	100.0	108.8	52
1967	235.5	129.1	106.4	45

there was a total population of some 159 million people, of whom nearly 29 million were urban. Nearly 131 million were rural, meaning that 82% were residing in rural areas and were largely engaged in farming, with the balance occupied in agriculturally related pursuits. By 1940, just before the outbreak of the Second World War, the total population had increased significantly. Similarly, the percentage of the population that was rural had diminished significantly and has continued to do so down to the present. Thus, the figures for 1969 show that the population of the USSR had increased by that time to some 239 million with a majority of the population now residing in urban areas and engaged in urban pursuits and, as we noted earlier, with only some 44% living in rural areas. This obviously reflects the industrial growth of the USSR since the 1917 revolution. However, two interesting facts need to be noted here, both pointing up the lack of development in the USSR when compared with other industrial nations. First of all, as stated earlier, although there has been this great reduction in the percentage of the population that is engaged primarily in agricultural pursuits, it still remains 44%—a surprisingly large 44% for an industrially advanced state. But second, there is the absolute figure. Until the period after the Second World War there was a significant drop in the total rural population, but not as great a drop as there was a growth in the urban population. Moreover, from 1950 on, in absolute terms there has been virtually no reduction in the rural population. In short, this reflects the problems of agriculture in the USSR which surely constitute the most painful of the Soviet domestic headaches.

Population figures also reveal another very important problem of the USSR, one that is often common to nations that are having

Table 2

Population in the Republics, 1967 (millions)

Armenia	2,253	Lithuania	3,026
Azerbaijan (1 AR, 1 AP)	4,802	Moldavia	3,425
Byelorussia	8,744	RSFSR (15 AR, 5 AP, 10 Nat. Dist)	127,312
Estonia	1,294		
Georgia (2 AR, 1 AP)	4,611	Tadzhikistan (1 AR)	2,654
Kazakhstan	12,513	Turkmenistan	1,966
Kirgizia	2,749	Ukraine	45,966
Latvia	2,285	Uzbekistan (1 AR)	10,896

difficulty with development; that is, the nationality problem. Today, the USSR is comprised of 15 republics and has, according to her constitutional description, a republican form of government. There were, incidentally, in the earlier years 16 republics, but after the Second World War the decision was made to absorb the Karlo–Finnish Republic into the RSFSR (Russian Soviet Federated Socialist Republics), and so the number was reduced to 15. Linguists estimate that there are many more than a hundred identifiable ethnic or national groups, all of which guard their identities, jealously. When the decision was made to create a viable state of all these elements, the most significant of them had to be recognized. In fact, this is the area in which Stalin first distinguished himself, for through his comprehensive study of the nationality problem, he gained Lenin's attention. As a result of his study, the USSR was divided into 16, and finally, 15 republics, some containing smaller autonomous regions, provinces, and national districts (Table 2).[4]

The RSFSR is by far the largest republic, containing over half of the total population of the USSR. Some 127 million people live in the RSFSR alone. Beyond it there are three other republics that have over 10 million people: the second largest, the Ukraine, has nearly 46 million; the Kazakhstan has 12.5 million; and Uzbekistan has nearly 11 million. The rest of them contain fewer than 10 million people. Much of the history of Russia and the USSR is concerned with the problems of the various national groups.

CHAPTER 2

A Capsule Summary
of Russian History

Origins
and Autocracy

MANY historians argue that a specialist studying a nation can cover in his lifetime, at best,
only five to ten years of that country's history.
Here, we shall cover some two thousand years of Russian history in
a single chapter. Needless to say, this summary is sketchy and distorted by its brevity. Nevertheless, students of Soviet government
must have some concept of the political roots of the USSR if they
are to appreciate the peculiar problems faced by the new leadership,
after 1917. Hopefully, the following will provide some sense of the
Soviet antecedents.

The prehistoric roots of the peoples that populate what is now
known as the Soviet Union are said to have gone back at least to the
eighth or sixth century B.C. From the beginning to the present, the
peoples of that area have been beset by long periods of invasion.
The Cimmerians, the Scythians, and the Alons came in from the
fifth century B.C. to the first century A.D.; the Goths came from the

second to the fourth centuries A.D.; the Huns, the Avars, and the Magyars from the fourth to the seventh centuries; and the Tatars in the thirteenth. Napolean invaded in the nineteenth century, and in the present century the Germans have invaded twice, first in the teens, under the Kaiser and later in the forties under Hitler.

In the eighth century, between the Magyar and Tatar invasions, the Slavs came into possession of much of the area that we now think of as the Soviet Union. The origin of Russia as a nation, that is, a meaningful entity going beyond the very loosely related nomadic hordes that had previously populated the area, is generally dated from the ninth to the eleventh centuries. Perhaps, the most important specific date with which to identify the origin of Russia is 980, the beginning of the reign of Vladimir I, who is credited with having brought Christianity to his country in about 988. According to legend, Vladimir examined the various religions and deliberately selected the Orthodox faith as practiced in Constantinople as the most suitable for Russian soil, or perhaps more correctly, for the Russian soul. St. Sophia's still stands in Kiev, and it is regarded as probably the first Christian church in Russia. Vladimir claimed supreme authority over the Church and promoted it as an autonomous Russian institution designed to fill the religious void that existed among the people. In time, the Church also came to be a major tool of the Tsarist system of rule.

One of the most significant early forces for social and political change arose out of the Tatar invasions that are believed to have begun in 1223. The Tatars swept across Russia's vast lands and even moved into Germany in about 1240. For 250 years, these Mongol hordes from the East maintained sovereignty over Russia. Their rule is credited with having effected a considerable decline in urban craft industry accompanied by expansion of settled agriculture, as contrasted to the nomadic tribal existence that had previously characterized life in the countryside. Starting at this time, agriculture became the predominant feature of the Russian economy. Another important change resulting from the long rule by the Tatars was perhaps best expressed by Napoleon in his famous remark, "Scratch a Russian and you will find a Tatar." Indeed, it is generally accepted that Lenin himself had Tatar blood in his veins.

Ivan III, often called Ivan the Great (1462–1505), is said to have been responsible for shaking off the already weakened Tatar rule, in 1480. However, not until another century had passed was full freedom from the Asian Imperialists finally secured. Moreover, on the political side, the Russian tsars adopted the Tatar practice of insisting upon communal responsibility for taxes, thus stimulating the growth of the village and its administrative entity the *mir,* about which we shall have more to say later. The Mongols also had trained the people to take orders, pay taxes, and supply soldiers without delay. To quote Professor George Vernadsky from his text on Russian history, "They continued to perform the same duties for their own grand duke, Dmitri Donskoy, who became their leader in the national struggle against the Mongols."[1] During the same early period, another of the roots of serfdom, which was to become the way of life for the vast majority of the Russian people, developed into the two means of economic control of the landlords over the peasants, the *barshchina* and the *obrok. Barshchina* were "services demanded by the landlord." Theoretically, a peasant worked three days a week for his lord, but actually, more often than not, he was forced to work five and six days a week. What little time was left over he could use to cultivate the scant bits of land left to the village for growing the food necessary to keep the peasant families alive. The *obrok,* "an annual tax or quit rent," was a fixed sum of money which was charged the communes, into which the peasants were organized, for the privilege of farming the land.

Ivan IV, better known as Ivan the Terrible (1533–1584), had an enormous impact on the evolution of Russia. By 1550, the evolving Russian nation had become strong enough to mount an effective counterattack in the steppes and had succeeded in conquering the khanates of Kazan and Astrakhan, thereby establishing Russian rule over the entire course of the Volga River—that vast waterway often referred to as the Mother of Russia. According to Prof. Vernadsky, since the expansion to these areas, the subsequent course of Russian history with all its variety has shown "one consistent and striking characteristic: steady growth in numbers and in territory."[2] This also is the period in which the Cossacks, so often romanticized in literature, are first mentioned. The term means roughly "free man" or "free adventurer." The Cossacks were bands of military men who were camped on the periphery of the settled areas of European Russia and organized into a kind of military democracy. Indeed, one group was a society of bachelors who would not allow women in their camp. They lived primarily by fishing and hunting. Their particular import in this portion of history is that they probably made the difference in the struggle for emancipation from Tatar rule. Indeed, although some of these adventurers were of Tatar origin, the major key to membership in their societies was a willingness to pledge loyalty to the Orthodox Church, which served to transform them into Russians. Finally, under Ivan IV, the *Zemsky Sabor* came into being. This was a "national assembly or advisory body of military men, landlords, officials, and traders," but it excluded the peasants. Individual members were appointed by the government.

Tsar Feodor (1534–1598) was the tsar who was dominated by that interesting figure of history, Boris Godunov. He was Feodor's brother-in-law and is regarded as having been the real ruler for fourteen years at a time when the tsardom was fighting a losing battle against the power of the nobility. Why? The nobility held direct power over the peasantry who not only formed the basis of the economy but also provided the recruits for military purposes, as well. This state of events had been encouraged by an *ukase* (a "decree" or "law") of 1500 that attached the peasants to the soil and prohibited their leaving without special permission from their lord. When Feodor died in 1598, Godunov succeeded him, but then committed suicide after a rise in terroristic practice throughout society, which ushered in the period called the "Time of Troubles." This period was marked primarily by famine and revolt which ended when Michael Romanov ascended to the throne in 1616, beginning the rule of the House of Romanov that lasted until 1917.

Michael was succeeded in 1645 by Alexander I, whose reign was punctuated by peasant uprisings, Cossack revolts, and the rise of a group of individuals who came to be known as "Westernizers" —that is, those who wanted to adopt Western ideas and institutions in Russia.

Perhaps at this point one should note a phenomenon which seems to have existed under the tsars and still to persist under the Soviet commissars, that is, a tendency for a strong, authoritarian, reactionary leader to be succeeded by one who exhibits much more liberal attitudes (toward individual freedoms, as well as concern for the general welfare of the population) and who is, in turn, followed by another reactionary leader. The Soviet leadership has demonstrated a similar pattern in that Lenin was relatively liberal, Stalin was extremely reactionary, Khrushchev again was more or less liberal, and although the record isn't written yet, Khrushchev's successors, Brezhnev and Kosygin, may be heading a more reactionary period.

Peter I, also called Peter the Great (1682–1725), opened a "door to the West." In many realms Peter attempted to adopt what he saw as good in the West. He reorganized along Western lines the courts, the military, and the government administration itself. Peter has been accused of having been utopian in his thinking, at least utopian for his time. He wanted, among other things, to emancipate the serfs, to introduce Western technology, and to create a great army. He was largely responsible for the introduction of modern industry into Russia. He also identified the Church with the state much more than had his predecessors. He encouraged the merchant class, and surprisingly he established the soul tax on the peasants, thereby increasing their bondage to the landlords. Thus, he is credited with having been largely responsible for the solidification of the Russian class structure that was to last until the revolution. The aristocracy was artificially created by the tsars, an aristocracy which, in turn, passed their economic and service burdens on to the peasantry. As practiced in Russia, this burden provided a major stimulus for the evolution of the mir and the commune, which extracted these services from the village community as a whole rather than from individuals as was done in the West. By Peter's time there had evolved in Russia some four classes or estates: the aristocracy, the clergy, the bourgeoisie, and the peasantry.

The next figure in Tsarist history we ought to mention briefly in passing is Catherine II, more often referred to as Catherine the Great (1762–1796). She was a German princess who established a French-type court and gave government lands to the gentry, a liberal herself, but one who tended not to allow liberal attitudes in others. Nevertheless, it is agreed that liberalism probably got its firm foothold under her rule. Unfortunately, however, the famed Pugachev Rebellion also occurred during her rule, and it lasted from 1772 to 1774. Pugachev, an illiterate Don Cossack who claimed to be former Tsar Peter III, proclaimed freedom for the serfs, and with this cry led the peasants in a revolt. To date, this was the worst of the peasant rebellions, resulting from peasant opposition to the growing institution of serfdom, really a form of rural slavery. Pugachev is said to have gathered together discontented Cossacks, Old Believers, and serfs, ravaged the Volga basin, and vowed to overthrow Catherine. The social upheaval was directed primarily at landlords and was an open effort to put an end to serfdom. Because of Pugachev's weakness as a leader, however, the royal armies put down the rebellion, but the gentry and the courts were left with a serious dread of another peasant uprising. Henceforth, the government stationed garrisons of troops among the people to forestall future rebellions.

Alexander I (1801–1825) was a ruler who was under the strong influence of his counselor Michael Sporansky, who served as his advisor during the early period of his reign. Some historians have implied that these two men developed a truly liberal approach to reform. Indeed, interestingly enough, a correspondence was carried on with President Jefferson on the principles of American government. Apparently, the goal shared by Alexander and Sporansky was the establishment of a constitutional government of the type that had evolved in Western Europe and the United States. Thus, among the early decrees there was one that worked to transform court ranks into purely honorary positions and another to limit the higher ranks of the civil service to university graduates or to those who could pass a competitive examination. In addition to these proposed changes, plans were fully drawn up for establishing, among other things, separate branches of government, a committee of ministers to assume control of administration, a limitation on the senate's responsibilities to judicial matters only and the formation of a house of representatives, the so-called state Duma, to handle legislation. However, all of these plans were halted by the Napoleonic invasion of 1812. Sporansky, accused of being pro-French, was cast aside. Although Alexander activated a few of his liberal ideas, including the abolishment of serfdom in Estonia, Kurland, and Livonia during the period from 1816 to 1819, he kept the rest secret, and they perished with him when he died of a fever, in 1825.

Alexander was succeeded by Nicholas I (1825–1855), who ruled during a period of growing misery among Russia's people under serfdom. As a result of this misery and the influence of the French and American revolutions, Russia's own band of revolutionaries expanded and became more active. Indeed, one historian has asserted that in a single year during this period, there were some 556 separate revolts in the countryside. Widespread confusion had resulted from Alexander's death, and a group of revolutionaries staged a revolt in 1825 known as the *Decembrist Revolt*. (In Russian affairs there is a tendency to name things after the months in which they occur.) The greatest concentration of this revolutionary attempt was in the St. Petersburg area, and some of the demands made by its leaders were the abolition of the monarchy, an end of the military dictatorship, the emancipation of the serfs, the communal possession of the land, and a reduction of the role of the clergy. Perhaps, one of the most interesting footnotes to this period of history is the observation that an important number of the leaders in the uprising were officers who had participated in chasing Napoleon back into Europe where they were exposed to Western ideas which they felt should be brought into Russia. These leaders tended to be either Slavophiles or Westernizers; that is, either those who felt that all that was good was rooted in Slavic history and culture or those who said that the path to progress was an adoption of all that was progressive in the West. Yet, whether they counted themselves as Slavophiles or as Westernizers, almost all were dependent upon Western writers and thinkers from Kant to Marx. But Nicholas answered the cry for change in his usual reactionary manner with his famed remark "autocracy, orthodoxy, and nationalism."

Peasants   Alexander II's rule (1855–1881) was im-
and Revolts   portant in many ways. Among the more
                    significant advances made during his reign
was the creation of *Zemstvos* (local government assemblies), in 1864. Although these were discriminatory in their representation, they were in the direction of responsible popular government. Another of the changes he introduced was the enactment of judicial reforms modeled after Western court systems. However, the most important change of all those made during his reign was the political emancipation of the peasants from serfdom, in 1861. Most historians would agree that fear of revolution was at least as strong as a desire for liberation in this reform. Nevertheless, it was an enormous step in the right direction, and had it been accompanied by additional measures, it could have turned Tsarist Russia along

the path of parliamentary democracy that was being followed in many of the Western European monarchies. Unfortunately, the reform did not also embrace the economic help that the peasant majority needed if their freedom was to be meaningful. Most of the land remained in the hands of the landlords, and the tiny parcels that belonged to the peasants were totally inadequate to guarantee them security, much less to afford them any opportunity to improve their lot.

The gross inadequacy of the emancipation was authenticated by the continuing peasant unrest and uprisings that were climaxed by the assassination of Alexander II in 1881 by members of *Narodnaya volya* ("People's Will"). The Narodnaya volya was one of several groups that sprang up in the latter half of the nineteenth century, which were known collectively as the *Narodniki* ("People").

One of the most important leaders of the Narodniki was Alexander Hertzen who, like many in these groups, was a Marxist. Others, not strictly followers of Marx, were Socialists of other orientation who rested their sympathies on the peasantry. In the main, the Narodniki asked for the establishment of a system of peasant socialism, hoping to create a constitutional assembly largely made up of peasant representatives. In spite of ruthless suppression, the Narodniki managed to establish the roots of the very important Socialist Revolutionary party that was formed in 1902.

Alexander III (1881–1894) reacted to the assassination of his father by pushing the pendulum to the opposite extreme of social and political reform, bringing to a halt the advances initiated by his predecessor. What he could not stop, however, was the movement of the opposition forces into parties. Thus, as will be enlarged upon subsequently, the end of the nineteenth century was marked by the creation of several political parties which represented varying degrees of opposition to the crumbling monarchy.

Some might argue that the last Romanov, Nicholas II (1894–1917), could have turned the mounting revolutionary tide. However, in this writer's opinion, the failure of emancipation to fulfill the people's economic needs had long since cast the lot for tsardom's inevitable destruction. True, Nicholas II did attempt a few moves toward reform, but given the setting and time none were adequate to save either him or the tsardom.

The year 1905 marked the beginning of the end. Russia's participation in the worldwide period of expansion and colonialism that marked the end of the nineteenth century resulted in her clashing with Japanese forces in Korea, and the Russo-Japanese War broke out which ended in a disastrous defeat for Russia. This defeat underscored the weaknesses of the system and the despair of the population, and widespread rebellion broke out. The events of the period were marked by the infamous Bloody Sunday Revolt in which a group of workers, led by the priest Father Gapon, marched unarmed to the palace to petition the Tsar. In spite of the relatively peaceful nature of the demonstration, an order was given to fire on the crowd, and the revolt started.

Although the revolt penetrated the countryside as well as the cities, and although the workers formed *soviets* ("councils"), the groups were widely dispersed and lacked disciplined and coordinated leadership. Added to this, the government forces remained basically loyal. As a result, the revolt stopped short of destroying the monarchy (as it did not do in 1917 when Lenin profited from the 1905 mistakes). Out of the event came a momentary promise of needed change, first in the early response to the October Manifesto (issued on October 30, 1905, under the initiative of Count Witte), and second in the attempts made under the Stolypin reforms undertaken between 1906 and 1911.

Briefly, the Manifesto called for the creation of a constitutional assembly and the establishment of a parliamentary system. Initially, Tsar Nicholas' response seemed positive in that the first Duma (elective Parliament) was elected in March of 1906 under the leadership of Witte. However, he was shortly replaced by Goremykin who was a puppet of the Tsarist forces, and the Duma was dissolved near the end of July. The second Duma of 1907 and the third that lasted until 1912 were more rightest and successfully resisted reforms, particularly the peasant-oriented reforms introduced by Prime Minister Stolypin (1906–1911).

In order to appreciate the potential import of the Stolypin reforms, an understanding of the mir and the peasant commune is necessary, for not only were these village institutions extremely important in Tsarist Russia but their influence carried over into Soviet Russia, as well.

Unlike their American counterparts, the Russian farm family did not live on an isolated farmstead. Agriculture was organized on a communal basis and the peasants' dwellings were clustered together in small rural villages. As with most institutions such as this, the origins of Russian rural collectivism are hidden in antiquity. That the roots are common to the collectivist tendencies found in most primitive societies is obvious. In Russia, as elsewhere, such tendencies seem to have originated in the need for mutual protection against the harsh vicissitudes of nature, as well as to provide media for establishing dates for the sowing of seeds, and so forth, which are so closely bound to the religious convictions of early societies.

Other than the family, the most important institution within the commune (that is, the "individual village society") was the mir. The major task of this latter institution was to administer the affairs of the commune. At the head of the mir was the *starosta* ("village elder"); membership on the mir belonged to the head of each *dvor* ("peasant family"). The individual peasant was by-passed by the mir in most matters of business, including tax paying. Although the land under cultivation was farmed by individual households, the commune owned the bit of land that the peasants had (including the family plot or kitchen garden), and the mir was responsible for such matters as collectively paying the peasants' taxes and, after the 1861 emancipation, for meeting the redemption payments to the landlords for the tiny parcels of land turned over to the peasants for their livelihood. These and other purposes for the commune and the mir are reflected in Sir John Maynard's description of these institutions in their "nineteenth-century form"

... an organ of village self-government: distribution among its members of the customary peasant duties of repair of roads and bridges, escorting of holy icons and the like, forming by collection from all a reserve of corn for insurance against need, allotting his subsistence farm to the priest, managing the communal field when there was one, organizing fire-fighting and protection against thieves, enforcing the patriarchal authority upon contumacious sons, and settling minor disputes among its members, it even made separation orders for quarrelsome spouses, regardless of the law, which gave the monopoly of divorce to the ecclesiastical courts—but the peasants were always half outside the law. It was the maid-of-all work for the miscellaneous demands of a busy administration, and we are not surprised that more tasks were soon laid upon it by the State.[3]

Professor Gerard Robinson, in his book *Rural Russia Under the Old Regime,* implies, however, that the most important egalitarian factor in the commune, the redistribution of land, probably originated no earlier than the sixteenth century, and certainly that the greatest growth of this practice came in the seventeenth, eighteenth, and nineteenth centuries.[4] Furthermore, an important influence for the spread of the practice was the state. Once adopted, however, partition of the land was handled by the mir in a manner designed to achieve the highest degree of egalitarian relationship among the peasants. Periodically, the cultivated land was redistributed among the dvor with the aim of eliminating any inequality which may have developed during the intervening years—a minimum period of 12 years was established by law in 1894. These redistributions excluded the household plots and the pasture lands which were used in common.

Although most scholars of agrarian problems probably sympathize with the egalitarian outlook that sponsored the redistributions, they do credit this system with being a major factor responsible for the relatively backward nature of Tsarist agriculture. In order to achieve the highest degree of equality possible, the land was usually allotted in long, narrow strips scattered throughout the farming area. As a result, much land was wasted in boundaries, and the peasant was sentenced to spending a large portion of his working time walking from plot to plot. In addition, knowing that a few years hence he would not be cultivating the same pieces of land, the peasant had little incentive to undertake long-term improvement measures. Finally, the communal system included the use of the discredited three-field system of rotations which, though certainly superior to no rotations at all, was far from adequate to replenish soil losses.

In analyzing the character of the Russian peasant, students of Tsarist history often overemphasize the mir, seeing in it the manifestation of a deeply-rooted collectivist nature. (This was the position adopted by Marx.) Such analyses fail to consider the various practical roots of the system, the strong encouragement it was given by Tsarist governments, and the fact that the combination of the mir and the commune was hardly the collectivist system which it might appear to be on the surface. For although it is true that the Russian peasantry depended upon the commune for protection and government, the sense of being primarily dependent upon one's own efforts to secure the daily bread had penetrated deeply. In the village commune, although the pastures were often held in common, the fields were tilled by the individual family, and no peasant doubted that his income came directly from his labors in the family enterprise. (The strong resistance of the Russian peasantry to collectivization in 1928 to 1935 was a measure of the depth of its independent nature.)

In a concession to the liberals in 1906, Peter Stolypin was appointed Prime Minister. Stolypin recognized that the major politico–economic force lay with the peasants and that central to solving their problems in a way that would work to strengthen the government was to build the peasants' economic position. The mir became his primary target, and thus the following were his key reforms:

1. The redemption payments were cut in half in 1900 and abolished in 1907.

2. Government policy was no longer geared to the mir, thus the peasant's individualism was encouraged.

3. Legal control of the *dvor* ("family") passed from the commune to the head of the family.

4. Loans were made available for private purchases of additional land.

5. Maximum holdings of the land were established to prohibit the monopolization of peasant land by a few powerful and ambitious families.

6. Measures were taken to end the system of strip farming.

In short, the Stolypin policy was meant to evolve a strong yeoman peasantry. As the Prime Minister saw it, commenting before the third Duma,

The government has placed its wager, not on the needy and the drunken, but on the sturdy and the strong—on the sturdy individual proprietor who is called upon to play a part in the reconstruction of our Tsardom on strong monarchical foundations.[5]

The late, great Naum Jasny recorded in his book *The Socialized Agriculture of the USSR* that, as a result of Stolypin's efforts and in spite of Stolypin's assassination in 1911, by 1913 five million households had left the commune. By 1917, he goes on to say, "Much less than half of all peasant households remained in fully unchanged repartitionable tenure," but "the Revolution of 1917 blew all the efforts of the Stolypins to pieces."[6]

Nicholas II was dominated by a strong-willed wife who was under suspicion as a traitor (falsely accused because she was a German princess) and who was, in turn, dominated by the "mad monk" Rasputin. The Tsar was hardly the man capable of saving the dynasty and the government. Beyond his own weakness, however, both the bureaucracy and the Church, which had become mainstays of the system, had grown ever more corrupt. All of this added to the devastating defeat at the hands of the Kaiser's armies spelled the end.

The Birth of Modern Politics   Modern politics came into being in Russia by a rather painful birth, at the turn of the century, when various groups representing a myriad of political and social opinions evolved into parties. The conception probably can be traced back to Peter's opening a "door to the West," a door through which came not only a drive for industrial construction but also new political ideas. As noted earlier, Western concepts of constitutional government and freedom had become increasingly attractive to many Russian intellectuals. Yet, although some of the tsars held relatively liberal ideas for their time and place, on balance, the government's response to the new social and political ideas was not accommodation but reaction and suppression. Thus, the political environment at the end of the nineteenth century did not encourage the development of responsible parties comparable with the loyal opposition parties that grew up in the West where such groups could anticipate the future responsibility of government. Quite to the contrary, the Russian parties were forced to become underground opposition groups which carried with them the irresponsibility of increasing negative criticism and action. In short, their only hope for a chance to govern lay in revolution.

The society was ripe for revolution. A great gulf lay between the masses on the one hand and the various levels of the bourgeoisie on the other. Industry was barely beginning to develop and the entrepreneur represented a small, insignificant minority. There was, however, an extensive group of professional people, doctors, lawyers, and especially bureaucrats, but as with all of Russia's intellectuals they were a world apart from the illiterate masses.* The nobility (gentry) owned most of the land and the bulk of the wealth, and they were even more removed from the peasants who carried out the work. Indeed, reflecting a widespread worship of things foreign, many of them hired French tutors for their sons and daughters. As a result, some of the nobility grew up unable to speak Russian. There was another kind of nobility that had become very important and which filled most of the ranks of the bureaucracy. This was the service nobility, a status awarded as a result of responsibility to the government. For most, rank in government was even more important than birth. But even the service nobility was hardly progressive, as it worked to block education and other needed social changes. Interestingly, Lenin was a minor nobleman, not because of any princely blood, but because his father had attained a rank in the bureaucracy. Some 80% of the society, that is, nearly all the peasants and most of the workers were illiterate. Thus, even those intellectuals, who saw the future of Russia in the hands of the peasants and were joining the conspiratorial groups, were far removed from the masses.

These conspirators could not communicate with the masses not only because of their ability to read but also because of what they were reading. Their authors were the foreign Socialists of the West; Montesquieu (1689–1755), the father of social science; Rousseau (1712–1778), the French philosopher and social theorist; Hegel (1770–1831), the German mystic; and, above all, Karl Marx. These were key figures among the thinkers who influenced

* According to the 1897 census, there were 700,000 professionals in the economy.[7]

the evolving leadership of the disloyal opposition: A leadership which would eventually produce one that could adapt these foreign ideas to Russia, make them meaningful to the masses, and provide the force and charisma to overturn the tsardom.

Let us examine for the moment the various parties that were centrifugalizing out of the opposition. Reading the political spectrum from right to left, the more important of the parties were the Octobrists, the Kadets, the Social Revolutionaries, and the Social Democrats.

The Octobrists' name was taken from the October Manifesto of 1905 issued by Nicholas II in answer to the uprising at that time. The primary aim of this relatively moderate party was the establishment of a constitutional monarchy. Indeed, the creation of the Duma was a major outcome of its work. In addition, in the Manifesto, the emperor granted such basic principles of liberty as the democratic franchise, the freedom of assembly and thought, and the inviolability of the individual. Furthermore, all subsequent law was supposed to arise only from the Duma. Unfortunately, the Tsar no sooner had made these concessions than he backed down. Perhaps even more important to the eventual demise of the party was that in spite of its relative liberalism, since the membership was drawn primarily from well-to-do merchants and bureaucrats, they were not actually too far removed from the political establishment at a time when the demands of the masses were increasingly being pressed.

The Kadets (a contraction of "Constitutional Democrats") were not far removed in their ideas from the Octobrists, although they were more liberal in the Western sense. Their key leader was Prince Lvov who served for a time as the head of the 1917 provisional government. This party was much more interested in working for modernization, and, as such, often worked with the Mensheviks, the more moderate wing of the Social Democrats (S.D.'s).

The Social Revolutionary party was the prime descendant of the *Narodniks* ("Populists") who accepted Alexander Herzen as their major spiritual founder, although they were also close students of Marx. The Social Revolutionaries (S.R.'s) were founded in 1902, and their most important leader was Alexander Kerensky who succeeded Prince Lvov as the head of the 1917 provisional government.

As Populists, the key distinction of the S.R.'s was their belief that the destiny of Russia lay in the hands of the peasant masses. Paralleling the passing notation of Marx and Engels that in the mir, Russia might have the base for passing directly from feudalism to socialism, the Social Revolutionaries believed that through nationalizing the soil and organizing the peasants, Russia could solve her politicoeconomic problem, progressively. Their major activity, therefore, was in the villages, and the available evidence indicates that through 1917 the S.R.'s had by far the greatest popular support. Like the Social Democrats, the S.R.'s were split into factions, particularly a moderate right and an extreme left. Perhaps, therefore, it is incorrect to suggest that they were not as far to the left on the political spectrum as the Social Democrats. Certainly, in the use of extreme measures, particularly terror, to gain their points in their formative years, the left S.R.'s outdid the Bolsheviks.

The Social Democrats were members of the Communist party, founded by George Plekhanov, in 1898. They, too, had Narodnik roots. However, as close students of Marx, the Party members had a strong tendency to believe that the development of capitalism (as a stage in the transition from feudalism to socialism) was both inevitable and necessary. Similarly, Marxist doctrine turned the thinking of the S.D.'s away from the illiterate peasants toward the working class and its asserted class consciousness—the motivating force of the classical Marxian revolution. Thus, in the beginning, under Plekhanov's leadership the group was known as *Osvobozhdenie truda* ("Emancipation of Labor"). An irony of historical truth is that a political analyst, in 1913, could well have concluded that the Social Democrats were wild-eyed utopians who could be ignored as impotent in the political arena. After all, they were building their hopes on an industrial proletariat in a Russia wherein the industrial workers constituted less than 2% of the population. Yet, after the split of the S.D.'s into the more moderate Mensheviks and the more radical Bolsheviks, the latter, under the leadership of Lenin, became the one political organization in Russia capable of seizing and retaining power in the chaos of 1917. Since the Communists were destined to succeed, they are by far the most important, historically. However, since Lenin was to dominate the course of events so completely, and more importantly, since no neat separation existed between his pragmatic and theoretical sides, the balance of an examination of Bolshevism's rise to preeminence will be left to the subsequent examination of Leninism.

The following simple diagram may be helpful in understanding the major political parties in the final years of tsardom.

Still, the questions remain: Why did parties arise when they did, only to help usher in both the demise of tsardom and the end of their own short lives? What did their brief existence mean for the future? Neither the historians nor the social scientists have offered fully satisfactory answers to these questions, but the following observations offer some explanation for the phenomenon.

Parties arose partly because they were the most successful instruments of organization, communication, and control that other European states had employed in their own political modernization. They promised to fulfill the political needs of their founders and adherents. They came into being, partly because near the end, tsardom was no longer able to block their advance, and the Duma seemed to forecast the evolution, in Russia, of still another European parliamentary system.

In a few short years, however, the parties died, or rather, they were eliminated by the Bolsheviks who remained the sole survivors of the short experiment in political pluralism. Russian parties enjoyed only a meteoric existence partly because the society did not

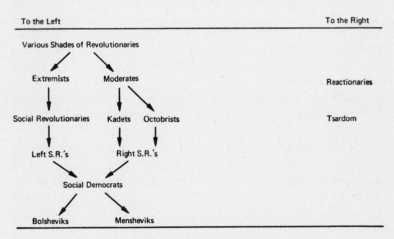

Figure 1: Parties under Nicholas II

support a political culture (i.e., a combination of knowledge, traditions, and shared attitudes) that led toward the kind of social pluralism essential for party life. In contrast, the whole historical thrust pointed in the direction of a new authoritarianism, capable of wielding the power that tsardom had lost. Moreover, most successful parliamentary systems depend upon large urban and industrial populations, but Russia remained primarily rural and agricultural. Furthermore, successful parliamentary systems depend upon the slow working out of compromises, whereas the enormous failures of the tsardom, combined with defeat at the hands of the Germans, created a sense of the need for strong leadership and decisive action, not party debate and compromise.

Parties came into being in Russia at the end of the century because for a short time there seemed to be a need and a future for them, but they died in their infancy because they were so much weaker, and, particularly, less resolute than the Bolsheviks, at a time when the tragedies of Tsarist history and that of Europe (i.e., World War I) combined to give them little chance for survival. In short, hindsight strongly implies that the political vacuum that developed in Russia at the beginning of the present century could be filled only by a highly disciplined dictatorship, if what had been Russia were not to be Balkanized into small, bickering, nation-states. The Bolsheviks quickly learned the lesson that for the forseeable future, a united USSR could not afford parties (or even "factionalism" within the single party). Unfortunately, however, no opposing party or faction was ever permitted to attain sufficient strength to prove that this philosophy might have been wrong.

Finally, the following points summarize some of the major political forces at work in the last years of tsardom—forces inherited by the new leadership that were to enormously influence both the successes and failures of the new system of rule:

1. Starting at least as early as Peter the Great, Tsarist Russia and, in recent years, the USSR have exhibited the schizophrenia of the Slavophile-Westernizer split. Both systems have looked to the West for ideas and examples, while, at the same time, they have rejected the West as evil and inferior to the great Slavic tradition of Russia.

2. Both tsarism and communism have been extremely author-

itarian, tending to see truth as monolithic and brooking none but a single party rule.

3. In close relationship to the previous point, in times of great stress both systems have stressed mass terror as a legitimate and necessary mainstay of rule.

4. Both systems have given evidence of a significant element among the intellectuals, particularly those with a literary bent, which has yearned for the evolution of a liberal society and state.

5. Under the tsars the peasants constituted the vast majority of the society, and they still remain its single largest segment. Agriculture was the major industry, and it remains the single most important element of the economy. Likewise, agriculture was and remains the most important domestic problem area. Thus, should political pluralism evolve, the rural inhabitants would constitute by far the most powerful political group in the society.

6. Under both the Tsarists and the Communists, Russia and the USSR have discovered that nationalism—e.g., the ethnocentrism of the Ukrainians or the Georgians—is an enormous thorn in the side of the attempt to achieve unified rule.

7. Both systems of rule have tended to see Russia (or the USSR) as destined to provide the way for the future organization of the world.

PART II The
Soviet
"Myth–Complex"

CHAPTER 3

Marxism

Origins THE working conditions in England, humorously and bitterly described by Charles Dickens, were also described by Karl Marx in *Das Kapital,* but there is little humor in his words.

William Wood, 9 years old, was 7 years and 10 months when he began to work. He "ran moulds" (carried ready-moulded articles into the drying room, afterwards bringing back the empty mould). He came to work every day in the week at 6 A.M. and left off about 9 P.M. "I work till 9 o'clock at night six days in the week. I have done so seven or eight weeks." Fifteen hours of labour for a child 9 years old! J. Murray, 12 years of age, says: "I turn jigger, and run moulds. I come at 6. Sometimes I come at 4. I worked all night last night, till 6 o'clock this morning. I have not been in bed since the night before last. There were eight or nine other boys working last night. All but one have come this morning. I get 3 shillings and sixpence. I do not get any more for working at night. I worked two nights last week."[1]

In the last week of June, 1863, all the London daily papers published a paragraph with the sensational heading, "Death from simple over-work." It dealt with the death of milliner, Mary Anne Walkley, 20 years of age, employed in a highly-respected dressmaking establishment, exploited by a lady with the pleasant name of Elise. The old, often-told story, was once more recounted. This girl worked, on an average, 10½ hours, during the season often 30 hours, without a break, whilst her failing labour power was revived by occasional supplies of sherry, port, or coffee. It was just now the height of the season. It was necessary to conjure up in the twinkling of an eye the gorgeous dresses for the noble ladies bidden to the ball in honour of the newly imported Princess of Wales. Mary Anne Walkley had worked without intermission for 26½ hours, with 60 other girls, 30 in one room, that only afforded ⅓ of the cubic feet of air required for them. At night, they slept in pairs in one of the stifling holes into which the bedroom was divided by partitions of board. And this was one of the best millinery establishments in London. Mary Anne Walkley fell ill on the Friday, died on Sunday, without, to the astonishment of Madame Elise, having previously completed the work in hand. The doctor, Mr. Keyes, called too late to the death bed, duly bore witness before the coroner's jury that "Mary Anne Walkley had died from long hours of work in an overcrowded workroom, and a too small and badly ventilated bedroom."

In order to give the doctor a lesson in good manners, the coroner's jury thereupon brought in a verdict that "the deceased had died of apoplexy, but there was reason to fear that her death had been accelerated by overwork in an overcrowded workroom, etc."[2]

Dr. Lee, Medical Officer of Health for Manchester, stated "that the average age at death of the Manchester . . . upper middle class was 38 years, while the average age at death of the labouring class was 17; while at Liverpool those figures were represented as 35 against 15. It thus appeared that the well-to-do classes had a lease of life which was more than double the value of that which fell to the lot of the less favoured citizens."[3]

Accounts such as these were well documented in the British press and especially in the Sadler Report, thus revealing the price that the Industrial Revolution was extracting from the British people.

In contrast to the evolution of Western democratic thought, the intellectual foundation of modern Communist political systems is said to have arisen, like Minerva, full-blown from the "scientific" analysis of Karl Marx (1818–1883) and his colleague Friedrich Engels (1820–1895). One should really say *nearly* full-blown, because the later interpretations of Marx by Lenin are believed to be enormously important. Western European and North American governments claim to rest upon beliefs evolved out of the Judeo-Hellenic past. Without a knowledge of the philosophical concepts of our forebears, one cannot make any sense of Western politics. Similarly, whatever position one may take as to the influence of Marxism–Leninism on present-day political decision-making, Marxist–Leninist ideology is the language of Soviet politics, and without a knowledge of this language, Soviet political literature is incomprehensible.

The famed *Communist Manifesto* was first issued in 1848; Volume One of *Das Kapital* was published jointly by Marx and Engels in 1867, and the second and third volumes were brought out by Engels in 1885 and 1894, after Marx's death. Marx was clearly the more important of the two partners, yet to speak just of Marxism is to withhold credit for the enormous import of Engels' contribution. Marx, the son of a German Jew, was a scholar who emigrated to England and carried out most of his work in the British Museum. In addition to supplying many of the funds to finance Marx's studies, Engels, the son of a wealthy German manufacturer, drawing on his experience in the industrial world, provided a practical balance to Marx's writing. *Das Kapital* is too often mistaken as only a dry-as-dust economic analysis. It is this, but it is also much more. Like all serious attempts to provide a complete philosophy of life, Marx's work, as reflected in the citations at the beginning of this chapter, is even more a socio-political analysis.

The nations of the West that are now known as the developed, industrial states were entangled in one of the greatest revolutionary upheavals of history, the Industrial Revolution. Societies were caught in a tremendous burst of development and change that destroyed many of the old ways, at an enormous personal and social cost for the great bulk of society. *Capitalism* was the term used by the Scottish economist Adam Smith (1723–1790) in his interpretation of the economic system that resulted from machine production, industrial organization, and the new forms of economic relationship that supplanted the old urban–rural system of production, ownership, and exchange.

In spite of the horrors Marx saw in industrial society, he was optimistic about the future of mankind. He attempted to explain man's position in the new environment, and in so doing, like other philosophers of merit, Marx had to rest his description on a clear concept of the nature of man. In spite of the obvious contradiction with strong threads of inevitability contained in his doctrine, Marx viewed man as essentially a rational being, one who was destined to control and determine his own fate. Therefore, Marx rejected God and religion and focused instead upon man as the center of the universe. The nature of his ideas was such that he may be considered to be one of the last great thinkers of the Enlightenment, even though that period in European intellectual history is dated in the previous century. There were, however, important innovations in Marx's thought.

Professor Alfred Meyer has noted that the essence of Marxism is his extreme radicalism (particularly, in criticizing his society), an optimism rising out of a faith in the inevitability of human progress (gnosticism), and a belief that the scientific method is fully applicable in explaining man's actions.[4] In my opinion, at least one additional element must be added to Meyer's essence of Marxism, that is, Marx's concept of man as essentially communal.

The pioneering anthropologist Morgan studied the American Indians, and believing he had found an example of man in his pristine state, he described a social organization in which ownership of material goods was common. Marx accepted Morgan's findings as a discovery of first order, one reflecting the very essence of human relationships. For Marx, the key element was the absence of the decisive factor of individual wealth; in such an environment there could be a full flowering of human communality. Not only did Marx reject Western views of man as essentially an individual (although with a great need for social intercourse— *à la* Aristotle), but he insisted that the dog-eat-dog existence under capitalism was a perversion of human nature. Moreover, since communal existence was man's true nature, he was destined to evolve into a new, higher state of being wherein he would return not only to the common ownership of material wealth but also to a common sense of identity. Thus the Marxian nature of man might be illustrated, from the psychological point of view before 1900 (i.e., before Pavlov's theories were accepted), by exploring why an individual instinctively withdraws his hand from a hot stove. Most Western psychologists, at one time, thought that man had built-in automatic responses in order to keep him alive and thereby to continue the species. A Marxist, however, might describe such automatic withdrawal from danger as a felt need to preserve the person so that he could maximize his contribution to the common good. Here, then, is a major part of the quarrel between Western democrats and the inheritors of Marxian communism.

Western philosophy does emphasize man's social needs, but even more, it stresses the triumph and, one might add, the tragedy of the individual. Thus Shakespeare's Hamlet wrestles with the human dilemma, "To be, or not to be?" whereas the Marxian Communist might well be asking, "To be a fully integrated member of society, or not to be?"

For Marx, all men carry such a nature in their beings, but the socioeconomic systems of feudalism and capitalism, which had followed man's fall from the grace of primitive society, had alienated him from his communality. Yet, this life force could not be denied. The common misery under capitalism imposed on the working classes by the Industrial Revolution was calling forth this latent force among the proletariat. Their common misery was so great, the need to set things right so demanding, that a class consciousness was growing by leaps and bounds. The renewed sense of communality would continue to grow until the working masses would no longer put up with the misery of capitalist existence. They would then spontaneously rise as one, cast out their exploiting bourgeois masters, and establish a new existence wherein class conscience rather than the capitalists' whip of economic deprivation would be the glue to hold the new society together. Here, of course, is a major root of the anarchical streak in Marxism, since in a society wherein *all* were both subconsciously and consciously for *one*, the negative aspects of political rule (e.g., the police and the army), essential for exploitive systems, would not be needed.

Here are Engels' words, reflecting what has been said above, in his description of the "fundamental proposition" of the *Manifesto*.

That proposition is: that in every historical epoch the prevailing mode of economic production and exchange, and the social organization necessarily following from it, form the basis upon which is built up, and from which alone can be explained, the political and intellectual history of that epoch; that consequently the whole history of mankind (since the dissolution of primitive tribal society, holding land in common ownership) has been a history of class struggles, contests between exploiting and exploited, ruling and oppressed classes; that the history of these class struggles forms a series of evolution in which, nowadays, a stage has been reached where the exploited and oppressed class (the proletariat) cannot attain its emancipation from the sway of the exploiting and ruling class (the bourgeoisie) without, at the same time, and once and for all, emancipating society at large from all exploitation, oppression, class-distinction and class struggles.[5]

The state is nothing else than a machine for the oppression of one class by another class, and that no less so in the democratic republic than under the monarchy.[6]

Feudalism, characterized by its rural slavery, had represented man's fall from grace. Capitalism was a step up the ladder of progress because some of its inventions, such as industrial-production processes and modern-production organization, carried discoveries that would also be utilized during the era of communism. Indeed, the population explosion, already hitting the world prior to the onset of capitalism, would surely have doomed mankind to mass deprivation if industrialization had not shown the way to multiply human output to a point where all of men's needs and legitimate wants could be met. Yet, some of the horrors of industrialization surpassed even those of the rural slavery of feudalism. In particular, the bulk of the workers no longer had the contact with nature that they had once enjoyed. Enslavement to the landlord had been supplanted by enslavement to the capitalists' machines under the hardest working conditions imaginable.

The new system of economics had forced men into two basic classes: the ever-smaller group of bourgeois exploiters and the ever-growing mass of exploited proletariat. The wealth of the bourgeoisie had allowed them to seize control of the government from the former landed nobility, and thus political leadership was merely a matter of manipulating society to the advantage of the capitalist owners. All institutions in the capitalist state as devised by the bourgeoisie served as instruments of control and exploitation. Religion and patriotism were but opiates of the people to maximize control. As we shall see from the social laws Marx evolved from his analysis of economics, private ownership of the means of production meant inevitably a movement toward monopoly with the resulting complete control by a small handful of society over every element but one—the burgeoning class consciousness, the catalyst that would eventually force the dialectic to produce the Communist revolution that would destroy the capitalist system itself.

Dialectical Materialism and Surplus Labor   Marx was a conscientious scholar, and he read widely in the philosophical works of his European forebears. The German philosopher Hegel, British economists such as Adam Smith, and the French Socialist thinkers were major contributors to his thought. For example, much of his view of labor as the source of all value came from the English economist David Ricardo (1772–1823).

The Marxian dialectic is the wedding of the long-standing concept of historical materialism to Hegel's dialectical movement of society. Karl Marx was, of course, a thoroughgoing materialist who believed that the only things that were real were those that could be counted and measured. *Ergo*, in accepting Hegel's concept of the dialectic, Marx threw out the view that a *volksgeist* ("people's spirit") was the root of evolutionary change and used instead what he (Marx) thought was a hardheaded interpretation of the material world—the struggle between the classes that was produced by capitalist society. For Hegel, human existence was a changing balance of antithetical forces; for Marx, it was the struggle between the bourgeoisie and the proletariat which would finally create the synthesis of communism.

In spite of Marx's claim to having made a "scientific" analysis, he was merely substituting a new mysticism for the old *volksgeist*. Searching behind Marx's explanations of the class struggle, one discovers that although he rejected the "people's spirit," he argued

that what made the class struggle work, and work in the direction
of his prophecy, was the spirit of the working masses. Max Eastman
has stressed this aspect of Marx's thought in his abridgement of
Das Kapital. Eastman tells us that Marx was a thoroughgoing
optimist in his "faith in the benign drift of his material universe,"
and that his thinking was a "relic of a religious attitude." According
to Eastman,

[H]e started in by deciding in general what the universe is made of
and how it operates, and then gradually worked down towards a demonstration that by the very nature of its being and laws of its operation
this universe is inevitably going to revolutionize itself, . . . in just the
manner outlined in his plan, and therefore as intelligent parts of a universe of such a kind it behooves us to get to work on the job.[7]

There is a tendency to describe the dialectic as a simple cause-
and-effect relationship. However, such an interpretation is unfair
to the balance of Marx's analysis, which was functional. Certainly,
Marx was well aware of the complexity of social relationships of
such forces as the feedback effect noted by modern behavioralists.
Marx was, in fact, a forerunner of modern social scientists in that
he too stressed the environmental influence over man and society.
This he implied strongly in his often-quoted observation that "Life
is not determined by consciousness, but consciousness by life." In
practical terms, this meant that without the proper economic relationship, which is the fundamental force of society, human consciousness must be wrong, was wrong under capitalism, and could
be corrected only by changing the relationship of society to the
means of production. Here, then, is the basis for the Marxian condemnation of ideas, nationalism, and religion.

Ideas, from the viewpoint of dialectical materialism, could
only reflect the distortions imposed by the economic environment.
Nationalism and religion not only were rooted in the capitalist
material relationships but also they had been fashioned and shaped
by the bourgeois masters to serve as opiates for the exploited working masses. One does not have to be a Marxist to see an element
of truth in these views. Throughout history, warlords, generals, and
ambitious politicians have exploited nationalism (the love of country) for their ends. Similarly, many historians would agree that the

leaders of feudal society utilized religion to calm the cries of mass desperation by pointing to the Church's promise of salvation after death. Viewing the misery of the urban industrial slums in the midnineteenth century, Marx argued that this practice had extended into the era of capitalism. God and religion were still being used as an "opiate of the people" designed to lead them into believing that there was relief for their misery, but only in another world and only for believers who remained faithful to the Church's teachings, accepting its dictates with docility.

Democracy, as practiced a century ago, was in Marx's eyes but another delusion of capitalist society. Although he believed that democracy was good and that the Communist society of the future would enjoy a kind of popular rule, he was convinced that under capitalism, real democracy was impossible, again because of the wrong relationship of society to the means of production. Because the economy was wrong, society was wrong, but the operation of the "laws" which Marx believed he had discovered in dialectical materialism would lead the workers of the world out of the capitalistic wilderness. To cite Lenin, "The doctrine of surplus-value is the cornerstone of Marx's economic theory."[8]

As noted previously, Marx accepted David Ricardo's argument that all material value stems from labor. Everything that man has is of value only because it represents a given amount of congealed labor. Let us take, for example, a laborer working at a lathe for ten hours a day in a capitalist plant. Let us say that in that time he fashions with his machine fifty table legs, and that the wood he uses to make the fifty table legs had already consumed another ten hours of labor in the felling of the trees, the rough cutting into lumber, and the transportation to the workman's bench. For Marx (and other adherents to the labor theory of value), the fifty table legs would be worth twenty working hours. Therefore, if just wages at the time were a dollar an hour, the true value of the fifty legs would be twenty dollars. This, however, according to Marx, was not the way wages and prices were set under capitalism. Continuing our example, the manufacturer probably would pay the lathe operator only fifty cents an hour, thereby robbing the worker of half his labor, five dollars per day. In such a situation the laborer in our example was spending half of each day "working for nothing," again using Lenin's words, "creating for the capitalist *surplus-*

value, the source of profits, the source of the wealth of the capitalist class."[9]

As Lenin points out, in the Marxian view, surplus-value extracted from the worker almost never is *equal* to profit. Returning to our example, the manufacturer may be in the midst of a business slump and forced to sell the table legs at an actual loss. Still, the worker is exploited by half his working time if he was paid only fifty cents an hour and the surplus-value remains at five dollars. Again, times may be good for the plant and wooden table legs may be in great demand. Under such circumstances the manufacturer may well sell the fifty table legs for forty or fifty dollars, in this case greatly magnifying his profit at the expense of his worker— but again the surplus value remains at five dollars. We see, therefore, from the Marxian point of view, that the evils wrought on the working masses arise from robbing the worker of his just wage, and that this extraction of surplus value is common to all firms, whether they are wealthy industrial plants or plants that are about to go into bankruptcy through failure to make any profits.

Marxian Laws   For Marx, there were inescapable laws regulating economic activity. Therefore, the degree of deprivation of the value which workers add to commodities is not accidental. Under capitalism, labor is but another commodity, one to be purchased at the lowest possible cost in order to maximize profits. Moreover, in such a system the worker is without any power. Marx did not see the full potential of trade unions or strikes as effective weapons. In his view, the worker was trapped in a position of having only his labor to sell, and the laws of capitalist competition determined that the price paid for that labor would be the lowest possible. Indeed, to cite Marx, in practice, the price actually paid the worker would be "the value of the means of subsistence necessary for the maintenance of the labourer."[10] Just as a farmer would not feed expensive oats to his draft horses if cheaper hay would sustain the horses' working power, the capitalist entrepreneur tended to pay wages only at the level necessary to sustain the workers' strength, and to allow them to live long enough to reproduce their kind so that there would always be an ample supply of workers.

As noted earlier, Marx considered industrial organization of production both a bane and a boon to mankind. In extracting surplus value from the proletariat, the bourgeois masters deprived the workers of their just due; yet machine production along with the "collective power of masses"[11] made possible the abundant production of human material needs. Marx's concept of the "collective power of the masses" is important to his promise for the future. It was his belief that a large group when properly coordinated could, in fact, produce and accomplish more than the same number of individuals could when working separately. We all know, for example, that two hundred men, each individually or one at a time, could never push over a tree two feet in diameter. Yet, with a long enough and stout enough rope, the same two hundred men could pull down the same tree. Similarly, by detailing the work in a plant making wooden tables, one worker turning out the legs on a lathe, another planing the boards for the top, and others sanding, varnishing, and polishing, all working separately but in unison, a group of ten men can manufacture more tables in a collective operation than the same ten individuals can produce working separately, each fashioning an entire table by himself. Here again, however, a great human price is paid for modern industrial methods. Under preindustrial conditions each worker was an artisan. The cabinetmaker made the whole table and had the satisfaction of creating an entire product, or in Marx's terms, a commodity. However, with the division of labor into detailed operations under modern manufacturing, the "detailed labourer produces no commodities"[12]; and deprived of creative satisfaction, the worker becomes a "crippled monstrosity."[13] Under feudalism the artisan produced the whole commodity, but under capitalism the worker becomes but an extension of the machine to which he is figuratively chained, being constantly required to repeat monotonous tasks. Here, then, is the basis for the Marxian "theory of alienation," which states that the industrial worker is completely foreign to both his work and the direction of society. One should not, however, lose sight of the point that Marx believed that the mode of industrial production is essential to human progress because it promises production in abundance.

Interestingly, whereas earlier Soviet philosophers tended to ignore or depreciate the Marxian concept of alienation, regarding it as a phenomenon confined to capitalism, in recent years there is strong evidence to indicate that the concepts may become vital to the evolving Soviet system of beliefs. Thus, as Professor Murray Yanowitch has demonstrated, the earlier reaction to the first complete translation into Russian (in 1956) of the young Marx's *Manuscripts* was that his stress on alienation was a result of his immaturity. Now, however, Soviet writers see the idea as having been important to *Capital*. More than this, there is at least a hint of recognition that even in Soviet Socialist society, factors may exist that appropriate a worker's labor, his output, and, thus, "his reason." Most important to the present author's conclusion that Marx's thought is a key component of an evolving Soviet belief system—and we wish to underline this point—is Professor Yanowitch's observation that in the USSR "the converging of both philosophers and sociologists—most actively on the part of the latter—on the concept of alienation is an act of self-recognition that has added *another note of seriousness to Soviet–Marxist thought* and represents a move away from its former purely ideological function."[14] (Present author's italics.)

As far as Marx could see (which was somewhat short of modern automation with its promise to free human beings from the tedious, repetitive tasks), the advent of industry meant that undesirable tasks would always have to be performed. However, not only did he maintain that justice would be done if all labor were recognized as equal in value but also he argued that no individual should be permanently chained to a particular machine. This Lenin was to emphasize in his *State and Revolution*: in the just society of communism, everyone would be educated equally; and more to the point of the discussion, all would take equal turns both at the tasks of tedium and at the more self-rewarding intellectual pursuits. In this same context we should also note the Communists' argument that if all were in an equal relationship to the means of production (thus, industry was owned by the workers), the worker would happily and eagerly turn to the machines since he would know that his entire output would be going to maximize his own and his fellow workers' well-being rather than lining the pockets of the exploiting capitalists.

As implied earlier, Marx viewed the worker's condition under capitalism as but a new form of slavery. To cite his words, "The Roman slave was held by fetters: the wage-labourer is bound to his owner by invisible threads. The appearance of independence is kept up by means of a constant change of employers, and by the *fictio juris* of a contract."[15] Furthermore, the lot of the worker was not destined to improve, indeed, quite to the contrary. As noted earlier, although not equal to profit, surplus-value stolen from labor was the source of the manufacturer's capital in a system wherein the accumulation of even more capital was the primary goal. Now since machines were even less expensive than laborers, the capitalists would utilize the funds derived from surplus-value to purchase ever more and superior machines, thereby replacing more and more workmen and expanding the rolls of the unemployed. But even here the oppression would not stop, for the increased competition among the workers for jobs would place the owners in a position of continually being able to reduce wages, and thereby increase surplus-value with which to buy more machines, and so forth. In short, however miserable his working conditions and his life, the proletarian really has only two choices: either to subject himself to the slavery of the capitalist or to perish, and eventually even that choice may be made for him by the capitalist.

The preceding are most of the basic observations of Marx, resting largely on his concept of surplus-value, from which he derived three, assertedly fundamental, laws. These are the law of fall in the rate of profit, the law of capital concentration, and the law of increasing misery, which are summarized by Prof. Meyer as follows:

1. ... competition forces the capitalist to accumulate capital in order to save labor. But by increasing the proportion of machinery to labor, the capitalist causes a fall in the rate of profits.
2. ... competition drives the weaker capitalists from the field, thus swelling the ranks of free labor, while concentrating capital in the hands of fewer and fewer capitalists who gradually turn into monopolists.
3. ... forced to compensate for the decline in his profits, [the capitalist] must intensify his exploitation of the workers by extorting more and more surplus labor from them [thus forcing more men out of work] increasing misery.[16]

Here again, in examining the basic Marxian laws, one can see that his philosophy (the Communists would say "science") is much more than just economic analysis. It is really an attempt at a thorough sociopolitical theory that explains the whole of human existence, for with the completion of the third and final step, mass misery combined with the greatly expanded class consciousness would reach the point at which capitalism would collapse, largely from its own internal weakness and with little or no push from the masses.

Lenin spelled out, in good Marxian terms, this argument that large-scale mechanized production is the key to the inevitable self-destruction of capitalism:

> By destroying small-scale production, capital leads to an increase in productivity of labour and to the creation of a monopoly position for the associations of big capitalists. Production itself becomes more and more social—hundreds of thousands and millions of workers become bound together in a regular economic organism—but the product of this collective labour is appropriated by a handful of capitalists. Anarchy of production, crises, the furious chase after markets and the insecurity of existence of the mass of the population are intensified.
>
> By increasing the dependence of the workers on capital, the capitalist system creates the great power of united labour. . . .
>
> And the experience of all capitalist countries, old and new, year by year demonstrates clearly the truth of this Marxian doctrine to increasing numbers of workers.
>
> Capitalism has triumphed all over the world, but this triumph is only the prelude to the triumph of labour over capital.[17]

Marxism Criticized: The Value and the Errors
Whatever criticisms one may have of the twentieth-century state systems created in the name of Marxism, one would be enormously shortsighted not to recognize the keen insights that Marx had into the nature of the society of his time. More than this, even though his major prophecy of a world-wide Communist revolution has failed to materialize, and even though none of the societies that have adopted Communist systems fit the industrial formula he prescribed as necessary for a "Socialist" revolution, few, if any, other social scientists have been as nearly correct as was Marx in many of the specific points of his prophecy. Forgetting for a moment that the following points were first presented in the *Communist Manifesto* of 1848, it is interesting to note how much of what he and Engels said was to be adopted

in the future state—has in fact even been adopted in one form or another in most advanced *non-Communist* systems:

1. Abolition of property in land and application of all rents of land to public purposes.
2. A heavy progressive or graduated income tax.
3. Abolition of all right of inheritance.
4. Confiscation of the property of all emigrants and rebels.
5. Centralization of credit in the hands of the State, by means of a national bank with State capital and an exclusive monopoly.
6. Centralization of the means of communication and transport in the hands of the State.
7. Extension of factories and instruments of production owned by the State; the bringing into cultivation of wastelands, and the improvement of the soil generally in accordance with a common plan.
8. Equal liability of all to labor. Establishment of industrial armies, especially for agriculture.
9. Combination of agriculture with manufacturing industries; gradual abolition of the distinction between town and country by a more equable distribution of the population over the country.
10. Free education for all children in public schools. Abolition of children's factory labor in its present form. Combination of education with industrial production, . . .[18]

In his abridgement of *Das Kapital*, Max Eastman used partly his own words and partly those of Engels in summarizing some of the more important insights of Marx.

[1] Marx discovered the simple fact (heretofore hidden beneath ideological overgrowths) that human beings: must have food, drink, clothing and shelter first of all, before they can interest themselves in politics, science, art, religion, and the like. . . . [H]ere then is . . . the foundation upon which the state institutions, the legal outlooks, the artistic and even religious ideas are built up. . . .

[2] There is little doubt that he did demonstrate the inevitability under a capitalist system of the recurrent crisis of over-production,

[3] [A]nd bound up therewith the inevitability of imperialist wars. His contribution to the understanding of business crisis and the causes of war will not often be denied today even by the most "bourgeois" economists.[19]

In his paper "The Communist Ideology," Professor John Plamanetz rates Marxism as being among the most serious sinners
against the advance of democracy. Nevertheless, Plamanetz has
looked at the reverse side of the coin to note that Marx, perhaps
more than any other man, must be credited with awakening the
industrial societies of the West to the evils within themselves that
needed to be corrected.[20] Marx was a major stimulant of the economic and social reforms of modern times. Marx also must be
credited with emphasizing the dialectic as an important analytical
tool and with pointing out the importance of class and class forces
in any attempt to understand society. Finally, and perhaps most
importantly, too much credit can never be given Marx for calling
attention to the enormous influence of economic factors on social
and political affairs, as he viewed society as a whole, made up of
all three forces. This point is difficult to appreciate today when we
hear such observations as: "People who are starving aren't interested
in democracy," or when the Supreme Court rules on matters related
to social science with evidence primarily based on the recognition
that economically deprived people cannot enjoy the equality promised by a democratic system. The point is that prior to Marx's day,
such social-science facts were virtually unknown. As implied earlier,
the promises of religion and the niceties of philosophy were accepted in ignorance of hard economic reality.

The debts modern society owes to Karl Marx are tremendous,
and intellectual honesty demands full payment. However, he was
far from a superman, and the weaknesses and shortcomings in his
analyses are also monumental.

As indicated in the previous capsule summary of Marxism,
the theory reduces all value to a matter of congealed working time,
thereby not allowing for any differences in skill. One might well
ask, "Why would a worker devote the time and effort necessary
for acquiring a skill if he knows beforehand that no additional
reward will result?" Perhaps even more serious was Marx's denial
of the import of managerial skill. His faith in the stimulus that an
aroused sense of communality would bring led him to argue that
most managerial work is unproductive. True, some small measure
of guidance and coordination of the work would be needed in a
society wherein class consciousness held sway, but this would be
minimal. Therefore, in his opinion the great bulk of managerial

effort under capitalism was really that of a slave master driving the reluctant workers to their machines.

In giving credit where it is due, we have asserted that Marx's identification of class as a vital social force was an important contribution to social science. However, surely one can argue that he greatly exaggerated the importance of class, especially class consciousness. Class implies permanence, the rigidity of inheritance and the lack of social mobility. Yet, in spite of the serious shortcomings of the Western open societies, there has continued to be a significant degree of movement both up and down the socioeconomic scale.

Surely there are identifiable urban blue-collar working groups in all industrial societies, but the argument that these people have a high (indeed, ever increasing) degree of solidarity, a growing consciousness of their common cause, has not been borne out by history. Here again, the anarchical streak in Marxism fails to represent political reality. Where the "proletariat" have been successful in effecting common demands, leadership, rather than spontaneous mass action, has most often been the key to advance. *The proletariat*, therefore, has proved to be much less substantial and much more mercurial than the Marxian analysis indicates. Indeed, following Lenin's lead, modern Marxian analysts have turned more and more to stressing nationalism (that cuts across the Communist concept of class) as the most potent revolutionary force in societies suffering mass deprivation. Factors such as nationalism and leadership, rather than the nebulous class struggle, seem to be the more important social elements behind popular stimulus for change in the modern world.

The forces Marx identified were not always as effective as he asserted them to be. In this connection, Max Eastman takes him to task for failing to distinguish between condition and cause in his analysis.[21] That is to say, Marx seems to be guilty of having decided on the ultimate goal first and then selecting only those factors and forces (e.g., the class struggle) which strongly seem to support his conclusion.

In our opinion, Marx's rejection of the force of ideas exhibited an enormous blindness to human behavior. Although is seems quite true that a hungry man is consumed with concern for his belly, once his stomach is full and his family is enjoying a reasonable

level of security, man everywhere tends to turn to ideas and beliefs to explain the unexplainable. The tremendous influence of the
idea of communism on the world today is major evidence that the
doctrine's attempt to rest entirely on material influence is self-
contradictory.

Closely related to the narrowness of economic analysis is the
criticism of the doctrine's vision of truth. From Marx to the present
day among Soviet ideologists, there has been the vigorous assertion
that truth is a single "scientific" whole. This view, perhaps as much
as any other factor, can be blamed for the insistence, in practice,
that all Communist states must be dictatorships. If truth is monolithic, then those who grasp its vision are morally bound to enforce
the correct way on those members of society whose class consciousness is insufficiently developed so that they cannot grasp the whole
truth. True, those whose consciousness lags behind will eventually
see the truth, but by pushing them ahead, society as a whole benefits more and suffers less as a result. Yet a major conclusion drawn
from modern knowledge, greatly buttressed by Einstein's discovery
that even in the physical world all is relative, points in the direction
that truth is not single but pluralistic. If this is correct, then the best
society is one that most successfully encourages the contest of all
ideas with the hope that the ideas most suited to the particular
needs of the time will prevail. In such a system, change would be
championed as the most positive of all universals, but forced change
would be rejected.

Surely a major weakness of Marxism is its unquestioned faith
in human progress (i.e., collectively, all social change will eventu-
ate in human betterment). One can certainly assert that enormous
progress in the material world has been achieved by the invention
of ever more sophisticated devices. Automobiles, for example, can
transport man from place to place much faster than horses could,
and atomic power can enormously strengthen the arms of industry.
However, horsedrawn vehicles killed very few travelers, and they
did not produce carbon monoxide to poison the air. Similarly, to
date, the most awesome use of atomic power has been to multiply
the destruction of war. There is no indication that either physical
or social change improves the human condition; moreover, if human
misery in absolute numbers is any measure of social advance or
decline, then there is no doubt that at the beginning of the 1970s

many more human beings are suffering physical deprivation (according to United Nations' statistics, a majority of mankind is ill fed) than at any previous time in history. And beyond the persistence of hunger on our globe, the slaughter and destruction of twentieth-century wars surpasses that of any previous human era.

Whether or not one believes in progress, however, the Marxian doctrine clearly outlined a linear forward march of mankind to a superior material welfare in a way and to a degree that has not occurred. The optimistic prophecy of Marx is as far from fulfillment as ever.

CHAPTER 4

Leninism

*The Role of
tne Party*
,

LENINISM might be taken to imply only Lenin's contribution to Marxist thought. But Lenin was a man of extraordinary abilities; he presided over the inauguration of the Soviet experiment in rule, and such a narrow connotation certainly would not do justice to his total impact on history. In our view, for good or ill, to date he has been the most influential man of the present century. Lenin was not only an enormously influential theoretician but also a highly successful politician who combined his writings and activities in such a way that to separate his ideas from his actions would distort the picture of this extraordinary leader.

Vladimir I. Ulyanov, later known as Lenin, was born on April 22, 1870. His father, a minor nobleman, was a bureaucrat who served as inspector of schools. Lenin, having taken his revolutionary name from the Lena River on which he was exiled, came to be by far the most important of an impressive group of conscious-stricken intellectual sons and daughters of the Tsarist establishment,

who built, fought, and finally directed the Russian Revolution of 1917.

One of the most important influences of his early years was the hanging of his brother, in 1887, for participating in a plot to assassinate Alexander III. His whole family came under suspicion, and Lenin was thrown out of law school (where he is said to have received only two grades: honors and failures). After his dismissal, he continued to study on his own, and in 1891 he passed the law examination with honors and was admitted to the bar. However, Lenin's formal studies had not occupied all his time nor all his thoughts, for he also joined subversive Marxist groups and became a leading figure in the Social Democratic party (S.D.), which had been founded by Plekhanov in 1898. Indeed, the history of the S.D.'s from the turn of the century until World War I became more and more the history of Lenin's talent in combining the theoretical with the practical.

Forced into self-imposed exile, if they were not to be imprisoned or exiled in Russia by Tsarist agents, many of the key members of the Party fled to Western Europe. Here, they carried on the increasingly disruptive factional struggles that eventually produced the Bolshevik–Menshevik split, which was marked by Lenin's domination of the Bolsheviks. In brief, the congresses being held in many of the key cities of Europe (Brussels, London, Stockholm, and Prague) were gravitating more and more into two opposing groups: the *Iskra* and the Plekhanovites. *Iskra,* the Russian word for "spark," was also the name of one of the Party's underground newspapers. More importantly, however, the word came to represent the idea that a revolt in Russia would spark a genuine Communist upheaval in the industrial nations of Western Europe, which the Marxists believed were ripe for a Communist revolution. Although many individuals were to change sides during the course of the debate, under Lenin's leadership the *Iskra* faction became the Bolsheviks when at one point in the dispute the *Iskra* side won a majority in a Party Congress vote. (In Russian, *bolshevik* means "majority" and *menshevik* means "minority.") After adopting the name *Bolshevik,* Lenin and his followers dubbed the Plekhanovites with the name *Mensheviks.* This name then stuck in spite of the fact that most of the time until after 1917, the Menshevik wing of the S.D. was actually greater in number.

By 1905 the split had already grown quite wide, largely as a result of an argument between Martov and Lenin over Martov's use of the phrase "one who accepts" in drafting the rules for accepting candidates for Party membership. Martov and his colleagues were willing to admit most anyone who so declared himself, but Lenin insisted that more stringent rules of discipline to the leadership should be imposed on the group. However, the defeat of the Tsarist forces by the Japanese and the events of the 1905 revolution brought the warring factions together momentarily at the so-called Unity Congress of 1906, which was held in Stockholm.

A fifth congress was held in London in 1907, and a sixth in Prague in 1912 when the break between the Bolsheviks and the Mensheviks again had widened. This split, that had originated in 1903 and that eventually was to prove fatal to the Mensheviks, was fought primarily over the nature and size of the Party. In a sense, a dispute over "one who accepts" implies ideological nit picking of the first order. Yet, out of Lenin's arguments was to come his theoretical conception of a tightly knit, highly disciplined Party. Not only was he able to impose this concept on such key *Iskra* men as Zinoviev and Molotov, but the theoretical conception enabled him to fashion a disciplined Party vanguard that eventually staged the successful coup of 1917, to fashion the Red army which under the guiding genius of Trotsky was to win the Civil War of 1918–1921, and to consolidate the Bolshevik rule that has continued to the present day. Here, then, is one of Lenin's two major revisions (a good Marxist would say "extensions") of Marx's thought; the other is his theory of imperialism. Together these two were so important that the Marxism–Leninism which guides contemporary Communist states is really more Leninist than Marxist. Indeed, the Bolshevik–Menshevik split reflects a breach that has continued in the international Socialist movement, a division of paramount importance both to the USSR and to the whole world.

As suggested in our earlier discussion of Marxism, there were inconsistent strains in Marx's thought. For example, although he believed democracy was a desirable goal, his narrow, doctrinal strictures have led to authoritarian dictatorships in the name of Marxian "science." By the turn of the century, Socialists all over Europe were forced to choose. Those who had no faith in parliamentary change chose the bloody path of revolution, and most shared Lenin's view of a hardened, disciplined Party vanguard that would force history in the direction Marx said it inevitably must go. In the industrially advanced countries, however, an increasing number of intellectuals who felt that the state must greatly increase its activity in order to improve the lot of the masses (and so called themselves Marxists or Socialists of some other persuasion) came to take a different view. Their faith in democracy and peaceful change through the ballot box helped to bring about increased government responsibility in many of the Western European states. Such is the history of the Labor (i.e., Socialist) party of Britain and many of the Christian or Social Democratic parties on the continent.

On balance, the Mensheviks of Russia followed the same path. True, they believed that conditions in Tsarist Russia were so impossible that a revolution offered the only solution. However, many of the Mensheviks had gone into the prerevolutionary Duma, and, after the tsar's resignation early in 1917, many worked in the Provisional Government. Significantly, they continued to champion the evolutionary aspect of the Marxian doctrine, and argued that the new system would have to evolve through the capitalist stage. On the other hand Lenin's arguments more often pointed toward skipping directly into the early stages of socialism.

Again, Lenin's view of the Party is key to understanding the Bolshevik position, and Profs. Meyer and Sabine have vividly summarized his concept of the Party's vanguard role. As Prof. Sabine noted,

The essential and distinctive quality of Leninism was the role that it assigned to the communist party. The moral attitude which Lenin passed on to the class-conscious Marxist—the attitude of a man with an insight and a mission—was far more that of a militant religious order than that which democratic countries associate with a political party.[1]

Professor Meyer's observations are particularly perceptive, for where Marx had viewed the proletariat as the "Chosen People," Lenin differed:

Perhaps Lenin's most conspicuous contribution to twentieth-century politics is his conception of the Communist Party as a creative history-making force and as the general staff of the world revolution. . . . [W]hereas Marx had believed in the spontaneous growth of working-class consciousness under the impact of capitalist realities, Lenin tended

to assume that the working man was forever doomed to insufficient consciousness, no matter how miserable his conditions.[2]

Thus, as Meyer underlines, the role of the Party is to lead the
proletariat in achieving its historical mission. It should not, as stated
in a 1921 Party resolution, "adapt itself to . . . the backward sections of the working class, but raise the entire working class to the
level of its Communist vanguard. . . . The Party exists for the very
purpose of going ahead of the masses and showing the masses the
way."[3]

At least two points should be stressed at this juncture: that
out of Lenin's concept of the Party a conception of an elite leadership, quite antithetical to Marx's original ideas, arose; and similarly,
that Lenin's view of the Party affected his view of the working
masses. Marx had pictured the proletariat as being a chosen people
who would find their own way to the land of milk and honey.
Lenin saw them as an instrument of history to be manipulated
carefully toward the goal.

The course of the Russian revolutionary movement of 1905 to
1917 became more and more controlled by Lenin's genius for combining theory and practice. To understand this growing together,
one needs to recognize that 1917 really encompassed three revolutions.

1. The first revolution marked the end of tsardom when
Nicholas II abdicated early in the year, and no one could, or would,
ascend to the throne.

2. The second was a peasant revolt which had been mounting
for more than a century; 1905 had witnessed peasant uprisings, but
now, starting early in the year, the peasantry spontaneously and
increasingly swept the countryside of the landlords, burned the
manor houses, and seized the land they had long claimed as their
right. As news of the revolution spread, the peasant soldiers voted
with their feet, deserted the front, and returned to the countryside
to join the revolt and claim the land.

3. The third revolution was only a beginning. The Bolshevik
coup d'etat of October (November by the new calendar) was really
only the displacement of the weak Kerensky government; that is,
primarily the seizure of Leningrad and other key cities by the Len-

inist forces who were unable fully to secure power. They did so, in fact, in 1921, only after three years of civil war, but even then their control over the countryside was highly tenuous.

Much of Lenin's writing between 1905 and 1917 had dealt with what had gone wrong in 1905. *Shto Deleyet* ("What Is To Be Done?") was his theme, and his answer was that a Russian revolution could succeed only if the workers were to join hands with the peasant revolutionaries. Interestingly, as we shall see, Lenin's view of the peasants' key role in the revolution was inseparably related to his second major revision of Marxism, his idea of imperialism.

*Imperialism, Peasants, and Wars of National Liberation**   Marxism should have died at the end of the last century. Had it done so and received a decent burial along with the other utopian schemes that preceded it, there would be no Communist states; the national uprisings that are now described by the world's Leninists as "wars of national liberation" would be called by quite another name, and their character undoubtedly would be quite different. In short, major revisions of Marxism by Lenin provided not only the basis for Marxism's revival but also a Communist interpretation of the struggles taking place in former colonial and underdeveloped nations. Therefore, contemporary Soviet foreign policy analysis regarding relations both with the West and with the developing nations, is rooted in Lenin's analyses of imperialism and nationalism.

Perhaps at this juncture we should stress agreement with the view that Lenin's roots in classical Marxist analysis were so strong that he never abandoned Marxism to the point of systematically outlining his own theory of international relations although this theory has come to be accepted by contemporary Marxist–Leninists.[4] Nevertheless, what he didn't systematize was clearly, if implicitly, there. Both Lenin's successors and Western analysts, therefore, can see the base in his writings for the present-day view of international affairs that is shared by the great bulk of the world's Communist leaders—regardless of the severity of their quarrels over how "West-

* This portion of the chapter is adapted from the author's contribution to the forthcoming study of *Wars of Liberation*, Professor Stephan A. Fischer-Galati (ed.). New York: Frederick A. Praeger.

ern imperialism" should be met. Indeed, the irony of their quarrels is that the leaders of the various nations—Yugoslavia, China, Rumania, Cuba, and the Soviet Union—attack their Communist brethren primarily on the points of asserted misinterpretations of Leninist thoughts, all while denying that there were any major revisionist elements in Leninist thinking.

The Leninist Base

Lenin had spent much of his effort during the 1905 to 1917 period analyzing the 1905 uprising. Out of this work came his recognition that in predominantly agricultural Russia, no Communist revolution could succeed without widespread peasant support. Tsarist Russia was an underdeveloped country. Only a tiny portion of the population fit the "proletarian" label. Thus, Lenin's search for a revolutionary base on Marxist lines led him to elevate the poor peasantry to a semiproletarian class. Lenin never argued that the level of peasant class consciousness had reached the heights of revolutionary solidarity believed to exist among the industrially oriented proletariat of the cities. Nevertheless, the poorest, land-short, and landless peasants were assigned a position analogous to that of the exploited urban workers. Lenin came to describe this segment of the peasantry as "semiproletarian."[5] Given strong Party leadership, a base existed for a common cause: joining of the peasant and the proletarian revolutions. Similarly, Lenin came to view the peasantry as the primary source of mass opposition to imperialism in the colonies.

Tsarist Russia was a predominantly agricultural, underdeveloped country wherein, long before 1905, peasant uprisings had demonstrated the existence of a rural revolutionary base. However, in wedding the peasant–worker revolutionary elements in Russia, until his death in 1924, Lenin remained faithful to his Marxism to the degree that he did not believe that the newly created USSR provided a base for building communism in isolation. Communism, as prophesied by Marx, could come only in the advanced industrial nation in which the predominant segment of the population comprised an exploited working class destined to suffer an increasing cycle of misery at the hands of the bourgeois masters. In effect, therefore, Lenin admitted that the Bolshevik coup of 1917 was an accident of history, an un-Marxian seizure of power made possible by the defeat of Russia at the hands of the Kaiser's armies. The new Soviet state was not the place for immediate Communist construction, but Lenin believed that the Bolshevik successes would provide the *iskra* ("spark") that would light the revolutionary fires in industrial Western Europe, which was ripe for revolution. Lenin never stopped believing that the revolution was imminent in such nations as Germany, England, and France, and that once the comrades had succeeded in these nations, they would turn their efforts to helping their Soviet brethen achieve the levels of industrialization necessary for the construction of communism in the USSR as well.

Why had the revolution not occurred earlier in industrialized Western Europe, without awaiting the ignition of the Soviet "spark"? Imperialism had allowed the "capitalist" states to postpone their inevitable demise. Lenin's analysis of imperialism as "the highest stage of capitalism," particularly the final wave of colonization in the latter part of the 1800s that resulted in virtually all of the remaining parts of the underdeveloped world being swallowed up as colonies, was central to his analysis of world affairs: an analysis that allowed him to breathe new life into moribund Marxism. Marx was a careful scholar who put no precise timetable to his prophecy. Nevertheless, the clear implication was that by the turn of the century the revolution should have been near at hand in the industrial West when, in fact, the growing signs pointed in the opposite direction. In this writer's opinion, what had happened was that the Marxian analysis had failed to account for the strength of the democratic process. Spurred ahead by the arguments of such social critics as Marx and Owens and the grimness of the reality described in the official British Sadler Report, parliaments and congresses were enacting wage and hour laws, child labor laws, and other reforms that were reducing the great ills wrought by the Industrial Revolution. Instead of the increasing human misery said to be inevitable by Marx, the working masses' conditions in the industrialized nations of the West were improving, and Marxism probably would have faded away *if* Lenin had not reevaluated the world and altered the Marxian terms of analysis.

Lenin's view, however, was that capitalism had found a temporary respite for its inevitable collapse. The great new wave of capital exportation to the colonial areas, with it the exploitation of vast new depositories of natural resources, and (most of all) the exploitation of huge additional reservoirs of labor in the under-developed regions of the world allowed capitalism momentarily to postpone its inevitable collapse. Specifically, the advance of the revolutionary class consciousness among the workers that should have been developing at an ever more rapid rate had temporarily been slowed down, perhaps even reversed for the time being. Why? The new wealth, stolen by the capitalist colonialists of the indus-trialized nations from the exploited masses of the colonies, was so enormous that some of this was even being allowed to trickle down to the workers. Most of all, he argued, this surplus of booty was being passed on to the workers' leaders. According to his "trickle down" theory, the proletariat in the industrially advanced states were being bribed.

As noted earlier, the improvement in the industrial workers' lot had coincided with a growth in many Western European Social-ists' faith in the democratic, parliamentary process. To a degree this development also took place in Russia. Therefore, some Russian Marxists, including Nicolay Bukharin, came to argue that the con-tradictions of capitalism that would have led to a Communist revolution were being resolved. As implied previously, however, Lenin emphatically rejected this point of view. The new vigor of capitalism was only a passing phenomenon. Shortly, the misery visited upon the colonial masses, combined with quarreling among the imperialists over the colonial holdings—where the benefits of the new wealth would rapidly be drained off—would result in a reappearance of the inherent contradictions Marx had described in capitalism. This time the ills of capitalism would appear on a worldwide scale, and there would be no new escape from the global disaster of the system.

In many ways, the conditions of the colonies were seen as similar to the conditions of Tsarist Russia. The 1905 Russian Rev-olution had not gone further because the leaders had ignored the impact of peasant discontent. Lenin redefined the class war and transformed it into a union of the classical Marxist struggle of the exploited industrial proletariat against their bourgeois masters in the advanced industrialized states with the increasing struggle of the semiproletarian peasant majorities, particularly in the underdeveloped nations and especially in the colonies. Thus, as one present-day Soviet academician observes, Leninism involves "a continuation of Marxism as an international doctrine."[6] The revolution became truly worldwide in a setting wherein the workers joined hands with the peasant majority in the underdeveloped nations. The struggle would be carried forward not only by a common sense of misery but also by a growing sense of nationalism in the colonies, fueled by a hatred for colonial masters. Here, then, Lenin was describing a new Marxist–Leninist class warfare, one quite different from that originally defined by Marx in his dialectical materialism.

Lenin did not live long enough to appreciate fully what his analyses implied, and Stalin turned policy considerations inward to the isolationism that characterized most Soviet foreign policy until after the Second World War and his death. Nevertheless, relatively independent Communist wars of national liberation in China, Yugoslavia, and Vietnam were built on Leninist theory and patterned after the Bolshevik model. Moreover, Lenin's revisionism provided not only the rationale for staging Communist revolutions in predominantly peasant nations but also the basis for supporting national uprisings when there is little or no immediate hope for the establishment of a Communist system. The importance of Lenin's alteration of the focus of world Marxists is stressed by Professor Roger Kanet in his study of Soviet relations with Africa. Thus, Kanet has emphasized the point that Lenin made in the last article he wrote before his death that in the long run the key to world revolution would be determined by such nonindustrial (at the time) nations as Russia, India, and China.[7]

War and Peace: The Split

As described by Soviet theorists, wars of national liberation are an important part of one phase of the present-day stage of the "world revolutionary process which involves the merger of three basic revolutionary forces."[8] Lenin characterized the modern era of capitalism as imperialism, and its "highest stage" as a point in history that marked the decline of the rule of capitalism throughout the world. Since Lenin, the "general crisis of capitalism" is described as having reached a "third terminal stage," a point where the capitalist nations are no longer even capable of effective military suppres-

sion "of the national liberation movement of colonial peoples."[9]
Clearly, therefore, wars of national liberation are the most progressive element of the present era of international relations.

The three fundamental revolutionary forces that have merged are "the world system of socialism, the international working movement, and the national liberation movement."[10] The first two are said to represent the vanguard of the revolutionary forces, whereas a particular national liberation movement may, or may not, be in the mainstream of the revolution, however positive and important this may be to a world revolution. When national liberation movements involve direct Communist takeovers (such as in the USSR and China), the movement itself is obviously in the mainstream. However, when national liberation actions involve uprisings such as occurred in Egypt, Lebanon, and Iraq, where Communist parties played no central role, they are a step removed from the vanguard.[11] More than this, the national liberation movement is viewed as a product of the process of history, producing a nonexportable mass-revolutionary consciousness that, as in Vietnam, may require war, whereas in other instances more peaceful means may be required by prevailing circumstances. According to Lenin, "no force would be able to destroy capitalism if history did not undermine and overtax it."[12]

Soviet hesitancy to advocate the universal use of force in the national liberation movement is a major point of contention in the Sino–Soviet split. Soviet writings and speeches in recent years indicate that the Soviet leaders have looked down the long gun barrel of a possible nuclear conflagration and have resolved to turn away in the direction of "peaceful coexistence" with opposing systems. However, such a resolve has in no way meant that the Soviet theorists have seen a lessening of the new class struggle described by Lenin in his 1905 to 1917 reappraisal of the world. Soviet observers stress Lenin's view that the changed world is one in which there has been a joining of the Marxian class struggle within the capitalist states with the class struggle of the oppressed peoples in the colonies and former colonies.[13]

As is so often the case in Soviet affairs, policy decisions seem to have arisen from a joining of both pragmatic and ideological considerations, which in this case have led to the conclusion that although great care must be taken to avoid local wars that might precipitate a third world war, if the time is ripe for revolutionary action in a nation, not only should war be applauded but also Communist nations are morally bound to support such struggles with spiritual and material aid alike. Chinese claims that the West, and particularly the United States, is as ineffective as a paper tiger are said to reveal a blindness to the danger of precipitating a new major war.[14] Not only are the former Chinese comrades acting foolhardy in the face of atomic cannons but also, in effect, they are repudiating the *primus inter pares* position of "the world system of socialism and the international working movement" in relationship to "the national liberation movement" as the third, but less advanced, part of the triad of the basic forces working for revolution in today's world.[15]

Not only have the Chinese downgraded the Soviet leadership role, but in so doing from an ideological point of view, they have also weakened the impact of the system of socialism on the total revolutionary movement. Even more importantly, the Chinese arguments reveal that Mao and his colleagues have adopted a false notion that the working classes in the capitalist countries "are losing their revolutionary character." Indeed the Chinese Communists have gone far beyond putting the first last in seeing the struggle for revolution as "exclusively" a matter of national liberation. They have turned both Marx and Lenin on their heads, and are acting as "opportunists of the left" who describe the current scene as one in which there is a war of "the world countryside against the world city." In short, they have arrived at a "nonclass" analysis that denies the revolutionary unity of the proletariat in the industrially advanced nations with the exploited peasants of the underdeveloped world, much less the "vanguard" role of the proletariat in that partnership.[16]

Workers' and Peasants' Nationalism

Marx and Engels and most of their earlier followers regarded nationalism, along with religion, as a major opiate of the people: a drug foisted upon them by their bourgeois masters. Lenin, however, in reanalyzing the world at the turn of the century, came to realize that from the Communist point of view, the national and colonial problems were fused as a "national–colonial question" as far as the people who suffered under the yoke of imperialism were concerned.[17] Present-day Soviet theorists have carried the implications of Lenin's analyses further. Even in the industrially advanced societies, nationalism is no longer regarded as all bad. Thus in the bourgeois society, there are really "two nations."[18] Of course, between the extremes there are all gradations of petty bourgeois types, on the one hand, and semiproletarians, on the other hand. Within the capitalist nations, however, an important distinction needs to be made between the nationalistic opiate fostered by the bourgeoisie and the revolutionary nationalism held by the working people. Not only is the latter seen as embodying a true revolutionary spirit but also it is said to include the element of international solidarity described by Marx. In short, the tortuous path of neorevisionism has been reflected in the description of some forms of nationalism as genuinely progressive and thus internationalist.[19] In analyzing the changing status of the peoples suffering under present-day colonialism and neocolonialism, the transformation has been even more tortuous.

Professor Kanet has observed that the progressive revolutionary forces in the former colonial areas may even include the national bourgeoisie.[20] In sum, Lenin's alteration of the slogan "Proletarians of all countries, unite," to "Proletarians of all countries, and oppressed nations, unite," which he made at the Second Congress of the Communist Internationale, reflects the view of the Leninists that virtually all nationalistic forces in opposition to the status quo in the underdeveloped nations must be counted as progressive, and that the most important of all the fuels feeding the revolutionary flames is the force of nationalism. According to one Soviet writer, nationalism has become then "the natural ally" of the world's "Socialist" movement.[21] True, whether a national liberation movement involves a nominally free, but "politically and economically dependent nation" (that is, "the semicolonies" or a nation still suffering under the total yoke of colonialism), there will be important elements of reaction feeding on the nationalist spirit.[22] Thus, nationalism can never be regarded as a purely Socialist revolutionary force. Nevertheless, even though a movement may start out to be predominantly national, according to the (former?) head of the Indonesian Communist party writing in *Kommunist*, it will "ultimately" turn to the true Socialist path.*[23]

The majority of the peoples in the colonial and former colonial areas of Africa, Asia, and Latin America are peasants, and their alliance with the working class is seen as "the most important force of the national liberation movement."[24] Furthermore, as noted earlier, the Soviet ideologists still claim that to be a Leninist is to stress the key role of the workers, whereas the Chinese have wrongly elevated the peasantry to first place. In this writer's opinion, however, although the Chinese may reasonably be charged with being less literally correct in their reading of Lenin, they have the argument of the history of their own revolution and that of the Soviet revolution as points of reference. Indeed, Mao is not all wrong in arguing that the major class struggle in the world is between the countryside and the cities. Moreover, drawing on the model of their own revolution, Soviet writers themselves sometimes speak of the possibility of by-passing capitalism, whereby underdeveloped, predominantly peasant nations can transform themselves directly from feudalism to socialism without the intervening stage of capitalism. Thus, one Soviet theorist describes this as a "new law of social development."[26] In short, although the differences between the two major powers on the subject of the role of the peasants in wars of national liberation seems large at first, a close analysis of the theoretical arguments implies that positions taken by the two sides are really not very far apart. Given the will, this ideological breach could be repaired easily.

Sacred Wars

In the Soviet analysis of the Leninist doctrine of imperialism, although all national liberation movements need not take the form of war, when they do, they become "sacred wars."[27] Virtually all wars

---

* However, as Prof. Kanet indicates from his most recent research, there is emerging a small group of Soviet analysts who are becoming more pessimistic in their evaluation of current developments in the "third world." Some even go so far as to question whether the national liberation movement will necessarily evolve into a Socialist movement.[25]

since the Second World War are regarded as conflicts of national liberation which add up to being a key factor in weakening the capitalist system.[28] However, this progressive force long antedates the Bolshevik Revolution; indeed, even the American Revolution is described as a war of national liberation.[29] The primary target of all such wars is, of course, imperialism with the major focus now on the United States which serves as world capitalism's "gendarme."[30] As in the Soviet model, at least as long as the fighting continues, a revolution, often a multiparty affair, may even include the national bourgeoisie.[31] The Bolshevik revolution was the most important model which provided not only the beginning of the "socialist" world but also the programatic legislation which all subsequent struggles would do well to copy.[32] Nevertheless, each revolution is special. Even the army, in many cases, specifically in Egypt, Burma, Algeria, and Syria, can be important.[33]

Like the Catholic theology and other ideologies that have managed to persist over time, Marxism–Leninism has shown an extraordinary ability to adjust its doctrine to fit changing circumstances. Marx described a world in which revolution was imminent because of forces of decay in the industrially advanced societies. Nationalism was considered to be one of the greatest of all human evils; spontaneous class consciousness was to be the bearer of change. Now, nationalism is equated to internationalism; disciplined parties play the vanguard role. Even though Soviet theorists still speak of the lead role of the workers in the world revolution, some of their analyses imply (and Chinese theorists assert) that the peasantry of the world are in the forefront of the class struggle. Neither Europe nor North America, but, according to the new ideology, underdeveloped Asia, Africa, and Latin America are the settings upon which the play of the future is being staged.

Lenin's wife Krupskaya summed up the importance of imperialism and much of the essence of Leninism in her observation that "To be able to study new situations and problems in the light of the experience of the revolutionary struggle of the world proletariat, to apply Marxist method to the analyses of new concrete situations—that is the special substance of Leninism."[34]

The Spark,
Democratic
Centralism, and
Critical Evaluation

As indicated earlier, Lenin never openly contradicted the Marxian view that a genuine Communist revolution would occur only in an industrialized setting, one in which a proletarian majority was ripe in its class consciousness for seizing power. True, the main thrust of both his actions and his words provided support for Stalin's later conclusion that socialism could be built in one state (e.g., the USSR) without awaiting the onset of the international revolution in the industrially advanced states. Yet Lenin did insist, as late as 1918, that "It is obligatory for a Marxist to count on a European revolution if a *revolutionary situation* is at hand."[35] To his death, therefore, although he had sown the seeds for a further revision of the doctrine, he retained an outward expression of a belief in the inevitability, indeed the immediacy, of a Europeanwide Communist revolution. The rationale, therefore, of staging a Communist *coup d'etat* in Russia in 1917 rested on the idea of the "spark" and the closely related Trotsky concept of the "permanent revolution."

As implied previously, the *iskra* theory was based on two premises: First, the proletarian class consciousness had reached such a point in Western Europe that the revolution would occur at any time. In fact, many of the faithful fully believed that rather than fighting in the first great "Imperialist War" (World War I), the working masses of Europe would join hands and reject their capitalist masters' bidding to the trenches. Second, since the tinder of Europe had reached the flash point, only the slightest encouragement would be needed to touch it off. Specifically, therefore, Lenin and his followers justified their takeover in Russia with the argument that the encouragement their action would give their Western brothers would act as a spark and ignite the Western revolution. Moreover, expressing the "international solidarity" of the oppressed masses, once the revolution had been achieved successfully in the industrial nations, the new workers' regimes would eagerly and massively come to the aid of their Russian brothers, helping them to pass rapidly and easily through the necessary period of industrialization. In essence, this would allow the merger of the capitalist and Socialist revolutions so that Russia could relatively quickly and painlessly travel from her late feudal stage into the early stages of socialism. Here, then, was a functional revolution with some states ahead, but less developed, others temporarily behind, but more developed, and a permanent sort of rapid change in that new, stepped-up revolutions would continue to develop indefinitely until that now unclear point in time when the whole world would be Communist.

Here again, the Leninist party, acting as a vanguard, was of vital significance. Only the national Parties, both guiding the particular revolutionary stage in the home country and working with the Parties in other states in the Internationale, could direct the intricate forces at work in the permanent revolutionary setting. It would be a difficult undertaking requiring strict Party discipline, and that is where democratic centralism would come into the picture. All comrades in the Party were theoretically equal. All decisions of importance, therefore, should be made by the fullest participation of the entire membership. Yet, in order to get the everyday tasks done and to remove all possibility of the internal dissension that had so weakened Parties elsewhere and had been responsible for the earlier breakup of the Social Democratic party, the comrades must agree not to question policy once it had been decided upon. Debate over policy-making should be completely open and free during the formulation stage, but key to the discipline demanded of a Leninist party member was the agreement that once a decision is made, all members must act in concert, as though the policy had been entirely their own idea in the beginning. Once policy was made, further criticism was encouraged, but only over how the policy was being carried out, or directed at individual failure in executing the policy, but never against the policy itself.

The impracticability of trying to join meaningful democracy with centralism as a principle of political decision-making reflects the nature of Lenin's most widely read work *State and Revolution* which, in fact, is the least representative of all his writings.[36] Although the balance of his work is hardheaded, shrewd, and practical analysis, *State and Revolution* is the product of a man dreaming of what ought to be. True, what he has to say about the future state does faithfully reflect the utopian element of Marxism, and its woolgathering may have been most important to Lenin, and certainly to his followers, as providing emotional attraction for the cause, but as the early weeks of Soviet rule proved, his outline of how to run a state was totally impractical.

In the tract Lenin stressed his conviction of the imminence of the European revolution. Indeed, his optimism carried him to the extreme of implying that Russia was prepared to become a democracy, enjoying the Marxian concept of popular sovereignty—i.e., a sociopolitical system that really would not be a state. Social cooperation would be so great that, for example, there would be no need for either an army or police force. Those few governmental positions that are essential would be filled by the general populace taking turns. After all, he argued, any female trained to do the accounting necessary to being a good cook could fit her talents to running society. The total lack of reality in the book and the fact that it was aside from the major thrust of Lenin's writings, is revealed by the discovery that the Communist party is not mentioned once in the entire work.

The study is important, however, because in the early weeks of Soviet rule, Lenin tried to make his dreams reality. This was during the "Honeymoon" period that ended in the full outbreak of "War Communism" (the 1918–1921 Civil War). In those early days the Bolshevik leadership's attitude was that Nirvana had arrived. For example, during the early part of the armistice negotiations with the Germans at Brest-Litovsk, the Bolsheviks were completely uncooperative. Their point of view was that states produce treaties, most of which are evil. In effect, they were saying, "We will not be a state; we are international; we will have no foreign policy and sign no armistice." Only after the German army renewed its advance did the leadership feel compelled to act as a state in negotiating with the Germans. Similarly, on the home front legislation such as complete wage equality was passed. Capital punishment was abandoned. The workers were told to form committees and run the factories. The time for utopia, however, had not yet arrived, and reality soon caught up with the leadership, forcing them to abandon *State and Revolution* as a guide to practical political affairs.

Lenin's place in history is hard to overrate. Whatever view one may have of his ideas and actions, no other man has had as much influence over the course of events in the twentieth century as Lenin. The vast majority of the world's Marxists think of themselves first as Leninists. All of the nations that have become Communist subscribe to Lenin's ideas, and when they quarrel among themselves, they argue that their policies are more truly Leninist than those of their opponents are. Many intellectuals and political leaders in non-Communist nations subscribe to Lenin's views, particularly in the realm of foreign affairs.

Whatever criticism one may have of the extremes of Lenin's analysis of imperialism, one must credit him with being a major figure in calling attention to its evils, now soundly damned by most of the world's political leaders. Starting with World War I and especially following World War II we have seen colonial nation after colonial nation abandon its empire, some only after revolution, some reluctantly, but some (particularly the British in several instances) with relative grace.

Lenin's stress on nationalism (instead of just the Marxian class warfare) as a major force for change in the world was highly perceptive. Prior to his writings, few appreciated the potential of this enormous emotional element that holds a nation together if for no other reason than a common hatred of former colonial masters. National leaders of nations, such as Nassar in Egypt, may well order the jailing of indigenous Communists and yet share with those who have been jailed a Leninist interpretation of international relations.

Finally, for millions of Soviet citizens, Lenin is the George Washington of Russian liberation from tsardom. Much in Leninism, of course, demands criticism. Imperialism has played a part in modern wars; but not all modern wars, certainly not the two World Wars, can be totally explained by the Leninist point of view. Lenin was a selfless person in his private life, but he was the one who adapted tsarist-like terror tactics and secret police to the Soviet system of rule. Stalin only developed further what Lenin had initiated.

Democratic centralism has its good points. Is it not, after all, what Western political parties attempt to practice, particularly Great Britain where a high degree of party discipline has been achieved? In a sense this is true, but the ruling philosophy of Western political systems is not monolithic. Opposition parties are encouraged as being essential for the preservation of the fullest possible contest of ideas. Therefore, even though dissension from a party policy may result in dismissal or resignation from one's party (Winston Churchill changed parties twice in his career), it does not mean automatic ruin of one's career, much less loss of liberty or life. In some cases, such as Churchill's, dissension may in the long run even actually further one's political career.

Much more should be said by way of critical evaluation of Leninism, but we shall conclude here by objecting to Lenin's insistence upon carrying to the extreme the authoritarian line in Marxism. Perhaps, if the Mensheviks had been the inheritors of the Tsarist throne, the USSR would have evolved into a parliamentary open society. Perhaps today Russia would closely resemble the democratic Socialist systems that characterize so much of Europe. Lenin, however, only extended the Marxist strain that truth was monolithic, stifling the pluralism that might have produced opposition parties and a parliamentary system. Leninism is a major root of contemporary Soviet ideology, and to the degree that ideas hold sway over history, Stalin should not receive the whole blame for the authoritarian nature of the Soviet political system. In short, unless Leninism is abandoned or at least drastically revised, one should not be too optimistic about the apparent liberal trends in the post-Stalin Soviet system. Leninism is essentially extreme authoritarianism.

CHAPTER 5

Soviet Nationalism

Stalinism:
Socialism
in One State

STALIN, unlike Marx and Lenin, contributed no seminal ideas to the doctrine of Communist rule. Therefore, a discussion of his contribution to the Soviet system in a section devoted to ideology may seem out of place. However, if one defines ideology broadly, that is, as the sum total of all the beliefs held by a society and its leaders, then Stalin's quarter of rule (1928–1953) must be recognized as having had an enormous impact on Soviet thought.

Ideology understood in this light consists of beliefs arising from deliberate theorizing as well as accepted interpretations of what has been done in the past. Indeed, perhaps most of what men do is based upon principle stipulated by theory and practice dictated by precedent. Actions are taken and decisions are made because they fit a familiar pattern that bodes security.

In Stalin's period of rule, little was left untouched by his hand. Moreover, much of what Stalin added to the Soviet system has remained, establishing a pattern of rule which has been altered only slightly since his death.

Yosif Dzhugashvili—later called Koba and then called Stalin (steel)—was born in 1879 in Georgia, in western Transcaucasia. He was the son of a poor, drunken shoemaker who, according to biographer Isaac Deutscher, left his wife to shift for herself and her son. Since Stalin's mother was ambitious for her son's future, and since they were very poor, she arranged for him to attend free Church schools, first at Gorki and later at Tiflis, where, as a good pupil, he remained until he was expelled at the age of twenty for reading subversive books and joining an underground debating society.

Like Lenin, Stalin's underground studies worked to transform him into a Marxist. In the early 1900s he often was in prison or in exile, although with the exception of one or two brief trips to the West, he remained within the country. His role became that of propagandist and agitator for the Leninist cause as well as supplier of Party funds through such activities as helping to direct a bank robbery in Tiflis.

Early, Lenin saw Stalin as a valuable contributor to the cause, and he appointed him to the Central Committee in 1912. Stalin's major achievement, in Lenin's eyes, grew out of a few weeks he spent in Poland where he produced a study of the nationality problem with special emphasis upon its relationship to the Party. This accomplishment seems to be the primary reason why Stalin was given the specific post of Commissariat of Nationalities when the Soviet government was created in 1917.

At the Eleventh Party Congress in 1922, Stalin was elected General Secretary of the Party, and the opportunities this position provided for control within the Party, combined with his enormous skill as an organizer, served him well in his quest for Lenin's mantle, which he finally acquired in 1928. Indeed, reviewing the history of the Lenin succession struggle, one realizes that Stalin, in the inconsistency of his positions, was really the most consistent of all those involved. True, Trotsky remained rather uniform in his more radical points of view, and others were relatively faithful to their conservative attitudes, but Stalin was completely consistent as a clever organizer aspiring to the leadership of the Party. He

played one side against the other, now joining the right to help
defeat the left opposition, then swinging to the left and using its
forces and arguments to defeat his colleagues on the right. This was
true, for example, on the key issue of forced collectivization of
agriculture. Prior to 1928, Stalin had opposed Trotsky's call for
forced collectivization, but by the end of the 1920s when Trotsky
had been eliminated as a contender for the leadership, Stalin became the prime mover of the forced collectivization campaign. In
fact, Stalin's final stand on this issue represented one of his major
ideological breaks with Leninism.

Perhaps, Stalin's employment of his zigzag tactics to the extreme ought to be described as the Stalinist syndrome for achieving
top leadership positions, particularly in an authoritarian system.
Over and above consistency in political philosophy, is not success
in making and breaking alliances that serve as stepping stones to
greater power a common trait among such leaders?

The Soviet leaders had inherited a predominantly peasant nation, and after the devastation of the economy by the Civil War
(1918–1921) following on the heels of the First World War,
Lenin realized that in some way the economy must be revitalized
and the peasants pacified if the Soviet Union were to survive. He
correctly read the seriousness of the revolt of the Kronstadt sailors,
who were predominantly peasant in origin and who had played
an important part in the 1917 takeover. Lenin's answer was the
NEP (New Economic Policy, 1921–1928), in which the guiding
line was his famed "one step backward for two steps forward"
could be taken to socialism. The liberalization and denationaliza-
tion that followed was primarily for the peasants and agriculture,
and Lenin's writings emphasized that however ideologically desirable agricultural collectivization might be, such a rural revolution could never be accomplished without gaining the peasants'
voluntary acceptance by convincing them that collectivized farming
was superior to family cultivation.

By the end of the 1920s, however, Stalin had gained control
over the Party, and he concluded that collectivization had to be
achieved through force, for both ideological and politicoeconomic
reasons. Collective farms would allow the Party to control the
peasantry and would provide a means by which the regime could
extract the peasants' produce, at a minimum cost, which would

pay for Stalin's all-out industrialization drive. Of course, the need to prove one's fealty to Marxism–Leninism remained, and so in his famed "Dizzy-with-Success" speech, Stalin's warning against excessive use of force sounded as though he had not ordered a bloody "revolution from above" (his own words).[1] Indeed, even today, the false myth is perpetuated that what force there was in the collectivization drive was initiated by the poorer peasants against the wealthy *kulaks* ("tight fists").* In spite of the pretense, however, the truth is surely much closer to Stalin's conclusion that the Leninist tenet of volunteerism was wrong, that once captured in *kolkhozy* ("collective farms") and *sovkhozy* ("state farms"), the peasant mass would quickly perceive their superiority over the old farming system. In short, the horse would change his mind about not wanting a drink once he was hurled into the river.

The instruments used by Stalin to achieve collectivization were known as "committees of the poor." These committees provided not only the rationale for the pretense that collectivization was voluntary but also the pattern for a key element of popular control still used in the USSR. Zealous comrades were sent from the cities to the villages. There they organized the poorer and less secure peasants into committees to form collective farms and to force the more well-to-do kulak peasants, who were reluctant to abandon private cultivation, into the collectives as well. Thousands of these committees were formed throughout the nation. They were so successful that Stalin became concerned with their excesses, and in his "Dizzy-with-Success" speech expressing the view that in pushing the drive too far and too fast, the zealous comrades had raised a widespread and dangerous animosity among the peasantry.

These committees were somewhat similar to the vigilantes who took law into their own hands in America's early West. However, whereas such groups are frowned upon in the present-day United States, they are still employed in the USSR to engender mass emotion and to encourage the use of ostracism and other means of social sanction against individual recalcitrants. The current "People's Militia" is an example. Another key difference is in their organization and leadership. In U.S. history, most such groups

---

* Thus, in the most recent denunciation of this writer's analyses of Soviet agricultural politics, a Soviet critic takes me to task for my asserted misuse of the term "force" in describing the creation of the collective farms.[2]

formed spontaneously, and virtually all were of local character and were regarded as extralegal, if not in actual violation of the law and central authority. By contrast, such groups in the USSR were and are initiated and directed from the center in order to accomplish aims prescribed by the top Party leadership.

Lenin had used force to capture the revolution, and he had used terror against his political opponents. Stalin employed both in the countryside to force the peasants into the collectives. The 1930s brought the mass purges of the Party, and terror became a weapon for eliminating internal Party opposition (even individuals only suspected of being possible opponents). Thus nationwide force and terror came to be regarded as essential instruments for saving the revolution and creating socialism in one state.

Stalin's decision to end the NEP was explained by the argument that since the possibility of revolution in Western Europe seemed to be receding, if Communist socialism were to be preserved in Mother Russia, it had to be a do-it-yourself project. Socialism (and, emphatically, a strong Soviet state, whatever its politics) was inconceivable without industrialization. Therefore, from 1928 until after Stalin's death, industrialization at all costs, under such slogans as "All Priority to Heavy Industry," became the preoccupation of the entire Soviet society and economy.

Stalin's successors speak of the "cult of personality" as having wrongly dominated his rule at the expense of Leninist democratic centralism. One assumes that Lenin recognized the self-contradiction in the concept, perhaps hoping that democracy might eventually come after the society had been strengthened by centrally led change. Stalin, however, eliminated democracy completely, emphasizing centralism to the point that Lenin's elite Party became totally subsumed under the ego of one man, the *vozhd* ("leader"). The bloody purges of the 1930s so seriously decimated the Party that Arthur Koestler's book *Darkness at Noon* echoed the truth in the imprisoned Rubishov's words, "The old guard is dead."[3] This was done in the name of Party unity and infallibility, but the practice proved that the only infallible Party member was the General Secretary. The will and the caprice of Stalin became the only reliable law in the USSR for more than two decades.

In the realm of world affairs, although the Communist internationalism of Marx and Lenin had clearly implied that world communism following a worldwide revolution should always be kept as the paramount goal, Stalin quite consistently practiced a foreign policy of narrow isolationism, until the capture of the East European states after the Second World War. True, fear of a Nazi invasion produced a period in the mid-thirties when the USSR called for League of Nations action against the Fascist threat. Moreover, the Kremlin-disciplined Internationale continued to function in many nations. Yet the flirtation with the League and the discipline imposed upon foreign comrades was all pointed at strengthening the security of the USSR, which was pictured as the base for an increasingly ill-defined, ever more distant world revolution.

Strengthening the Soviet system, while at the same time extending Stalin's control over it, required the tightest knit organization possible. Thus, while asserting that bureaucracy (a negative capitalist phenomenon) had been rooted out of the USSR, Stalin proceeded to fashion the most powerful, all-encompassing bureaucratic system known in the history of mankind. All but the kolkhoz peasants (who Khrushchev was to capture in the mid-fifties) were subsumed under the hierarchy of controls and rewards at whose peak stood Stalin.

The government setup was not the only leviathan. Stalin encouraged the "gigantomania" that came to influence so much of the Soviet attitude. Russia's leaders had long expressed a pride in vast expanses; Russia was huge and capable of any achievement. Stalin welded this traditional feeling of unlimited potential with the optimistic streak in Marxism–Leninism. Communist science was said to be capable of transforming nature itself. Similarly, the best farms and the best factories were supposedly the largest. Machines designed for cultivating Soviet fields were huge alongside their counterparts in other nations. The industrial way was said, by definition, to be large scale. Industrialization was to be adapted to virtually every phase of Soviet production, and gigantomania came to dominate much of Soviet life.

"Stalinism" brings to the minds of many, rule by terror. Stalin did institutionalize terror as a prime instrument of Soviet rule for a quarter century, but as we have tried to emphasize, Stalinism was much more than just terror, and most of the institutional forms and practices that he emplanted still flourish in the USSR. His "cult of the personality" has been damned, and yet the force of precedent combined with Khrushchev's personality allowed the latter to repeat this sin against the Leninist principle of collective leadership. Terror is gone, but under Brezhnev and Kosygin, repression in the literary realm probably was greater at the end of the 1960s than at any other time since Stalin's death in 1953. The all-encompassing bureaucracy now includes the kolkhoz peasants, as well. Isolationism is no longer practiced to the extent of maintaining an "iron curtain," yet, restrictions on travel both to and within the USSR remain enormous. The Stalinist pretense that the collective farms are based upon internal "kolkhoz democracy" remains. Heavy industry no longer receives virtually all priority, but it is still the most heavily favored segment of the economy. In spite of the drive for decentralization, expressed in such innovations as the Liberman proposals, extreme centralism still rules.

Change in the USSR is real, and in recent years the rate of that change seems to be accelerating. However, with the major exception of the downgrading of terror, the beliefs and practices that became ingrained in the system during Stalin's rule still predominate.

*Current Beliefs**   Although many Western observers of the USSR question the importance of Marxist–Leninist theory in current Soviet society, this writer has found considerable evidence that it does, indeed, still provide a meaningful basis for the sociopolitical beliefs of the Soviet Union. In the first place, budget-conscious Soviet leaders appropriate millions of rubles each year for promoting the virtues of Marxism–Leninism among the populace. Although the Soviet people undoubtedly exercise some selectivity in response to the Soviet brand of advertising, they are deluged with Soviet ideological propaganda dispensed by skilled hucksters with a virtual monopoly over the market. How could the citizenry avoid a certain amount of receptivity? Furthermore, Soviet leaders cannot ignore this market, since common beliefs are the essential strands for binding a society together in peaceful relationships. No society ever has become stable without having evolved a common public myth. Soviet society is relatively stable,

* The balance of this chapter incorporates much of the material the author first published in an article in the journal *Soviet Studies*.[4]

and if Marxism–Leninism is not central to the national beliefs that cement it together, what is? The Church certainly does not play the adhesive role in Soviet society that it does in Western Christian states.

One point should be made quite clear, however. If Communist dogma ever was a rigid ideological guideline for the Soviet leaders' actions, this is no longer the case. Marx as the god is dead! Indeed, the probable date of the fatality was the end of the "honeymoon of the revolution," in early 1918, with Lenin as the executioner. Lenin's highly pragmatic political sense, coupled with the early discovery that utopia could not be realized just because a society had experienced a revolution in the name of Marxism, surely inspired a growing awareness that Communist doctrine is an insufficient guideline for organizing and managing society. Yet, throughout his life, Lenin always thought of himself as a good Marxist.

The pragmatism of the Soviet leadership has spoken louder than their doctrinal fealty, but the scholar, attempting to understand Soviet affairs, should resist the tendency of swinging to the opposite extreme in an attempt to impose upon the Communists a standard of rigid adherence to doctrine that has not been observable in other belief systems. God may never have been, but, at least since the Reformation, devout Christians have openly quarreled over the content of their dogma. Indeed, the very churchmen who today join the argument that God is dead do so while simultaneously expressing a conviction that facing up to new reality will help to strengthen the Church. Although a modern theologian may believe that Christ was mortal, he also believes that Christ's ministry was inspired teaching that still provides the best possible direction for human relationships. Left out by too many atheist–agnostic critics of Christian societies and un-Marxian critics of the USSR is an adequate accounting for the reality that universally in most cultures, men, by necessity, have been believing animals, forced by their emotions to create personal and social myth-systems which may, or may not, be scientifically verifiable, but which do provide the tentative answers and guidelines necessary for coping with the problems of life. As the pioneering psychiatrist Jung observed, these myths (his term was "the great religions") have always been essential for the preservation of individual sanity. Moreover, when key elements of such myths are collectively shared by the members of a society, the warp and woof of meaningful communication is supplied from which the fabric of a community or nation can be woven. Everywhere, men are hypocritical in the name of immediate wants and needs. Yet, when serious disagreements over beliefs arise among segments of a society, the seeds of revolution are sown. If the proponents of the functional approach to political science are correct in concentrating upon the process of political socialization (i.e., the development of a viable polity through the successful employment of methods by which political values, attitudes, and knowledge are transmitted within a society), then surely the most important inputs are those which help to create and to maintain a common belief-system.

Obviously, as Professor Alec Nove pointed out in his article "Was Stalin Really Necessary?"[5] there were important economic reasons for Stalinist terror, yet the most important (though unspoken) reason behind Stalin's method of rule may have been that fear was the key ingredient which would allow the Bolshevik leadership to hold the potentially revolutionary elements of Soviet society at bay until a new society-binding myth of Soviet nationalism could be created. By 1953, enough of the strands of a new belief-system had been created for Soviet society not to fall apart when Stalin's successors abandoned terror as a key element of Soviet rule.

Western social scientists should spend more time identifying the strands of the new Soviet nationalism. Nevertheless, there is enough evidence at this point to conclude that the key sources of the new myth are traditional Russian nationalism (largely allowed to be revived by Stalin during World War II), Marxist–Leninist doctrines, and axioms derived from the pragmatic lessons of Soviet success.

Undoubtedly, the Party leadership is disturbed by such findings as that of a sociological survey of a representative agricultural area in which 57% of the ordinary, collective farm members were found to have icon corners in their homes. (However, in the homes of the skilled agricultural workers, only 7% had such icons.) The surprising point to the Western observer is that evidently approximately half of the rural society (perhaps the most dissident segment of Soviet life) gives evidence of having evolved a new belief-system.[6] Moreover, even among those who retain their icons, there is reason to assume that important elements of the Communist propaganda have been absorbed. After all, Western anthropologists have repeatedly discovered that among once-pagan peoples converted to Christianity, there almost always exists an amalgam of beliefs in which the old gods still play an important part. More to the present point, the extensive Harvard interviews of early post-World War II Soviet émigrés revealed that even among this most disenchanted element of Soviet society, a remarkable number of Communist values were carried over into their new lives.

Again today, as in Tsarist times, there is evidence of widespread dissent among the intellectuals, as expressed in private conversations and the underground circulation of manuscripts. Here again, however, the careful observer will discover that not all the new Soviet values are being discarded. Indeed, a favorite theme seems to be an agonizing over the failure of the leadership to live up to the ideology's promises. Any society's patterns of belief must be altered if the challenge of changing circumstances is to be met, but where is the example of a society that, without a prolonged and bloody revolution, engaged in a wholesale abandonment of the beliefs championed by its political élite for as long as half a century?

Certainly in 1917, only a small number of revolutionaries subscribed to Bolshevism. However, the area of common Marxist belief, possessed not only by the Bolsheviks and Mensheviks but also by most of the revolutionary groups, was impressive. Surely the Soviet ideology has been transformed, but hardly to the point where Marxism–Leninism has become relatively meaningless. Soviet society cannot take Marxism–Leninism lightly when in but half a century the leadership has guided the transformation of backward Tsarist Russia into the world's second major power—all in the name of the ideology. Moreover, with all the serious failings in the system and the inhuman sacrifices imposed by Stalin, the lot of the individual citizen has improved. The beliefs that sponsored the sacrifices for improvement cannot be repudiated or easily forgotten. Undoubtedly, both the doctrinal rigidity and certain specific elements of the earlier doctrine are now privately doubted by many, if not most, of the citizens and leaders alike. Yet, short of another revolution, Khrushchev surely was right in asserting that the Soviet Union will abandon communism "when shrimps learn to whistle."

Some Western observers of the Soviet scene believe that

Khrushchev's secret speech on the crimes of Stalin destroyed not only the deity of Stalin, but since so much of Soviet history had been Stalin's brand of Marxism–Leninism, the ideology may well have been destroyed as well. But one must ask again: If Stalin's wrathful, Old Testament Marxism is dead, what new social myth has taken its place? Soviet ideology may be undergoing radical change, yet now that the flames of the fire ignited by Khrushchev's speech are dying down, the new body of Soviet beliefs that is emerging may prove to be strikingly similar to the old phoenix.

There are those who believe that ideology has had little import upon Soviet policy that, for example, it has had no positive impact upon agricultural policy where, at best, the influence has been negative, merely limiting the range of possible decisions.[7] A closer look at decision-making in that area, however, suggests that ideology has, after all, played an important positive role. True, in the most crucial of all Soviet agricultural decisions, Stalin did use a lie in attempting to prove Leninist support for forced collectivization. However, although a review of Lenin's writings will show that he repeatedly argued that collectivization could be satisfactorily achieved only by persuasion, i.e., without coercion, he also emphasized that the need to adopt large-scale collective and mechanized agriculture constituted an "indisputable theoretical truth." Therefore, although collectivization offered Stalin an attractive economic promise for extracting from the peasantry the necessary capital for industrialization, collectivization also was a doctrinal imperative that sooner or later must be carried out. Had Lenin lived another score of years without bringing the peasant majority of society into some form of a collective system, such a failure surely would have destroyed any meaningful argument that the new system was building communism.

As implied earlier, a closer look at the evolving Soviet agricultural myth will reveal roots in the growing amalgam of pragmatic experience, traditional nationalism, and Marxist–Leninist doctrine. For example, the tradition of the mir, the commune, and the very village way of life was so strong that important distinctions existed between Russian peasant culture and that of the more individualistic Western farmers. Marx was not entirely wrong in seeing parallels between Communist prognostications and Russian rural experience under the tsars.

In this writer's opinion, Western observers of the Soviet scene tend to ignore ideological motivation in Soviet agricultural decision-making. Although it is true that for every major agricultural decision, economic or political explanations can be found, this fact does not prove that material or power considerations have always provided the prime motivation for agricultural decisions. The more tangible nature of economic and power factors may make them seem to be more important than they actually are. The following incomplete list contains examples wherein such relatively tangible explanations seems so weak, or where the actions taken seem to be so contrary to the alternatives which a relatively objective outsider might have selected as best serving the needs of the system, that Soviet myths must be credited with having provided the primary motivating factor:

1. If ideology were the prime determinant of policy, one might expect the more ideologically pure state farms to have dominated the countryside from the beginning rather than the less pure collective farms. Yet, in the early years, Stalin did set up huge "state grain factories" which failed. Furthermore, although the asserted ideological superiority of the sovkhozy ("state farms") over the kolkhozy ("collective farms") has been played down somewhat in the post-Stalin years, there is still indication of a widespread belief among the Party leaders that the sovkhozy are at least somewhat closer to the ultimate agricultural form. However, when state subsidies and other preferences given to the sovkhozy are allowed for, there remains no indication that they have been more efficient as production units than the kolkhozy. Furthermore, not since the heavy infusion of the Party into the collectives in the 1950s has there been any indication that state farms are more politically responsive than collectives. Nevertheless, in the period after 1950, the sovkhozy were greatly expanded, largely (although not entirely) at the expense of the kolkhozy. What more satisfactory explanation of this phenomenon is there than that to a great extent ideological belief has guided the decision-makers?
2. Both the size of the farms and the size of the brigades serving as work units can partially be explained by the need for controls over the peasants and their product. However, and especially in view of evidence indicating a much higher level of effi-

ciency in the small *zveno* ("link" or "team," composed of about a half-dozen people) work units, there is hardly any compelling economic argument for maintaining the present huge brigades (each probably averaging over 100 individuals) as the most desirable form of work unit. A review of the evolution of both the farms and the brigades into ever larger units supports the conclusion that agricultural gigantomania—rooted both in Marxian and traditional Russian beliefs—has been the primary motivating factor.

3. A combination of the authoritarian leadership's insatiable seeking of even tighter controls and Stalin's decision to concentrate virtually all effort on industrial growth was probably behind many of the post-World War II rural administrative reforms. Will such factors, however, account for either the frequency of the reforms or the fact that each time such reforms were announced, the leadership indulged in grandiose predictions of success, thereby exposing itself to later criticism when they failed? Of course, the Western observer would be partially right in answering, "But this was a form of irrationality. Have not Khrushchev's successors finally admitted that agriculture has long needed a substantial increase in investment?" Irrationality, however, is the point. Since science cannot provide men with all the necessary answers, other less supportable elements of the web of belief must fill in. Surely, many attitudes toward rural reforms can be explained only by the leadership's conviction that the kolkhoz–sovkhoz system really is superior; therefore, if only the magic formula of ordering local (and local-central) relationships can be found, the system will achieve the Communist promise.

4. Finally, in our opinion, the most important of all the myths that must be regarded as having an influence over Soviet agricultural decisions is the belief, fashioned from scientism and the asserted science of Marxism–Leninism which reached a peak in Lysenkoism,* that science can apply its magic formulas and solve all the major problems of society.

Surely there is a basis for worry over the growth of scientism in the West; too many believe that just as the natural scientists have used their mathematical disciplines to build super weapons

---

* Lysenko was the Marxist–Leninist biologist whose doctrines dominated Soviet biology for so long.

and produce wonder drugs, so such precise techniques can be employed to solve the problems of human relations. Yet, in addition to the optimism in the West there is a long tradition of religious and philosophical scepticism involving a belief that there are limits both to the knowable and to human achievement because man is not perfect. In contrast, communism is dominated by faith in material and human perfectibility. Perhaps most of the contemporary Soviet leaders no longer believe in the utopian dream of communism, but the over-optimistic belief in the promise of progress seems to remain.

Lysenkoism and the accompanying distortion of genetic theory may at last be laid to rest, but not all the other extravagant promises of science for agriculture. For example, his assertions about decisive advantages to be gained from a wholesale adoption in agriculture of manufacturing production processes and industrial administrative forms constituted one of Lenin's major claims to being a scientist of administration. From his time to the present there has persisted a belief that industrial experiences are wholly adaptable to agriculture. Moreover the belief persists that when such a marriage has been successfully consummated, the union will give birth to a wealth of scientific discoveries the exploitation of which will result in a growth in agricultural production rivaling the rates of growth achieved by industry. Perhaps the Soviet adherents of scientism are right, but such views are not in line with those of Western agricultural authorities who point to the relative limitations on rates of food-production growth. For example, in a pin factory in which the plant area is confined to only an acre of land, modern machinery will out produce the output rate of production-by-hand by the millionfold. In comparison, an acre that had been producing fifty bushels of wheat, even if put under glass and tilled with the use of all known scientific aids, cannot be induced to increase its output by as much as ten times. Undoubtedly, if confronted with such a statement of the relative promise of dimensions of growth, the individual Soviet agricultural scientist (even the individual Party leader) would admit its validity. Yet, the past and present records lead one to expect that the stress upon the promise science holds for food production has been out of proportion to similar expectations in the West.

After half a century of Communist rule, the official Party

ideology cannot claim a monoply on Soviet beliefs. Nevertheless, for any foreseeable future Marxism–Leninism cannot be ignored as a vital, perhaps the most important, source of the Soviet public myth. Furthermore, the political beliefs of Soviet nationalism are probably more important, more passionately held, and yet more passionately doubted in the USSR, than are comparable beliefs in the more stable Western societies.

If the ideology of a system is broadly defined as a combination of what the leaders see as obligatory for the future, theorists' attempts to describe present reality, and the citizens' common core of beliefs, the following might represent a partial catalogue of the more important elements of contemporary Soviet political thought, a major part of Soviet nationalism. Indeed, reading the Soviet press will reveal that the following beliefs are widely championed by one or more of the mentioned sources. There is no intention to contend here that any of these elements of belief are held unanimously by a majority. Nevertheless, they do seem to have an important impact on Soviet society and on political decision-making by the leaders.

1. Socialism, defined in terms of nationalized industry and public services, is believed to be beneficial, since it is regarded as the prime factor that has enabled the USSR to evolve into the world's second most powerful state.

2. Socialism in the form of collectivized agriculture is seen as desirable, since it is regarded as satisfying the need to bring communism to the countryside, as providing an instrument of control over the peasants and their product, and as creating the basis for advancing industrialization of the farms. Gigantomania (drawn both from traditional Russian views and the views of Marxism–Leninism) is an inseparable part of the faith in industrialization and is primarily responsible for the hugeness of both the collective and state farms.

3. Togetherness (based upon the Marxian–Morgan view that man is essentially a communal animal) is viewed as an important element in today's society. Thus, for example, a key feature of an ultramodern apartment complex planned for Moscow would be a common dining room instead of individual kitchens. Assertedly, Soviet women don't want to be bothered with preparing meals for their families.

4. In spite of the implications for profound change that many Westerners see in the implementation of the Liberman proposals (e.g., the adoption of profit as a key motive for production), these tend to be viewed as a Leninist "one step backward for two steps forward." Comprehensive centralized planning is still regarded as a key to organizing the Soviet economy and society.

5. The USSR is seen as being in a transitional stage between the final stage of socialism and dictatorship of the proletariat and the initial stage of communism. In the present stage, such ills of capitalism as classes and bureaucracy have been eliminated, although vestiges of these capitalist institutions still linger in individuals to plague the advance of communism.

6. "Freedom is the perception of necessity"—in other words, a joining of the individual will with the collective will that can be realized only under full communism.

7. Science is viewed as the key to future advance. This view is strongly wedded to the element of optimism inherent in Marxism–Leninism. As a result, a belief in the perfectibility of man and society is much stronger in the USSR than it is in the West.

8. Although there may be a trend to reduce the demand that natural scientists must square their work with Marxism–Leninism, the social scientists are still largely confined to basing their observations on the orthodox.

9. The Party is the infallible depository of truth. Therefore, any errors that are made are never seen as Party faults but rather as faults arising from individual shortcomings.

10. In furthering its monolithic view of truth, the Party is obliged to use the courts, educational institutions, and the media of communications as important instruments of rule, a use that is quite contrary to Western constitutional views of the role of these institutions.

11. The impressive rate of economic growth the USSR has been able to maintain will allow her to catch up with and surpass the USA in the not too distant future.

12. When the USSR has outstripped the USA, the balance of the nations in the world will see the inevitable superiority of the Communist way and will rapidly turn to adapting the Soviet model to their system as the best means for organizing a state and society. In short, with all the tinkering left to be done before perfection

has been achieved, the Soviet paradigm is believed to be the model for organizing human relationships in the future by all mankind.

13. Although dangerously possible, war between the Communist and capitalist states is avoidable. The USA, as the major capitalist state, is increasingly revealing symptoms of its impending doom (e.g., reverses in Vietnam, race riots, student uprisings, and increasing crime rates), and even if war can be avoided, it will collapse as a result of its own inner contradictions.

14. Capitalism has a grip on the non-Communist world that can be broken only by revolution. Thus, the claim of Western states to being democratic is but one of the most important opiates (along with religion and nationalism) that are used to fool the exploited masses.

15. The fires of nationalism that are on the increase in the colonial areas of the world are producing attitudes among the peoples of the underdeveloped nations that are linked with the drive to world communism.

This sampling of Soviet political thought reveals that much change has occurred. Yet, it also reveals that Marxist–Leninist doctrine still has a strong grip. What may the future hold? Marx and Lenin probably will continue to be revered. Nevertheless, as we will argue in a later chapter, there is evidence that the Soviet leaders may have opened Pandora's box in their repeated call in the late 1960s for the development of social sciences in the USSR. Social sciences, as evolved in the West, not only are pragmatic, but are also empirical. Moreover, Western social-science findings have strongly supported pluralistic political systems. To the degree that these findings are the product of true science, the Soviet leadership's call may precipitate the greatest force yet for fundamental change in the Soviet system of rule.

PART III The
Administrative
State

CHAPTER 6

The Hierarchy
and the Political Elite

GOVERNMENT in any political system is carried out largely by the institutions responsible for functions which the political scientist has identified as administrative, legislative, and judicial. In most states these functions are fulfilled by direct agencies of rule, that is, formal institutions which in modern times usually are described in a constitution. As important as such direct institutions of rule may be, however, additional organs of government plus informal public institutions and practices also comprise an important part of the total political process. Therefore, the student of political behavior must search far beyond what may be prescribed constitutionally for an understanding of political reality. This observation holds true for the United States (e.g., political parties are not mentioned in the US Constitution), and it emphatically holds for the Soviet Union wherein the constitution is not a limiting factor on political action. Moreover, the USSR is unique in having evolved the first system of rule wherein virtually the whole of society has been enmeshed into a single bureaucratic hierarchy of rewards and punishments.

Mature Totalitarianism versus a Monohierarchical Polity

In his book *The Machiavellians*, James Burnham attempted to prove that in the final analysis the seeking of power after power is the basis of rule even in assertedly democratic systems. Seen from this point of view, the party system in the United States is merely a sham designed to fool the public into believing that they have some choice of leaders, when in fact the system is merely an arrangement allowing two different segments of a permanent ruling elite to take their turns at filling high public offices. Therefore, in Burnham's eyes the American system is but another authoritarian governmental form.[1]

There are, however, important differences among systems and even among subsystems of the same general type. Certainly, Professor Robert Tucker's charge that too many scholars have been guilty of loosely bandying about the word *totalitarianism* is well taken. Authoritarian regimes of quite a different class from that of the Nazi and Stalinist systems (e.g., Peron's Argentina) have been indiscriminately labeled totalitarian. As Tucker states, the "novel forms of authoritarianism that have arisen... in this century" are better described as "mass-movement regimes."[2] In her book *The Origins of Totalitarianism*, Hanna Arendt maintains that Nazi Germany and the Soviet Union have been the only truly modern totalitarian systems. "Even Mussolini, who was so fond of the term 'totalitarian state,' did not attempt to establish a full fledged totalitarian regime...." Although at the time of the revision of her study, Miss Arendt implied the belief that Communist China had not as yet attained that highest level of authoritarianism, the People's Republic of China surely must now be counted in the exclusive circle.[3] Much work needs to be done in the field of comparative government to expand our understanding of the various forms of authoritarian rule. Nevertheless, just as few students of comparative political systems would deny that the United States' presidential system represents an important subspecies of the modern democratic form, so would most students agree that Germany under Hitler and the USSR under Stalin each constituted an important subspecies of the authoritarian class, which has been correctly called totalitarian. However, under changing circumstances the Soviet Union is, perhaps, better described as monohierarchical.

Western students of politics recognize that some minimal degree of social homogeneity is required before a democratic system can operate. Not only must differences be tolerated, but tolerance of dissent is actually necessary to keep such "open-societies" in operation. Nevertheless, differences among the populace, too great, too deeply held, and (especially) involving fundamental principles, can result in social disintegration and civil war. There are no unamendable clauses, as such, in the American Constitution, but should the American people ever fall to serious quarreling over such basic rights as the freedom of speech, religious worship, and assembly, democracy would be seriously threatened.

Majority rule is essential to democracy, but equally important is the requirement that such systems be so open that no majority can expect to remain permanent. Large, vocal, and tenacious majorities concerned with changing fundamental principles of democratic rule also can be of great danger. Indeed, such early democratic thinkers as Mill and De Tocqueville warned that authoritarian systems could well develop out of democracies if the call for change were buttressed by popular discontent. At least in its inception, such a system would not need to rely on the use of naked force to any greater degree than do modern democracies.

Although history has as yet to provide an example of a true tyranny of the masses arising out of a constitutional democracy, the revelations of modern social scientists concerning the subtle forces that may be employed to effect mass conformity provide cause for thought. In a sense this is a major lesson in the writings of such men as David Riesman ("the other-directed man") and William H. Whyte ("the organization man"). At the present juncture such findings seem to be particularly valuable to an analysis of the Soviet political process. Without terror, how is it that the Soviet Union continues to exhibit such a high level of social and political conformity among its citizens?

As implied earlier, students of comparative politics are still far from fully agreed on all of the basic characteristics of what have been called totalitarian systems, for they are both too new and too few in number to allow a highly sophisticated delineation of

their workings. In our opinion, however, the presence or absence
of totalitarianism should be gauged by two fundamental criteria:
intent and accomplishment. If the ruling philosophy of a society
attempts to encompass every facet of human existence within its
explanation and direction, and the leadership has achieved a notable
level of success in this aim, the system is totalitarian. Terror was
once thought to be a *sine qua non* of totalitarianism. However, the
post-Stalin leadership in the USSR has been able to maintain a
high level of conformity to a monolithic view of truth, without
terror, and since this is the case, we suggest that although terror
is probably essential in the developmental stage of a monohierarchical polity, it is not necessary once a high level of development
has been achieved. True, the Soviet Union can be described as a
"mature totalitarian system." However, as noted in the Introduction,
if "totalitarianism" is an epithet of the cold war, and past usage
of the term has inevitably linked the concept with the imposition
of mass terror on the populace by the leadership, perhaps a new
description is more desirable.

We are, after all searching for an understanding of the Soviet
political system, searching for answers to questions about the location and use of power and authority. "Who gets what, when, and
how?" Inevitably the answers must lie in the knowledge of such
factors as how political relationships are arranged, how decisions
are made, what are the supporting attitudes and institutions for the
use of power and authority.

In the narrow sense, of course, government is the combination
of institutions and practices that fulfill the administrative, legislative, and judicial functions of a polity. Every system must fulfill
these necessary functions if the disaster of anarchy is to be avoided.
Beyond these realms, however, modern political scientists have
increasingly demonstrated that the impact of citizen attitudes and
practices, the operation of nongovernmental organizations such as
parties and pressure groups, and the interactions of those in positions of authority and power, can be as important to shaping the
course of the political process as the three traditionally recognized
branches of government.

As implied, the particular character of any given system will
be determined by many crucial factors. Within the political culture
itself, important determinants will include historical experience,

fundamental beliefs, and attitudes sponsored by levels of economic development. Therefore, before a given system can be described, an analysis of all of these factors as well as particular institutional arrangements should be taken into consideration. Specifically, therefore, the view taken here is that the nature of the Soviet political system after more than half a century of experimentation has been profoundly shaped by several crucial factors that in total describe a unique environmental setting. Key among these crucial factors are the following:

1. Neither the present citizens of the USSR nor their forbears ever enjoyed the fruits of an "open society." Therefore, authoritarian rule is part of the Soviet political culture.

2. Closely related to the history of authoritarian rule is the pattern of personal relationships. Whether we look to the present pattern of cramped city dwellings or the tradition of the *mir* ("village unit") in the countryside, contrasted with other cultures (particularly that of the United States), close interpersonal dependences, as opposed to more individualistic life styles, are found to be the rule among Soviet citizens.

3. Fertilized by the "authoritarian" history, an ideology has thrived that insists upon one view of truth and one uncontested political elite.

4. Economically, the USSR is neither developed nor underdeveloped. Perhaps, it is best described as both. It is the second largest industrial power in the world, and yet it supports a very inefficient and underdeveloped agrarian system. Therefore, Soviet politics are influenced by factors common both to developed and underdeveloped political systems.

5. Politically, the USSR has undergone a process of modernization, but this has not always been characterized by changes considered common to other modernized societies—e.g., the evolution of parties in Japan.

6. Multiple demands, particularly economic (i.e., "all priority to industrial development") and political (i.e., the Party is interested in "everything") have served to fashion an ever-growing, all encompassing hierarchy of controls and rewards that peaks in the hands of the top Party leadership and spreads out to encompass nearly every human activity in the Soviet Union.

7. The dictatorship's desire for all-encompassing controls has worked to fashion institutions (most of which are familiar in other societies) and practices (less common elsewhere) that infringe upon the private lives of the citizenry in a way that these "adjuncts" to the system of rule (as we shall describe them here in Part IV serve to capture the whole of the Soviet citizenry in a single-minded state purpose.

As just highlighted, the most significant characteristic of the Soviet political system is the network of administrative relationships binding all economic and political activity together into a single chain of command. At the bottom is the worker in the plant or the peasant in the field. At the second level is the foreman or director, who must answer to an immediate superior who, in turn, is directly under a district official. So the chain of relationships continues until the ascending line of power and authority culminates in the politburo and the hands of the general secretary of the Communist party in the Soviet Union. As noted elsewhere, under Stalin there were at least three such hierarchies: the Party, the secret police, and the governmental agencies. Moreover, in theory, and in a sense, in practice, the Party and the governmental hierarchies still remain separate entities. However, a review of the changes that have occurred in recent decades, particularly since the death of Stalin in 1953, reveals a trend toward an ever increasing blurring of the lines separating governmental and Party responsibilities. Thus, at the beginning of the 1970s more than ever before, the vast majority of key posts that are strictly governmental are, in fact, held by key Party personalities. Thus, unless a major reversal in the direction of change should occur, for all practical purposes, Party membership has come to identify those who in other systems of rule would be the key governmental leaders.

Again, we do agree with Prof. Meyer's doubts about the continued value of the totalitarian model. Moreover, this view is widely shared by many other political scientists in the field, certainly by Profs. Armstrong, Jacobs, Kautsky, and Sharlet, who joined Prof. Meyer in a 1967 symposium on "Comparative Politics and Communist Systems."[4] Furthermore, the model we offer here incorporates many of the same elements that Prof. Meyer stresses in his bureaucratic model, which he uses to illustrate the comparability between the USSR incorporated and Western bureaucratic systems. Yet, we also agree with Prof. Jacob's strong caution that, however valuable the search for comparison may be—and our intention is for this study to be one in comparative politics—we must not lose sight of important differences peculiar to the USSR.[5] True, as several scholars have suggested, the USSR fits into the phenomenon of modernization, and the drive to industrialize—so vital to the evolution of the Soviet system—is probably the base upon which political modernization is built. Indeed, Soviet industrialization is seen as a key to the present monohierarchical paradigm, but the evolution of Soviet politics has encompassed significant deviations from what elsewhere are usually considered to be characteristics of modernization. Thus, the USSR offers a special model, which, in common with other models, is undergirded by industrialization and marked by bureaucratization. But also (and peculiarly) it is marked by the great extent of bureaucratization, the domination by a single political elite, and by the nature and import of the "new Soviet nationalism" (i.e., Marxism–Leninism, traditional Russian nationalism, and lessons gleaned from experience).

Where there is but one party the political process is quite another thing from that in pluralistic systems. The element of contest among organized opposing groups, which is an essential characteristic of nonauthoritarian systems, is absent in the USSR. Moreover, within the limits posed by the impossibility of perfecting human institutions, the USSR has carried the potential of unitary rule to the extreme, and it differs from other authoritarian systems and even other Communist systems; e.g., the impact of the Church on politics in Poland provides a kind of openly organized opposition that is unheard of in the USSR. Here, then, are significant reasons why the Soviet system probably is best described as the paradigm of a monohierarchical polity. Even the "adjuncts" to the system (e.g., the schools and the communications media) are plugged into the hierarchy at various points of articulation.

The Communist Party   At least to date, Western democracies have rested upon the tradition that man is at once a social being and an individual. He is neither wholly a creature of his environment nor entirely an island unto himself. Governments are not just necessary evils. They are positive instruments serving the common good of all members of society. Yet, whether formally written or merely understood, effective constitutional government is required to remind the rulers that there are private realms of human activity from which governments are banned. Constitutional democracies serve to preserve the free contest of ideas—today's unpopular opinion held by a minority often is tomorrow's truth held by a new ruling majority. Political pluralism, therefore, is the essence of democracy. For the Soviet Marxist, however, there is only one truth. Tomorrow something new may be added, but it must always be squared with the ideology as presented in the most recent authoritative pronouncement by the Party leadership, for all is part of a monolithic whole that rules out either differing views or organized political opposition.

Democratic Centralism in Practice

Lenin had some glimmer of the advantages to be gained from the open contest of ideas. This awareness must have been part of the impetus behind his championing democratic centralism as essential to the Soviet decision-making process. Assertedly, the paradox inherent in the concept could be solved by allowing a matter to be freely and openly debated when first presented. However, once answers were found, they would become a part of the Party's collection of truths, and henceforth all debate would cease. Not even those in the Party could raise further question.

Unfortunately for the possibility of free inquiry in the USSR, no such seemingly reasonable scheme would, in fact, eliminate the paradox, and *democratic* centralism has never really worked. Almost from the beginning, the insistence that the Party is infallible left everyone below the very top with the necessity of searching, not for new truths, but for an understanding of the new points of view held by the leaders. Time and again in Soviet history, various theses outlining new courses of action have been submitted to Party and/or public debate in the name of democratic centralism. Yet in virtually every instance, no significant changes have been made; indeed, in the final draft of a new program even the dotting of the i's and crossing the t's is usually the same as it was on the original document. Thus, public participation in the decision-making process, whether it be in the Supreme Soviet (Council) in Moscow (its two houses, the Soviet of the Union and the Soviet of the National-ities, resemble in structure our two houses of Congress) or in a local Soviet, is not a matter of deliberation but one of rubber-stamping the views already expressed by the central Party leader-ship.

For example, in 1961, Khrushchev, the First Secretary of the Party reported that "over nine million Communists, the entire Party," were only part of the 73,000,000 Soviet people who par-ticipated in the public discussions of the new Draft Rules of the Party released in July of that year. He added that more than 4,600,000 people spoke on the draft rules and that the Party, and the various communications media received more than 300,000 letters and articles on the subject.[6] Yet, the final document was essentially the same as the draft rules under discusssion. Moreover, on the surface, Congresses of the Communist party of the Soviet Union are somewhat similar to Western party conventions in that they constitute periodical gatherings of Party leaders acting as representatives of the entire Party membership and charged with representing the whole of the people in picking the key leaders and establishing a platform for future action. If democratic centralism were to work, in practice, this is the time for it to operate. Again, however, although in October of 1961 there were nearly 4,500 delegates to the Twenty-Second Congress, their task was not delib-eration; no important changes were made; nothing, not already agreed upon by the central leaders, was implemented. In short, that Congress's job was the same as that of all other Party Con-gresses—to ratify decisions previously taken by the Politburo, the handful of key Party men who rule the USSR.

Perhaps to remind any citizen who might have concluded that the relatively mild treatment meted out to the "anti-Party group"* did not mean any encouragement of the free contest of ideas, Party Secretary Kozlov, in a speech before the same congress, again emphasized the rules of the Soviet game.

The strict subordination of individual Party organizations to the center, and of lower organizations to higher ones, is an indispensable condition for the Party's fulfillment of its historic tasks.

---

* Although composed of key Party members, this faction had been work-ing for the ouster of Khrushchev.

The Party fights against all manifestations of parochialism, against all attempts to approach problems of Party policy from a narrow, departmental standpoint, for it considers them to be alien to Marxist–Leninist Party principles. Lenin stressed that "refusal to accept the direction of the central bodies is tantamount to refusing to remain in the Party, it is tantamount to disrupting the Party. . . .[7]

The Party as a Ruling Interest Group

When government is not encumbered by a constitutional requirement that it be limited and when it is unvexed by attempts to maximize popular participation in its process, that government is but a system of rule from above. True, in the USSR, as in other states, a crucial problem of politics is that of balancing the will of the ruling party with the desires of the ruled; but in the Soviet Union this is not complicated by the encumbrances found in democracies. As stressed earlier, Soviet political culture is very different from that known in Western democratic systems.

"Freedom of assembly" in the USSR, whether for civic reasons or for forming a philatelist society, is allowed for only one purpose. In some way every organization must show that it will serve the health of the state, as defined by the Party. Hobbies and athletics are regarded as healthy pursuits, and organizations for these purposes are encouraged because they serve the needs and wants of the citizenry; but proportionate to the size of the organization, key posts will always be held by loyal Party members whose major function (beyond personal interest in the group's activity) is to guarantee that the group always conforms to the wishes of the Party.

Political parties as created in, and defined by, the West do not exist in the Soviet Union, where there is only a single ruling group that calls itself "The Party." Organized pressure groups and interest groups which are so important to the functioning of Western democratic political systems do not exist (although the potential for their being is great. Moreover, every effort is made to assure that such pockets of possible opposition are allowed to develop.

True, in recent years some Western students of Soviet politics have carried out studies, employing new statistical analyses, which imply that there is more than just a potential for the evolution of interest groups both within and without the Party. Thus, Prof. Lodge as well as Profs. Schwartz and Keech place particular emphasis upon the role that they perceive is played by such specialists as engineers, teachers, and administrators. Unfortunately, since Prof. Lodge's work first appeared, criticism of the base for his statistical findings has resulted in his partial retreat, suggesting that perhaps his first conclusions went too far. Of course, there is truth in his general conclusion that the USSR as a monolith is a "myth," in the sense that many have read the use of the word in absolute terms rather than in the relative (i.e., to other political systems) sense meant here. True, in their examination of the outcome of Khrushchev's educational reform, Schwartz and Keech do convincingly demonstrate that opposition by specialists at lower levels may play a role in policy formation. Yet these gentlemen still stress a conviction that key top colleagues in the Party, not pressure groups, were primarily responsible for defeating Khrushchev's educational reform. As they point out in their study, the more modern a society, the more it must depend upon experts (who do constitute a powerful potential for political opposition). But to date, the influence of Soviet experts upon policy emphatically remains "when higher [political] powers seek their judgement."*[8]

A student new to Soviet affairs is tempted to conclude that a history of the Soviet Union is primarily a history of the Soviet Communist party, that a study of the political process in the USSR is a study of the Party's machinery, and that the Party is the Soviet government. Yet, in spite of the all-pervasive character of the Party, as the chapters that follow will illustrate, it is far from everything in the USSR. After all, only some 4 to 5% of the population belongs to this select, highly disciplined political elite. (Moreover, as we shall see later, youth groups, the educational system, and the communications media comprise some of the additional institutions that are vital to the Soviet political process.)

By Western definition, a party cannot exist by itself in a state system. At least two such political entities must exist to provide the voter with a meaningful choice in the matter of selecting policies and leaders. The Soviet Communist party is not a party, but

* Although Schwartz and Keech were making a generalization about modernizing systems, they certainly were including the USSR, which was the subject of their research.

neither is it a new Russian nobility. Along with Milovan Djilas, many have concluded that the Party itself in complete denial of the original revolutionary intent—that it has become not only a new self-perpetuating ruling elite, but the new exploiting class in the USSR.[9] In a very real sense, the Soviets have employed Orwellian doublethinking in their assertions that the USSR is the first classless, or nearly classless, society. Certainly, the Party is jealous of its power; it is the Party membership, or at least the "non-Party active" (those persons who have completely identified their interests with the Party), that makes the decisions, wins the trips abroad, possesses the country *dachas* ("summer cottages"), and can pull the strings for its children to get better places in the schools. The Party elite and the ordinary workers are miles apart. But, at least, the USSR is not yet a rigid society in terms of social mobility. The peasant's, or coal miner's, son does receive a genuine opportunity as well as considerable encouragement to achieve a high position. To date, the Party leadership has reflected an awareness that the best way to assure the Party's continued monopoly on power is to keep its ranks open for all of the best Soviet talent —that is, all who are willing to subsume their will to the Party's dictates.

The Party is not everything, and the Soviet political process is something more than the workings of the Party. Primarily, the Party is the sole interpreter of Marxism and Leninism, and thus the sole depository of all truth. The Party is the focal point for both central and local decision-making. Since the major focal point of the monohierarchical model presented here is an administrative state that has increasingly combined Party and state responsibilities (which are normally separated in other political systems), treating the Party as a distinct entity would only serve to distort our analysis.

When compared with parliamentary political systems, the Party may be considered to be the only special interest group that is allowed to exist in the USSR. In spite of the constantly repeated Soviet assertion that "the Party must be interested in everything," the Western definition that a special interest group is held together by a single common interest or goal can be said to hold true for the CPSU (Communist Party, Soviet Union). True, outside of multiparty states such as France, in constitutional democracies political pressure groups usually do not attempt to gain public office because their members realize that they are a minority who must compete with other groups with conflicting interests. Expending a political interest group's energies in capturing the few political posts it might win would not be using its resources to best serve its single-minded purpose. Not so in the USSR, for here the conditions are such that the reverse is true since the primary interest of the CPSU is to maintain and expand the Party's monopoly over political power. All else is subsumed under this goal, an illusive goal that can never be completely attained. In short, a common characteristic of Western political parties is that they tend to encompass several interest groups within their ranks, whereas the so-called Party in the USSR denies the need for separate interest groups and attempts to confine all social, political, and economic interests within a single pressure group that monopolizes leadership in the monohierarchical structure.

Organization and Composition

The Party is a highly disciplined segment of the administrative hierarchy; at its peak is the Politburo consisting of ten or more of the nation's key leaders. In Stalin's day, the very fact that he was the General Secretary proclaimed his supreme position. After his death, this title was not used by First Secretary Khrushchev. Brezhnev, however, has revived the title.

According to the Party rules, the Politburo (for a time known as the Party Presidium) is an executive committee elected by the Central Committee, which consists of a few hundred top rank leaders. In practice, however, the Politburo has been self-appointed, and thus controls the Central Committee. Similarly, the Central Committee is technically a creature of the periodic Party Congresses, which assertedly are the depository of all power. In fact, however, the Congresses have followed the lead of the Politburo, rubber-stamping its wishes, with the Central Committee operating both as the second level of leadership and as a depository from which tomorrow's Politburo members will be chosen.

In 1967, according to a Party publication called *Party Life,* below the national level, there were 14 Central Committees of Union Republics, 6 territory committees, 133 province committees, 10 regional committees, 747 city committees, 417 borough committees, and 2,746 rural district committees. This, then, is an accounting of the Party hierarchy, which parallels the state hierarchy, but even more it is an accounting of the focal points of decision-making in what is essentially a unified administrative system. In practice, the day-to-day leadership of the economy and society at the local level is carried out by the 338,000 primary organizations (formerly known as cells) that now exist in "almost all collectives of working people."[10]

Soviet statistics reveal that the average primary Party unit includes thirty members. About one-fifth of the members are women. Slightly over half of the membership is under forty years of age. Continued stress is placed upon membership drawn from the working classes (e.g., workers and peasants). Yet, an "employees and all others" category (including administrators, engineers, professional and service people) comprises nearly half of the total membership.[11]

As indicated previously, only 5% of the total population in Soviet society are Party members. Thus, as shown in Table 3, in 1967, out of a population of 234 million people, there were 12,135,103 full-fledged Party members and 549,030 additional candidates for membership. Well over half of these Communists (7,840,292) were Russians, with the second largest national group being Ukrainians (1,983,090).[12]

Soviet statistical compilations do not usually directly reflect the observation that virtually all key administrative posts are in the hands of Party members (although past statistical compilations have indicated that virtually all industrial plant managers and, since the 1950s, virtually all farm chairmen and directors are Party members). However, some indication of both the changed character of the Party and its lead role in Soviet society is reflected by the following. In 1927 only 0.8% of the Party members had a higher education (university training or its equivalent) and only 8.6% had a secondary education, whereas by 1967, more than half of the membership had higher, incomplete higher, or secondary education. Most important of all, however, among secretaries of district, city, and regional Party committees, 91.0% had higher education and 97.6% of the secretaries of province and territory Party committee and the Central Committees of Union-Republic Communist parties had higher education.[13]

Table 3—The CPSU in Figures[12] (As of January 1)

Year	Population of the USSR	Party Membership*	Members as a % of Population	EDUCATION			OCCUPATION				Number of Primary Organs
				Secondary & Incomplete Higher	Higher	Total in %	Industry	Construction	Transport	Agriculture	
1918	—	390,000	—	—	—	—	—	—	—	—	—
1927	147,000,000**	1,212,505	0.8	104,714	9,614	9	—	—	—	—	38,978
1937	163,800,000***	1,981,697	1.2	276,175	108,256	20	537,843	43,104	176,550	296,886	102,475
1947	—	6,051,901	—	1,461,045	453,288	32	1,188,758	78,128	364,492	1,042,407	296,568
1957	201,400,000	7,494,573	3.7	1,963,272	869,582	38	1,786,273	205,132	550,268	1,442,571	344,325
1967	234,400,000	12,684,133	5.5	4,319,104	2,097,055	51	3,195,718	666,380	838,019	2,336,412	337,915
1968	236,700,000	13,180,225	5.6	4,561,139	2,274,182	52	—	—	—	—	349,060

* Including candidate members.
** December 17, 1926 (interwar territory).
*** Boundaries as of September 17, 1939.

In the early years of the USSR, most who had achieved advanced education under the tsars were excluded from posts of political importance (although their economic talents often were harnessed for the new regime). Today, however, the USSR is run by a trained elite, people with advanced technical and professional training, but their education does not end there. In the 1966–1967 academic year alone, more than 8,000,000 Party members (two-thirds of the membership) studied in the Party's political educational system in the more than a score of Party schools.[14] Those in the West who conclude that the increased technical training of the Soviet party members bodes a managerial revolution, tend to ignore the enormous forces the Party utilizes to assure the "ideological-theoretical" training and fealty of the Party membership. Put in broader terms, much speculation is offered about the existence of common modernization forces, which will work in the direction of convergence so that some foreseeable tomorrow most of the significant differences between a huge industrialized USSR and a huge industrialized USA will have disappeared. True, an accounting of the key political leadership in a Western constitutional system also would reveal that only a small portion of society (perhaps 5%) is responsible for important political decision-making. After all, in any given organization there can be only so many chiefs; therefore the rest must be Indians. Yet, beyond such similarities, strikingly important and persistent differences exist between the Soviet monohierarchical model and pluralistic political systems and cultures. Some of the most important differences are as follows:

1. In contrast to the political single-mindedness of the Soviet leadership, included among the totality of political chiefs in democratic polities, are individuals and groups who outspokenly differ not only in philosophical persuasion but also in their commitment to political constituents.

2. In contrast to the cooptative (that is, selected from above) system of recruiting new members into the political elite in the USSR, direct participation in governmental policy-making in constitutional democratic systems is determined by periodical electoral contests between two or more individuals or parties.

3. In contrast with the unified political and economic administration system in the USSR, the various leaderships in a constitu-

tional system head up many relatively distinct public and private political, social, and economic institutions and constituencies.

4. In contrast to the inseparability of the Party leadership from governmental leadership in the USSR, a US president (even a British prime minister) must heed the demands of several openly competing elements, including constitutional prescriptions, party loyalties, and interest-group demands.

Political parties are, after all, an invention of the parliamentary political process, and a hallmark of their existence is a regularized contest for the seats of power. Ironically, therefore, although the Communist party in Italy and the Communist party in France are political parties in every sense of the term, the Communist party of the Soviet Union is not a political party, but rather a highly disciplined interest group, whereby a self-perpetuating elite is able to maintain its monopoly over political decision-making.

CHAPTER 7

Leadership

SOME CHARACTERISTICS OF THE MODEL*

Bureaucracy: BUREAUCRACY has become an integral part
The Key to   of the modern authoritarian leadership sys-
a Maturing   tem. As we have seen, both today's democ-
System   racies and authoritarian governments alike
depend upon bureaucracies to bring some
order out of the complexity of contemporary social and economic
existence. As between man and woman, however, it is the seemingly
small differences that are all-important and that differentiate the
democratic bureaucracy from that of the dictatorial. What are these
differences? As reflected in the stress that most Western scholars
have placed on the monolithic character of Soviet society, perhaps
the most important difference is in the single, highly uniform,
bureaucratic structure that characterizes the monohierarchical sys-

* Most of the material in this chapter is drawn from an article by the
author, "Some Characteristics of the Soviet Leadership System: A Maturing
Totalitarian System?" *Midwest Journal of Political Science,* Vol. X, No. 1,
February 1966, pp. 29–38.

tem, as contrasted with administration in a Western democracy that is dependent upon a multitude of relatively independent bureaucracies. Thus, the pluralism of a modern democracy is significantly (although not entirely) supported by such institutional arrangements as the frequently stressed independence of the judiciary (which is an integral part of the Soviet bureaucracy), as well as by the relatively separate existence of the central administrative departments, on the one hand, and by entities such as either the British Broadcasting Corporation as a self-governing corporation or the American independent regulatory agencies, on the other. Moreover, in the West there are the relatively independent, local governmental units and the quite independent but very significant, nongovernmental bureaucracies such as DuPont or General Motors.

In the USSR, however, the all-pervasive, Party-led and Party-dominated bureaucracy is the institutional foundation upon which the Soviet system rests. It is also the source of many of the key differences that allow for a meaningful distinction not only between the USSR and the democracies but also between the Soviet system and other authoritarian regimes. As will be stressed in Part IV of this study, the Party's monopoly over all political activity and the communications media, its close control over the educational system, and its sponsorship of the "voluntary" citizens' organizations that so adroitly utilize social pressures to achieve conformity are all-important adjuncts to Soviet monohierarchical rule. However, these means of assuring a maximum degree of mass conformity are only as effective as the administrative base upon which such relatively indirect instruments of absolute rule rest.

The term *mature* seems to best describe the stage of development of the system in post-Stalin USSR. Not only has the Soviet system been in existence for over half a century, a period that has allowed a number of institutional forms and practices to become fairly well established, but the post-1953 era has been marked by a degree of stability that was unknown under Lenin or Stalin. Khrushchev presided over the elimination of fear as a key element of rule, and, in addition, he made up for much of its absence by extending the bureaucracy to the countryside, by completing Stalin's unfinished revolution.

Although the administrative changes which Khrushchev wrought in rural Russia were the most significant and widespread that have occurred in recent years, paralleling these there have been other significant, if less obvious, innovations in the system of rule. As noted earlier, the immature system that existed under Stalin enjoyed something at least remotely akin to the separation-of-powers principle that operates in the American system. Under Nikita Khrushchev, this principle became less important while, at the same time, the Party became more active in the day-to-day direction of Soviet affairs. Still another example of the maturation of the Soviet system of rule, one not noted earlier, is the change in the role of the Procuracy (the Office of the Attorney General) that has occurred since 1955. In his book analyzing this office, Professor Glen G. Morgan reveals that although the post-1953 Procuracy must be credited with lessening the caprice in the conduct of Soviet administration, at one and the same time it must be charged with heightening the conformity of local administration to the central will.[1]

To anticipate Chapter 8, although Max Weber's work was completed before the dawn of the Soviet system, his observations on the nature of bureaucracies have become most valuable for interpreting what has been occurring in the Soviet Union in recent years. Thus, as he noted, although democratic societies have the problem of struggling against the inclination of bureaucracies "to be unresponsive to the elected political authorities," the leadership in an authoritarian system tends to be free of this problem in that it is itself a part of a seemingly "unshatterable" bureaucracy and not separate from the hierarchy as elected leaders are.[2]

If one implies that recent changes in the USSR have constituted a significant move away from total controls, then one ignores the enormous implications of Khrushchev's having completed Stalin's unfinished revolution, that is, the full incorporation of agriculture within the administrative system. In Weberian terms, Soviet bureaucratization has now been "completely carried through." Beyond this, barring defeat by an external enemy, any force capable of countering the tendency to self-preservation (strong in all governments but, perhaps, even stronger in an authoritarian system) can arise: (1) only where a very large segment of society has been welded together by a revolutionary spirit; or, (2) only within an aroused leadership that, for extraordinary reasons, has resolved to destroy the very system which has enabled it to rise to the pinnacle of power.

Stalin and Khrushchev (and even Lenin) reached their positions of power because they were first of all organization men, particularly well adapted to the Communist system of rule. Few would dispute that in his efforts to improve industrial and agricultural output, Khrushchev sincerely strove to allow greater individual initiative among the leaders at the production level. Yet, in the unfolding of the Khrushchev reforms, the left hand consistently took away whatever power the right hand attempted to devolve to the lower levels. Even without the actions of the left hand, however, there was no evidence of any desire on Khrushchev's part to attack the bureaucracy, directly. Constant tinkering within the system to make it more responsive to the central will and to stimulate greater economic output is the rule of Soviet administrative leadership, but nowhere is there any apparent lessening of confidence in the fundamental system.

As mentioned earlier, the abandonment of terror has been a highly significant reform in the Soviet system. In the first edition of his study *How Russia Is Ruled*, Merle Fainsod described terror as the "linchpin" of the Soviet system.[3] In earlier days when the couplings on trains were less sophisticated, the linchpin was the instrument that held a train together. The linchpin eventually passed from the scene, but it was replaced by a new, more complicated mechanism which was needed to assure the secure linkage of a train. Perhaps, such an analogy is helpful in understanding the changes going on in the Soviet system. Khrushchev presided over a pulling of terror as the "linchpin" of Soviet rule, and although it conceivably could be returned to its former position, the "linchpin" has not seriously been missed because, along with other changes, the now tightly woven, all-encompassing fabric of the bureaucracy has helped to provide a more comfortable framework for a maturing leadership system that may well enjoy a greater degree of actual conformity to a single purpose than did the Stalinist system.

The Price of   Superficially, the authoritarian leader seems
the Bureaucracy more powerful than his democratic counterpart. A Stalin could, and did, order the execution of untold numbers of Soviet citizens. Khrushchev's views, such as his opinions on the importance of corn and the desirability of eliminating the machine tractor stations, were expressed in

speeches that were quickly transformed into binding decrees having an enormous effect on the course of events in Soviet society.
The power of a Western president or prime minister (other than
in wartime, when they assume virtual dictatorial powers) seems
pale by comparison. Nevertheless, there are very real limitations
upon the effective power of a monohierarchical leader. The initial
restrictions placed upon such a leader's actions by the unwieldiness
of a huge bureaucracy, are further compounded by the impossibility
of any single individual leader being able to adequately perceive and
act on all matters of state and social interest. Indeed, as Weber
noted:

> The absolute monarch is powerless opposite the superior knowl-
> edge of the bureaucratic expert—in a certain sense more powerless than
> any other political head. . . . When a constitutional king agrees with a
> socially important part of the governed, he very frequently exerts a
> greater influence upon the course of administration than does the abso-
> lute monarch. The constitutional king can control these experts better
> because of what is, as least relatively, the public character of criticism,
> whereas *"the absolute monarch is dependent for information solely
> upon the bureaucracy."*[4]

Although the democratic leader's actions are restricted by the electorate, the electorate is still pluralistic in its makeup and desires;
and thus clear majority points of view are relatively rare. By contrast, the major source of pressures on the monohierarchical leadership is the bureaucracy (in effect, its electorate), marked by its
relatively monolithic view of public affairs. Therefore, Soviet leaders may be even more fettered by institutional and historical pressures, that at least in some areas can leave them with fewer
alternatives to choose from, than Western prime ministers or presidents are.

Paranoids and   Another major change since Stalin's death
Sycophants   has been the increasing level of technical
                         training among Soviet administrators at all
levels, but especially in agriculture which as usual had been well
behind the urban economy.[5] Does this mean that the experts in the
Soviet system have a greater influence over the course of events
than do their democratic counterparts? Probably not, since in the

Soviet system the most talented administrator–politician is the man most apt to rise to the top of the hierarchy, and it is his kind (e.g., Lysenko and his long reign over Soviet biology), rather than the best experts, who have a monopoly over deciding what technical advice will, or will not, be pressed upon the key Party leadership. This situation was, of course, the major point of complaint in Dudintsev's novel *Not By Bread Alone*. In contrast, as evidenced by the use of American presidents' "kitchen cabinets" and various independent advisory boards, the democratic leaders have always had important sources of advice (political and technical) that are quite independent of the administrative bureaucracy.*

Premier Khrushchev had no independent court or legislative body to correct his mistakes and no loyal opposition to offer new ideas in areas in which he may have been uninformed or lacking in talent. Moreover, as Stalin's rule demonstrated, and as was becoming increasingly evident under Khrushchev, the jealousies of a monohierarchical ruler and his inevitable encirclement by sycophants tend to result in growing conviction on his part that he really knows better than anyone else what the "correct" decisions are in all areas of human activity. And a monohierarchical leader must be vitally interested in precisely everything. Even though the monohierarchical ruler may at first recognize his own shortcomings, ultimately, only he can make key decisions; therefore, in coping with all of the problems of his society, he is soon forced to pretend that he knows all of the answers. Moreover, evidence from both the Nazi and Soviet systems indicates that in significant areas, the leader becomes more and more separated from reality. As Hannah Arendt has observed:

> Practically speaking, the paradox of totalitarianism in power is that the possession of all instruments of governmental power and violence in one country is not an unmixed blessing for a totalitarian movement. Its disregard for facts, its strict adherence to the rules of a fictitious world, become steadily more difficult to maintain, yet [totalitarianism]

---

* To take another example, an interesting chapter in the history of American administrative decision-making could be written on policy guidelines which such agencies as the State Department have received, guidelines drawn not from official state reports and analyses, but resulting from the President's (or one of his close advisor's) reading of the *New York Times*.

remains as essential as before. Power means a direct confrontation with reality, and totalitarianism in power is constantly concerned with overcoming this challenge.[6]

Significantly, in the period of leadership transition, Khrushchev seemed genuinely aware of this weakness in Stalin's rule; and thus, since the myth of "collective leadership" is deeply ingrained in Soviet thought, there was a real attempt to establish such a system.[7] However, the demands of a monohierarchical system for a single focal point of all power and authority proved to be irresistible, and Khrushchev, like Stalin, succumbed to the pressures of the system and his own human weakness. There seems to be an overwhelming force that works to shape monohierarchical leaders into paranoid personalities.

During the honeymoon of the transition, the Politburo, if not the Central Committee, very probably presided over the decision-making process, but this was only transitional; and when the period had passed, only Khrushchev could create the "theses on industrial reorganization." Another example of the demands on a monohierarchical leader produced another Khrushchevian thesis resulting in the reorganization of the educational system. Nowhere, however, was the egomania essential to monohierarchical rule more evident than it was in Soviet agriculture, and nowhere was the blindness (the inability of a single man to perceive the needs of a vast and complex society) of Khrushchev's rule more in evidence. This blindness is surely another major factor that limits the actual range of choice for a Soviet leader.

A Fundamental Flaw in Monohierarchical Leadership   In his 1957 address to the agricultural workers at Gorky, Khrushchev himself presented an interpretation of monohierarchical leadership that could result only in considerable harm to the system: "We the leaders are responsible for everything. Therefore, we must understand everything, recognizing right from wrong and good from evil, supporting the right way and vanquishing the wrong way."[8] The head of the bureaucratic body, the Party elite, must pose as the depository of infallible truth. Therefore, since the Party can never admit to being wrong, once an error has received the stamp of Party approval, all of society, even scientists and the technicians, are forced to affect the same blindness as that of the leadership. As a result, years will pass by and the havoc be wreaked because officially sanctioned falsehood as truth cannot be discarded. For example, a myopia shared by the leader and the Party had resulted in the year-after-year promotion of the William's crop rotation system as a major way of increasing badly lagging yields. Finally, the William's system was discredited, but the president of the Ukraine Republic Academy of Agricultural Science, P. A. Vlasyuk, had the audacity to suggest that in his past propagandizing of the grass-crop system, he had only been carrying out Party instructions.* In his role as the symbol of Party infallibility, Khrushchev had to refute the implication that the Party had been wrong. He did so in a speech to the agricultural workers in Kiev where he noted that even he himself might possibly be in error, but he spoiled it all by making clear that an agricultural scientist's first task is to convince Khrushchev that Khrushchev is wrong. As Khrushchev had noted previously, only the Party leaders are capable of "recognizing right from wrong." Thus, in the final analysis, it is the leader who must verbalize the Party's knowledge of truth. As such, "understanding everything," he is left with the awesome responsibility of passing final judgment on everything, including the validity of the findings of a scientist. The following excerpt from his Kiev speech (almost a poignant plea) is surely a revelation of the impossible position of both the scientist and the top leader in a leadership system that demands infallibility.

Comrade Vlasyuk's statement (that the Party was at fault) shows his lack of principle. Comrade Vlasyuk, you will now cite my words and say: "Comrade Khrushchev said thus and so." Am I the highest authority in agricultural science? You are the President of the Ukraine Republic Academy of Agricultural Sciences and I am the Secretary of the Party Central Committee. You must help me in these matters, and not I you. (Applause). I might be wrong, and if I am, you, as an honest scientist, should say: "Comrade Khrushchev, you do not quite

* In the opinion of this writer, although the William's system certainly had been pushed too far, it is well suited for current needs in many parts of the rural USSR. Therefore, the leadership made a new error by totally abandoning the system.

understand this matter." If you explain things to me correctly, I will
thank you for it. Let us say that I was wrong. But you will say, "Comrade Khrushchev said this and I supported him. . . ."[9]

In closing this discourse, Khrushchev condemned the Soviet scientist for "toadyism," but as his own description of an imaginary
course of events reveals, especially for the scientist working in a
controversial area, there was no other choice.

If the USSR has successfully carried out an experiment in
government, its leadership system ought to exhibit particular characteristics. This indeed seems to be the case, at least in the sense
of special weaknesses exhibited by the system, which can be listed
as follows:

1. An all-encompassing, monolithic bureaucracy seems to be
the key to a maturing monohierarchical system, but such a bureaucracy is a mixed blessing to the leadership, for although it provides
the means for nearly complete political and economic control, its
innate conservatism and unwieldiness make it reluctant to change
and slow to react to the leadership's direction.

2. The Soviet Party chief is the symbol, and a most effective
mouthpiece, for the most awesome concentration of political power
known to the history of mankind. Nevertheless, hemmed in by the
particular determinants of a monohierarchical system with its extensive bureaucracy (particularly a maturing system), the Soviet
leader probably has much less latitude in decision-making on matters that will affect the course of affairs than many Western analysts have suggested.

3. Monohierarchical leaders, once established in power, tend
to retain their positions much longer than do their democratic
counterparts. Therefore, the blindness of such leaders to those
problems related to their personal weaknesses increases as the
forces that produce sycophancy and paranoid personalities mount.

4. The impossibility for a single man (already severely restricted by the bureaucracy in his range of choice and experimentation) to possess the knowledge to make wise decisions in all realms
of social and economic affairs further contributes to the tendency
for a monohierarchical system to concentrate its efforts in a relatively narrow area of constructive activity. This, coupled with (and
really inseparable from) the concept of a totally planned economy,

implies that the Soviet Union may never be able to rid itself of its priority system and the unbalanced economy wherein impressive production records in a narrow range of heavy industry are contrasted with serious and chronic shortages of consumers' goods.

5. As a result of the factors described in the two previous points, the longer the monohierarchical ruler's tenure in office, the more seriously compounded the problems created by his particular myopia will be. Therefore, particularly in those realms in which decisions should draw heavily upon the best available expert advice, the monohierarchical ruler's need "to know everything," combined with the power of the professional administrators over the channels of communication, must place him at a far more serious disadvantage than his democratic counterpart.

6. The areas of a monohierarchical ruler's lack of perception are not necessarily (perhaps not usually) inherited by his successor. Therefore, although stable monohierarchical systems do not enjoy the important advantages of orderly leadership succession, they do tend to produce new leaders who are intent upon correcting their predecessor's errors. However, because of the damage caused by the lack of orderly transition, and because of the difficulties described in points 1, 2, and 4, one seriously questions the relative value of this built-in corrective tendency.

All of the weaknesses raised are based upon observable human failings, and as such can be discovered, to some degree, in any leadership system at one time or another. However, the tendency to these weaknesses does seem to be particularly strong in the maturing Soviet model, and they can be expected to continue to plague the experiment.

CHAPTER 8

Bureaucracy
"Completely Carried Through"

RECOGNIZING the extent of Party power in Soviet affairs often leads the student to believe that since the Party is all-powerful, its members hold all key posts, and nothing else needs to be known to understand the Soviet system of rule. Stalin did say that "cadres decide everything," and all important cadres are in the Party, but no matter how important political leadership may be in the USSR, as stressed earlier, the Party is not everything. Thus, the bureaucracy itself, the most important of all the Party's means of control, exhibits demands of its own.

Some observers have argued from time to time that the power of the army has been a decisive political force. Certainly, in the early years of War Communism (1918–1921), the army was a power to beware of, also again during the Second World War. However, such assertions fail to perceive the dissimilarities between the Soviet system and other species of the modern authoritarian dictatorship. Many of the "mass movement regimes" are highly dependent on the army.[1] Often (as in Egypt and several Latin American states), the army has played the decisive political role. In Nazi Germany, Communist China, and the USSR, however, the Party leadership has made certain that loyal Party officials have a decisive influence over politically related decision-making in the military. Trotsky inculcated this principle in the Red Army that successfully defeated the Whites, and it has remained intact.

Regarding the police, in Stalin's day, Soviet rule was perhaps best described as an arrangement in which the governmental apparatus was charged with the day-to-day tasks. The Party was responsible for checking on the government, and the secret police checked on both the government and the Party. Excepting the time of the Great Purge of the 1930s, however, even under Stalin the police seem to have been relatively limited in their authority over the Party.

Soviets and *Ministries*	Although a study of constitutional documents is only part of the study of Western democratic systems, descriptions of institu-

tions outlined in such documents are crucial guides to the political decision-making process since the constitutions delineate many of the responsibilities and limitations of governmental agencies. Descriptions of institutions in the Soviet Constitution also are meaningful, but in the sense that they reveal part of the system of centralized controls and not in the sense that Stalin's Constitution of 1936 outlines effective limitations on authority.

At one time, Western political studies were largely concentrated on explaining the structural forms of government as rigidly outlined in a constitution. Today, political science has matured to the point of recognizing that much of the political process is not inscribed in such documents. To succumb to using a structural approach in a study of the Soviet political system would be disastrous.

An analysis of Soviet rule in terms of the hierarchy of the elected Soviets ("councils," or legislative bodies), as outlined in the Soviet constitution, is meaningless. Soviets (as asserted legislative bodies) exist at all levels; and although their candidates are elected, this is done without opposition which would be in violation of the principle of "democratic centralism." Yet, the Party and state administrative organs that exist at all levels of the USSR in association with the Soviets (councils) are the backbone of the mono-hierarchical paradigm (see Fig. 2).

Federalism, somewhat on the model of the American system, is reflected in the claim that the USSR is composed of fifteen republics, each with independent powers. Indeed, theoretically they have a right to withdraw from the Union. Stalin and others, how-ever, made it quite clear that any expression of a desire to secede could emanate only from anti-Communist, antirevolutionary sources. Ostensibly, the Soviets (councils) of the individual republics have deliberative powers, but, in fact, the whole mission of government outside of Moscow, whether at the republic, regional (*oblast*), or district (*rayon*) level, is that of serving as an administrative arm of the central will. Soviet federalism does not encompass any con-cept of the separation of powers, either between national and repub-lican levels of government or between the divisions of government at the national center. In this sense, the Soviet system is federal in name, but unitary (as is the British system) in practice—that is, there are no limitations on actions that the central government might take.

In the Khrushchev years, attempts to create a greater ra-tionality in the articulation of the administrative needs of the economic area resulted in more than a hundred new administrative subdivisions as substitutes for the old divisions resting largely on national claims. These creations were known as *sovnarkhozy* ("So-viet people's economies"). Since Khrushchev, the sovnarkhozy have been abandoned. Then as now, however, neither the central offices of the sovnarkhozy nor the reconstituted ministries have depended upon republic and lower units to administer all affairs below the national level. Many central agencies beyond the ministries have dealt directly with local affairs.

Reflecting Stalin's recognition that the national aspirations of the Ukrainians, Uzbeks, Kazakhs, and others could not be neg-lected (although the eventual goal has always been complete assimilation of all groups into a single Soviet identity), the 1936 Constitution established both a Soviet (council) of the Union and a Soviet (council) of the Nationalities. Thus, as in the American House of Representatives, the number of deputies to the Soviet of the Union depend upon a population principle. In terms of repre-sentation, the system of the Soviet of the Nationalities is similar to that of the US Senate, although the republics and other "autono-

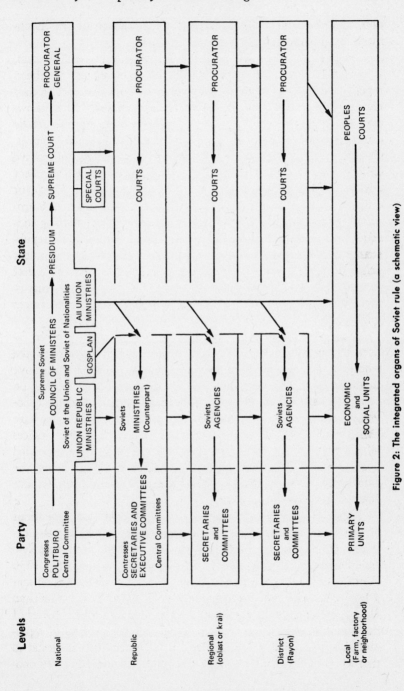

Figure 2: The integrated organs of Soviet rule (a schematic view)

mous national regions" represented in the Soviet of Nationalities
are designed to reflect national subdivisions rather than geographic
entities like the fifty states in the United States Senate. Of course,
a substantial majority of the members of the Supreme Soviet are
Party members.

Reflecting the scheme used for electing the members of the
Supreme Soviet, the Council of Ministers is divided into two sets
of functional ministries, the All-Union Ministries and the Union-
Republic Ministries. Thus, whereas the latter have had their counterparts at the republic level, the former have not, since they act
directly at all necessary levels. Not surprisingly, there has been a
tendency for the ministries in the All-Union Ministry to constitute
the more important areas. These ministries have had their own
offices at the local levels. As implied, the ministries are the administrative agencies that direct and coordinate the whole of the Soviet
economy and society.

Perhaps, the legislative role of the constitutionally described
Supreme Soviet is best revealed by the fact that, in practice that
body meets only twice a year for a two- or three-week term to
ratify what has already been decided by the Council of Ministers
under the guidance of the Party Politburo. Many conclude, therefore, that the Soviets (councils) are quite meaningless. Certainly,
the Soviets as policy-determining legislative institutions are without
power, but not so the individual members of the Supreme Soviet
in the other offices they hold in the Party and the government. Not
only is the Supreme Soviet a pleasant pageant but also it is a great
award to be selected by the Party to be elected to a council, particularly the Supreme Soviet. Such nomination is in recognition of
past service to the state and/or confirmation that one has been
selected to wield power elsewhere. In this sense, membership in a
Soviet is a signal badge of political and social worth, since virtually
all of the top leadership figures also are representatives from an
election district. Members of the Council of Ministers and the
Presidium of the Supreme Soviet are formally drawn from the
Supreme Soviet, but actually they are nominated by the Party and
as such, are men with important positions. Members of the Politburo are all members of the Supreme Soviet.

The Presidium of the Supreme Soviet is an important deliberative body that remains active the year round; the Council of Min-

isters represents the administrative heads of the various divisions of Soviet Government, but the final power of policy-making rests in the hands of the Politburo whose members hold key government posts because they have top Party posts.

Courts and Paralleling the hierarchy of administrative
Procurators units is an inseparable (since there is no division of powers) hierarchy of courts and procurators (public prosecutors). In Moscow, at the center, is the Supreme Court, complemented by a procurator general. At the very bottom of the legal hierarchy are the people's courts and the local prosecutors. Although Western students of the Soviet legal system indicate that some move toward the Anglo-American concept of an assumption of innocent until proved guilty has occurred over the years, Western concepts of law and justice are of limited help in understanding the Soviet legal system. By and large, Western systems are based upon the principles of the rule of law and the assumption of the innocence of the charged party. Both of these reflect the concept of constitutionally limited governments existing primarily to serve today's individual citizen. As we have seen, however, Soviet government is oriented to serving state-determined ends in the name of the citizenry. Maximization of power in the name of strengthening the state and promoting the future realization of communism has been the Soviet *raison d'état* and law, like all else, must serve this goal.

The rule of law in the West implies that all are equal before the law and that only laws arrived at after due deliberation are enforceable. Thus, the British or American citizen has a maximum opportunity to predict whether or not his course of action will be adjudged in accordance with the rules of the game. Since Stalin, more often than not, the Soviet citizen has had an opportunity for prediction, but Soviet practice does not guarantee prediction. Antistate crimes are the major crimes, and above and beyond the laws on the books, these crimes are what the state officials of the moment say they are. Similarly, since today's citizen is but a servant of the future, and only the state knows what paths must be taken to achieve *nirvana,* the person charged with crimes against the state must prove his innocence. One must remember that under the system of democratic-centralism, only individuals, and never the state, can be wrong. Thus, the state is presumed to be right when a citizen is charged with a crime. If he should prove himself to be innocent, then the individual official who made the charge, not the law or the state, would be in error.

A Power   The key to the Soviet experiment in rule
Instrument of   is the articulation of Party and government
the First Order   functions into, for all practical purposes, a
                     monohierarchical bureaucracy that encompasses the whole of society in a descending network of punishments and rewards, thereby creating a total administrative state. Thus, for example, an official that one day is a key Party secretary in a regional office may be promoted the next day to an important state post at the republic level, since there is completely free movement between Party and state agencies.

Bureaucracy is essential to complex, modern, industrial systems in order to coordinate their activities, and as such, it is a neutral tool of government. Nevertheless, like a tool, it can be used for various purposes. A jackhandle is used to elevate the jack, but it can also be used as a handy weapon for bludgeoning a man to death. Bureaucracy is a necessary instrument of modern democratic rule, but it is also the major key to modern authoritarian rule. Bureaucracies come to have their own demands; therefore, at times, they may thwart the will of the citizens or the leadership. In damning the state, all states, the early Bolshevik leaders recognized bureaucracy as the backbone of the modern state, and since they rejected the state as evil, they also rejected bureaucracy. Lenin recorded in *State and Revolution*:

The bureaucracy and the standing army are a "parasite" on the body of bourgeois society—a parasite created by the internal antagonisms which rend that society asunder, but a parasite which "chokes" all its vital pores.[2]

Since bureaucracy is a major characteristic of the capitalist states, one sees the repeated Soviet claim that their administrative system has shed itself of bureaucracy, as such, and almost completely of any bureaucratic tendencies. However, by Western definition, the Soviets have established the most awesome bureaucratic system ever created.

Bureaucracy is one of those broad descriptive terms including so much that a simple, concise definition is probably impossible; however, in their *Dictionary of American Politics*, Smith and Lurcher have identified several characteristics:

The highly centralized, autonomous, and quasi-military type of administrative system developed in France after the First Napoleon, the principal units of which were called bureaus; hence a government dominated by permanent administrative agencies and inclined to be unresponsive to the political authorities of the government and to public opinion. Bureaucracies tend to reduce administration to the application of a set of rigid rules and formulas and to insist on a slavish devotion to routine, with the effect of exasperating the people and delaying public business. They are inclined to be satisfied with existing methods and are not disposed to experiment with new ones.[3]

Although modern political studies have added to our understanding of administrative patterns and relationships, Max Weber's pioneering analysis of bureaucratic organization is still valuable, particularly in attempting to understand how authoritarian political systems work. According to Weber's observations on the import and role of bureaucracies, they are inclined "to be unresponsive to the political authorities." Therefore, they can be particularly frustrating to democratic systems, blocking the initiative of the elected authority who is, after all, apart from the bureaucratic system. In an authoritarian regime, however, there is no separation of the leadership from the administration, and Weber tells us, "Where the bureaucratization has been completely carried through, a form of power relation is established that is practically unshatterable."[4] Weber further observes that once it becomes entrenched in a state, a bureaucracy is one of those structures of society which is hardest to destroy. In an authoritarian state in which bureaucracy has been completely carried through, as far as political power is concerned the political authorities are not elected, they are coopted and thus are not outside the system; therefore, they are not just part of the bureaucracy. Indeed, they are at its pinnacle because, as Stalin so clearly demonstrated, such leaders have learned to manipulate its apparatus. The bureaucracy's apparatus is a nearly perfect instrument for manipulating society and every individual in it. Although Weber wrote before the rise of the modern totalitarian state, he clearly perceived the awesome potential of the modern bureaucratic system when coupled with modern means of communication.

Bureaucracy is the means of carrying "community action" over into rationally ordered "societal action," therefore, as an instrument for "societalizing" relations of power, bureaucracy has been and is a power instrument of the first order—for the one who controls the bureaucratic apparatus.[5]

As described here, the Soviet system is the paradigm of a mono-hierarchical polity in a political system that boasts of a monolithic view of truth coupled with a high degree of success in "societalizing" all power relationships. Hitler's Germany was totalitarian, but neither Nazi Germany nor any other modern authoritarian system has matured to the degree that the USSR has since Stalin's death. As stressed earlier, Soviet administration encompasses virtually every activity of every citizen within its hierarchy.

Prior to the early 1950s, an important segment of the Soviet citizenry remained, not wholly outside of, but somewhat on the periphery of the total Soviet bureaucracy. These were the peasants in the *kolkhozy* ("collective farms").* In 1949, there were nearly 250,000 collective farms on which one-third of the total Soviet population lived and worked. Collectives with Party members as chairmen were in a minority, and only through relatively indirect outside controls could the state be assured that the decisions of many of the farm leaders would conform with the state's desires. As demonstrated by widespread peasant neglect of the collective fields during the Second World War and by occasions when peasants actually failed to accept the leaders (farm chairmen) selected by higher outside authorities, during the relatively lax years immediately following the War, the extent of control over agriculture did not begin to satisfy the desire for total central control. However, a complex series of agricultural reforms, presided over by Khrushchev from their inception, were started in 1950.

* Prior to the end of the 1960s, in practice, the major difference between the kolkhozy and *sovkhozy* ("state farms") was that the state-farm workers received a guaranteed wage as state employees, whereas the kolkhoz peasants' incomes depended upon the farms' economic success. At the end of the 1960s, however, a move to provide a guaranteed kolkhoz wage was instituted.

Paralleling economic changes involving increased investments in agriculture sufficient for the average peasant to notice an improvement in his standard of living, Khrushchev brought the kolkhozy fully into the bureaucracy by securing Party control over the farms. Previously, the principle of a highly disciplined Party composed of a carefully selected elite had meant that not enough Party-member officials could be spared to man the key posts on the quarter of a million collective farms. Enough Party members to fill the post of chairman on each farm might have been spared, but assurance of maintaining Party discipline requires additional Party units, which today average thirty members, to support the Party secretary (the title of the key Party figure at a given level of administration); thus, the dispatch of several million Party members to agriculture would have been necessary to satisfy the Soviet administrative scheme.

Beginning in 1950, the key to the Khrushchev reforms was the amalgamation of the smaller farms into large units. By the end of the 1960s, there were only some 37,000 kolkhozy and 12,000 sovkhozy, or a total of fewer than 50,000 farms,[6] and virtually all of these are now administered by Party chairmen served by active Party units. Moreover, the total number of Party members on the farms increased by more than 230,000 from 1954 to 1958 alone, as a result of one of Khrushchev's campaigns.[7]

Almost from the beginning of Soviet rule, nationalization of industry had allowed Party leaders to be placed in key urban posts. Long before World War II, most important industrial directorates included Party officials and factory Party units. When Stalin forced the peasants into the collectives in the early 1930s, he laid the foundation for including agriculture in the administrative system, but his insistence on giving all priority to industrial construction had prevented him from completing his "revolution from above" in agriculture. This Khrushchev accomplished, as he noted in his address to the Twenty-Second Party Congress: "There are 41,830 primary [Party] organizations at industrial enterprises, 10,427 at building sites, 18,398 on railways and in other transport services, 44,387 on collective farms . . ." and he continued, "The success of our course depends in great measure on the level of the organizational and political work in these lower units of the Party."[8] By 1967, Soviet statistics revealed that 2,300,000 Party members were in agricultural work. The implication, therefore, is that the average farm now has more than forty Party members.[9]

As already pointed out, beyond intent, the Soviet model, in practice, requires a highly developed industrial system that provides the means for instantaneous communication in all parts of the realm and a bureaucracy that encompasses the whole of the citizenry. The German peasant was never brought under Hitler's bureaucracy, and as we have seen, the Soviet peasant was only partially within the Soviet administrative hierarchy, prior to Stalin's death. Today, however, Soviet Russia is the first authoritarian system in all of history to succeed in including virtually all its citizens within the same bureaucratic administrative hierarchy. With the addition of the kolkhoz link, Khrushchev completed the chain. Today, therefore, only an insignificant number of Soviet citizens are outside the monolithic hierarchy of rewards and punishments which spreads over the whole of society and peaks in the hands of the General Secretary of the Communist party.

In a sense, the still immature system that existed during Stalin's lifetime enjoyed something at least remotely akin to the "separation-of-powers" principle that operates in the American system. This was the business of the Party checking on the government and the police checking on both. However, under Nikita Khrushchev and his successors, perhaps a most important transformation in the scheme of rule has been the increased monopoly of the Party over day-to-day direction of affairs, as well as policy-making. The police have been demoted, and the state bureaucracy, once relatively separate, has been more efficiently integrated with the Party system of direction. In short, heeding the observations of Weber, we see that the Party has steadily become the "one who controls the bureaucratic apparatus" in a model wherein Party activity is inseparable from state activity.

Some Principles   An examination of statistics on the careers
for Party   of Party members in administrative posts will
Administrators   give some indication of the growth in the
integration of the Party in day-to-day affairs of the state. Unfortunately, statistics on Party members serving as plant directors and in other key urban posts are not as freely cited as one might wish. Nevertheless, official statistics reveal that, "As

early as 1936, 97 percent of plant managers, 82 percent of chiefs of construction, 40 percent of chief engineers were Communists."[10] We also know that the post-1938 purge years saw an increased emphasis on recruiting the "intelligentsia" (which includes all with higher education) into the Party.

Whatever the exact situation in urban and industrial administration, the post-Stalin emphasis on agricultural problems resulted in the publication of some most interesting figures (see Table 4,)[11] which include documentation that by 1960 more than 95 percent of all kolkhoz chairmen were Party members.

Recognizing that virtually all industrial managers have long since been Party members, that the rapid turnover rate of industrial administrators is probably slower than it was in early days, and that the average plant manager most probably has more technical training than his collective-farm counterpart, the figures cited will help to support some observations on the demands upon the kolkhoz administrator that probably hold true throughout Soviet administration. These may be regarded as the three principles necessary for a successful Soviet administrator:

1. Unless one is assured of becoming a member of the Party, he might as well forget any aspiration for an important administrative post. The days have passed when skill alone could give promise of achieving a significant directorship.

Table 4—Kolkhoz Chairmen

Chairmen in the Party, their education, and length of service (in percent)

	ON JULY 1				ON APRIL 1		
	1952	1953	1956	1957	1958	1959	1960
Chairmen of kolkhozy							
Members and candidates to CPSU	79.4	79.6	90.5	91.2	92.6	93.5	95.3
Those finished with higher and secondary education	15.1	18.0	37.1	36.0	37.2	50.4	55.6
Higher education	—	2.6	7.8	7.4	7.8	11.8	—
Secondary education	—	15.4	29.3	28.6	29.4	38.6	—
Term as chairman of kolkhoz							
To 1 year	23.5	23.8	29.7	16.9	17.3	4.6	4.3
From 1 to 3 years	36.1	35.6	33.9	41.0	33.7	38.9	39.1
More than 3 years	40.4	40.6	36.4	42.1	49.0	56.5	56.6

2. Up or out is the rule. In the West, the bulk of the economic activity remains in private hands, and competition still brings about a fairly high degree of turnover in the corporate bureaucracies, particularly among sales and production administrators. By contrast, in governmental work, civil service protections leave the administrator fairly sure of maintaining his position. In the USSR however, virtually all work is governmental, and the protection of the state employee in his class is nil. In the West, many political leaders express the fear that rigidity and loss of efficiency results from an expansion of governmental bureaucracy. Such a fear is absent from the USSR. No civil service system protects the Soviet administrator, who is in a position similar to that of a young instructor in some of the highly competitive institutions of higher education in the United States. If the Soviet plant manager fails to meet plan, or to satisfy his Party superiors, he can expect to be demoted to a less important position. Under Stalin, many were prosecuted as criminals. As seen in Table 4, although a somewhat greater stability in agriculture was achieved near the end of the 1950s, still nearly half of the kolkhoz chairmen could not expect to retain their posts for more than three years. Of course, some were advanced in the hierarchy, others were shifted to another farm, but the bulk, having failed to make the grade, probably were demoted to lesser positions.

Western students of Soviet affairs have long since noted the interrelated phenomenon of the lower level administrator serving as the safety valve for frustrations that develop in the system. Since the Party is never wrong when production shortcomings develop or local antagonisms mount, a lower level administrator must carry the blame, sometimes in the form of a public reprimand, often at the cost of his career. Indeed, if the failure is serious enough, even a very high level administrator must suffer. One example of this was Khrushchev's removal of V. V. Matskevitch from his post as minister of agriculture, in 1960, reflecting the increasing awareness of the serious shortcomings of Khrushchev's agricultural reforms.

3. Appointment to high posts depends upon loyalty to the Party before all else, even before technical competence. Although the statistics that have been cited are not the only reason for noting a third principle, they do rather dramatically illustrate an important reality all ambitious young men in the Soviet Union must face. Two

gods must be served, Plan and Party. Failure to serve either will result in a ruined career, but as important as the Plan may be, adherence to the will of the Party as voiced by one's superiors is even more important. A plant manager or a farm chairman can fail to meet the demands of the plan and, through support of higher Party officials, survive to try again next year, but if he fails to meet the demands of the Party, he is finished. Statistically, a basis for such a conclusion is provided by the lag that exists between the percentages of chairmen with higher education and those who are Party members.

As noted in the earlier accounting of the educational level of the nation's Party secretaries, increasingly, key posts are held by Party people who also have a higher education. Nevertheless, the evidence remains that the man appointed to a key job is the best Party man among the better technicians available for the post, and not the reverse.

Planning   The demands of complex, modern industrial societies make planning to some degree a necessity in all systems if the possibilities of economic chaos are to be reduced to a minimum. In the Soviet system, however, total planning has been the imperative. Where democratic socialism has been adopted by West European governments, the recognition that total economic planning at the center would probably destroy political democracy has placed outer limits on the degree of planning adopted. Moreover, most Western economists in the past (and now some Soviet economists following the lead of Professor Liberman) have recognized that by itself total planning is a most unsatisfactory means of determining all economic output, particularly consumer items. If the Soviet citizens want wool stockings but most stockings manufactured are cotton, a lot of merchandise will remain unmoved on the shelves of the state stores, or, more likely, many customers will be dissatisfied. Belatedly, Soviet economists have begun to recognize that allowing for consumer demand is essential to rationalizing output. The needs and wants of more than two hundred million people cannot be adequately forseen months and years ahead of time by Moscow planners. Whether the problem will be solved by Liberman-like economic reforms within the demands of such a centrally controlled system, however, remains to be seen.

Marxist ideology strongly rejects the concept of interest rate* (which, after all, involves a reward for investments made in areas of greatest demand). An economy that bases its investment decisions on interest rates must recognize competition; therefore, it is by necessity decentralized—at least to the extent of several independent centers of decision-making. In contrast, the Soviet leadership's demand for central control over a local official today, tomorrow, and next year goes directly against attempts to decentralize. Indeed, total planning seems to be an imperative of the Soviet model. As Lenin recorded, "Socialism . . . is inconceivable without planned state organization, which keeps tens of millions of people to the strictest observance of a unified standard in production and distribution. We Marxists have always spoken of this. . . ."[12]

Stalin pushed the Leninist precept to the extreme. However, the administrative reorganization schemes championed by his successors have revealed an awareness that centralized decision-making in matters of local detail has been an impediment to efficiency in the operation of the Soviet economy. Liberman's call for using profit as a success indicator is a move toward decentralization. Similarly, Khrushchev's creation of more than one hundred regional *sovnarkhozy* for industrial administration and many of his own reforms and his successors' reforms in agriculture represented attempts to achieve a measure of decentralization in order to enjoy the advantages of local initiative. Unfortunately, most of the attempts to decentralize seem to have failed. The dictatorship's insatiable desire for maximum power and control over what it would describe as the essentials has canceled out effort after effort to achieve decentralization. Not only do the requirements for strict subordination of lower to high officials in the administrative hierarchy destroy such efforts, but the planning system itself does so, as well, if it is to remain internally rational.

Planning in a scale and to a degree unimaginable in Western societies is an essential ingredient of the Soviet total administrative

* Although indices, which are crude interest rates in disguise, have been used.

state. This is part of the rationale behind the Soviet penchant to regard plans once drawn up as already fulfilled. Perhaps a major impetus for this latter phenomenon is in the importance of futurism in Marxist–Leninist psychology. Insecurity in men is born of not being able to reasonably predict their positions in the future. Security for a Marxist tends to lie in an assurance of achieving secular materialistic goals much more than it does for people in societies in which religion works to placate fears of the future. Particularly under Stalin, the citizens' yearnings for material advancement were answered with the promise of a better life for future Soviet generations in the way that the medieval European peasantry were told to bear their lot because of the promised reward in heaven.

Whatever may be the motivation, plans once made have been regarded as law, and more than profit, more than quality of workmanship, more than observing lesser laws, "fulfillment and over-fulfillment of plan" has been the Soviet "first commandment." Indeed, extralegal shortcuts to successful plan fulfillment are unofficially sanctioned as long as these violations do not harm controls or upset the balance of the economy. At least in the past, nearly every enterprise has had its part-time, and the bigger ones a full-time, *tolkach,* an individual who is supposedly an internal administrator but who is actually a man with connections who uses his influence (*blat*) to make extralegal deals with other enterprises which will assure that both parties (through trade of short materials, loan of machinery, etc.) will be able to meet plan.

Not surprisingly, the lack of any rational means of neatly separating planning and administrative functions has had considerable effect upon the administrative system. Almost from the beginning, the need to coordinate all planning activity required the establishment of *Gosplan* ("State Planning Agency") separate from the Council of Ministers. Many of the ups and downs of the Soviet economy and the dictatorship's worries over the possible evolution of separate pockets of power have been reflected in the periodic redefinition of the powers of Gosplan. Thus, for example, near the end of Stalin's rule, his apparent worry over Gosplan's exercising too much administrative power was responsible for his ordering the execution of Voznesenski, the Gosplan head at the time. Certainly, this act was followed by his shearing the agency of much of the power it had amassed. Since Stalin, there has been a considerable revival of the powers of the State Planning Agency, but its stormy history is certainly far from completed.

Not that a reminder was necessary for his comrades, but Khrushchev recounted the importance of planning for the future Communist society in his address to the Twenty-First Party Congress.

Naturally in a Communist society there will be planned and organized distribution of work according to various branches of production, and social regulation of working time, with special reference to the specific characteristic of production processes. Machine production has a definite rhythm which is impossible to maintain without corresponding planning of human work.[13]

The material world, in this case the machinery of industry, has its own rhythm, and man, as viewed by the Marxist–Leninist, has no choice but to adjust himself to the demands of his machine-made environment. How unrealistic is it to envisage a Soviet future in which efficient machine production is analyzed and the results are fed into a computer which, in turn, is programmed to determine the citizen's place and his duties in the all-encompassing bureaucracy?

CHAPTER 9

Policy Control

A STUDY OF ONE INSTITUTION*

SOVIET administration is highly complex. The institutions of rule are many and varied. Never-ending reorganization on a scale unknown in other systems renders today's description of the structural configuration obsolete tomorrow. Indeed, the MTS (Machine Tractor Stations) discussed here, were abolished in 1958. Nevertheless, most of the institutional patterns are similar throughout the Soviet system of rule, and continued reorganization is evidence that most of the problems remain. Therefore, the following relatively detailed account of the history of one Soviet institution should provide insight into the workings of the administrative system.

* Much of the material in this chapter is derived from an article published by Roy D. Laird and Kenneth E. Beasley, "Soviet Tractor Stations—Policy Control by Auxiliary Services," *Public Administration Review*, Vol. XX, No. 4 (Autumn), 1960, pp. 213–218.

The MTS as an   Auxiliary services providing specialized as-
Auxiliary Service   sistance to the line units in such fields as
                      typing, printing, purchasing, and public re-
lations have a clear place in Western administrative theory and
practice. On the whole, auxiliary service units are to serve the line
almost as though they were outside agencies hired to do so. In
practice, however, auxiliary services often exploit their power to
control the timing of programs and to modify the method, with the
result that at least occasionally, program content also is modified.
The central purchasing office, set up to save the agency trouble and
to provide expertise in seeking out the best product at the lowest
price, and the personnel office, established to provide professional
advice on recruiting and training, in practice, often control these
activities, and this control can strongly affect program content.

The Soviet Machine Tractor Stations were famed not only as
a system for channeling scarce and expensive capital equipment in
order to achieve greatest output, but even more as the eyes and
ears of the central government in the field (also, in this case, in
the fields). In short, the MTS was designed primarily as an auxiliary
service agency.

Origin of the MTS   In the late 1920s, the newly enthroned
                      Stalinists created Machine Tractor Stations in
an attempt to improve the efficiency of agriculture, an industry
woefully short of machinery. The stations soon demonstrated the
advantages attributed to auxiliary services:

1. increased efficiency as a result of grouping this "common
activity,"
2. expert advice for line officials—in this case the kolkhozy
(collective farm) leaders,
3. closer supervision of farming, and
4. scarce resources (farm machinery) rationed with a national
view.

More importantly, the stations became a policy arm of the
central government. In addition to the dictatorship's need to find
a means of controling the peasants, agriculture was the major source

of investment capital with which to broaden the industrial base, and the semi-independent system of peasant farming did not allow for efficient and speedy extraction of enough of the peasants' produce. Finally, Stalin and his colleagues saw the need to maximize production with minimum input and, equally important, to achieve the dictates of Marxian doctrine that agriculture be socialized, and to find a means of controlling the activities of the rural population, which in the early years amounted to some 120 million farm people, eighty percent of the total population at that time.* The MTS satisfied all of these needs.

The number of Machine Tractor Stations grew rapidly after the first MTS, the "ten-tractor" Schevchenko station, was started in 1927. For the first few years the stations were technically owned by the collectives. In 1931, when they were taken over by the central Soviet government, there were 1,131 stations. By 1957, a year before their abolition, there were more than 8,000. A statement made in 1954 (the best information available) set the number of permanent employees for all stations at more than 1,250,000, and virtually all of the cropped land was serviced by them.[1]

Lines of Authority Formal and clear lines of authority are regarded as one of the essentials of administrative efficiency in the Western world. In contrast, Soviet authorities created in the MTS a system of *formal* multiple lines of authority. Therefore, in Soviet administration under Stalin *doubt* was institutionalized, and interwoven hierarchies were regarded as an essential guarantee of conformity to the central will, (i.e., the formal state organization, the Party, and the political police). Under this arrangement, political decision-making and administration are joined and yet separated.

Structurally, the stations were an extension of a department of the national government. Although they were directly under the charge of the Ministry of Agriculture, other federal agencies, such as Gosplan, exercised considerable influence over them. Each MTS director was immediately responsible to the Union-Republic Min-

* The opportunity the MTS offered for control over agriculture was so important that Stalin's move to forced collectivization awaited the invention of the MTS.

istry of Agriculture, he was employed and dismissed by that agency (see Fig. 3). Of course, in routine matters regional offices of the ministry supervised the direction of agriculture. As the administrative head and as a government official, the station director was held primarily responsible for the fulfillment of the economic plans not only of his MTS but also of the collective farms it served.

Chief Agronomists   The chief agronomist of each MTS was a coordinate authority and at the same time, along with his subordinates, an auxiliary service to the auxiliary service. He was responsible basically for the methods and techniques of field crop production and soil management, but what made his position unusual was his joint appointment and dismissal by heads of provincial agricultural administrations and by the ministries of agriculture of the republics. Also, although he could be compared with the agricultural extension worker in the United States who advises and counsels with farm producers, the chief agronomist, according to a 1953 decree, was a state inspector, checking on the quality of collective farm work, and he was empowered to issue orders correcting malpractice. According to that directive, his "instructions and orders...on problems of farming methods and quality of agricultural work must be carried out and can be countermanded only by province and territory agriculture and procurements administrations and by republic ministries of agriculture and procurements."[2]

Under each chief agronomist were field agronomists and zootechnicians. Soviet authorities, caught in the dilemma of distance versus identification, vacillated as to whether these field personnel should be closer to the MTS or to the kolkhozy. Prior to 1951 they were part of the staff of the MTS, but in that year they were advised to live on the kolkhozy. In 1953, they were transferred back to the MTS. Two years later they were placed on the kolkhozy again so they could more easily become a "part of the kolkhoz." There they became subject to a rather standard type of dual supervision, subordinated to the officials of the kolkhozy except, according to a Soviet agricultural editorial, "in questions of crop and livestock servicing of collective farms [when] they are obligated to follow the instructions of the chief agronomists and chief zootechnicians."[3]

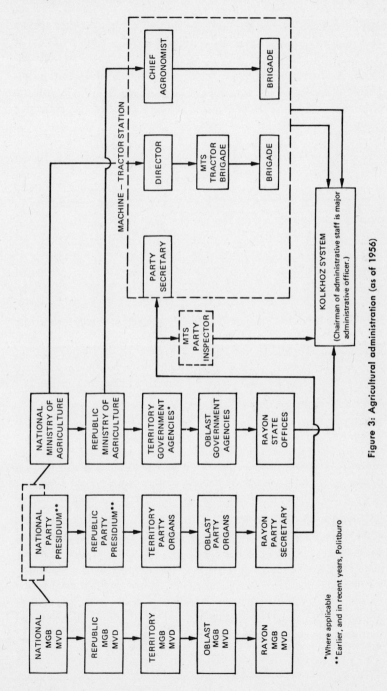

Figure 3: Agricultural administration (as of 1956)

*Where applicable
**Earlier, and in recent years, Politburo

Tractor Brigades   Actual tractor work on the collectives was
                          handled by the tractor brigades (five to seven
tractors) under the immediate command of the MTS director.
Members of the brigade were divided into three groups:

1. brigadiers (the brigade leaders and their assistant and some
"auxiliary inspectors") who were responsible for care and maintenance of equipment,
2. tractor drivers and other equipment operators, and
3. service squads (fuel and supply carriers).

Prior to 1953, these workers were members of a kolkhoz and were
temporarily attached to an MTS. Because of the large annual turnover stemming from this arrangement (estimated at 30–35 percent), a 1953 order of the Party and government provided that
"tractor drivers, . . . , brigade leaders [and helpers], . . . , excavator
machinists [and helpers], and chief accountants are permanent
[MTS] workers. . . ."[4] The decree further specified that seasonal
workers were to be assigned to the stations during harvest and could
not be assigned other work without the consent of the MTS. The
tractor workers exercised less initiative to help the kolkhozy in
unusual situations not covered in the plan after they were assigned
to the MTS permanently, and this motivation problem was never
fully solved to the satisfaction of Soviet authorities.

Control   The stations, controllers of agricultural op-
by the Party   erations, were themselves held to central
                       policy by the Party. A Party secretary, repre-
senting the local district government, was a "coordinate" to the
director. A most graphic statement of his function is found in a
1933 resolution of the Joint Plenum of the Central Committee:

The political departments of the machine and tractor stations . . . must
act as the eye of the Party and must guarantee control in all fields of
work and life on the machine and tractor stations . . . as well as on the
collective farms served by the machine and tractor stations. Guaranteeing the quality of seed during the sowing season, preventing the theft
of seed, supervising the correct execution of the threshing operation,
combating misappropriations of threshed grain, fighting against ab-
sentees from work, guaranteeing proper care of the livestock and other
property of the collective . . . farms, expelling all pernicious anti-Soviet

and anti-collective-farm elements from the collective . . . farms, selecting the best tested cadres for the collective . . . farms—such and similar are the problems that must constitute the focal point of the work of the political departments.[5]

Although the Party secretary, in 1933, was formally a deputy director of the MTS, further provisions of the same resolution explicitly stated (in apparent contradiction to the above) that the political departments within the MTS were to supersede neither the directors nor the local district Party committees. The MTS was to be governed by the principle of one-man management, and thus the director was to be clearly in charge, but the political departments (the full-time deputy Party director and any other Party members primarily engaged in production work) were to "aid in the solution of the tasks confronting the directors and were to supply the district committees with periodic information about the work of the stations." The Party spokesman was also to "explain to every mechanizer the nature and import of the Party and government directives."[6] These Party functions remained throughout the years although the formal relationship of the Party representative was changed when the position of deputy director was abolished, and a Party secretary established as a "co-equal" with the director in 1953.

Party influence on administration is not alien to Western administrators. The political party is expected to have an interest in, and be responsible for, administrative policy. But American parties have no formal role in administration as the Communist party has in the MTS, and, as emphasized in previous chapters, the parts that are played by the parties in both systems are almost opposite. In the United States, administrators are held responsible through successively higher supervisors, culminating in responsibility to an elected official. Although this system possesses unquestioned advantages, control of lower levels of the bureaucracy is often weak, and repairing mistakes in policy or procedure is usually delayed. In the Soviet Union, the Party is authorized to inspect and to intervene at the lowest administrative level, and it places spokesmen in official posts in units of government, such as the MTS.

In a Western democracy, it is the minority political party that checks on administrative practices, which, at least theoretically, are the responsibility of their rivals. In the USSR, prior to the post-Stalin blurring of the lines between the Party and the state, a major role of the single party was to play the "loyal opposition" to the administrators. Moreover, the Party probably has served to provide administrative uniformity in this activity. In the MTS, the responsibility was split between the national government (which appointed station directors) and the respective republics (which named chief agronomists). Of course, the need for coordination under the Soviet system, in which federalism is meaningless, is less than would be true in the United States.

Separatism and   The advantages of separating this auxiliary
Centralization   service from line control must have been
                                matched by the confusion that sometimes
resulted. For example, when a spring snow surprised one MTS, its leaders refused to switch from tractor plowing equipment to snowplows so the collective could ship its meat quota to market. The MTS already had fulfilled its quota of work and did not need to do any more. One writer complained:

Just think how many contradictions there are in our life. Just take this dispute with the collective farm chairman about clearing the roads. It seems like a triviality, a misunderstanding. But you try to solve it! For some time now the collective farms have been granted the power to plan their work and use their own initiative. But what kind of initiative is there here! The plans for tractor work, on which the whole prosperity of the collective farm depends, continue to be handed down from above by the province agricultural administration, and usually these plans exceed the needs. What does the MTS do? In pursuit of formal fulfillment of the plan in conditional hectares of soft plowing, it naturally begins to look for work that is "advantageous" of itself, large-scale work with a high coefficient, such as cultivation of fallow land, although often this endless cultivation—why hide our sins—only harms matters; while the MTS avoids such "trivial," "unprofitable" work as clearing the roads, even though it may be crucial to production. . . .[7]

There also were signs of overcontrol from the central government which was a growing problem as tractor stations increased in number and size and the potential for central control was fully recognized.

Until modest reforms were adopted in 1955, not only the total volume of tractor work but much of the detail work assigned to each MTS and the production of each collective were centrally planned. As Khrushchev himself admitted, this kind of planning was devised ". . . without any consideration for [local] soil o. climatic conditions and failed to develop the initiative and creativity of the MTS workers, agricultural specialists, collective farm leaders, and the whole mass of collective farmers."[8] Attempts to allocate machinery on a national scale also resulted in "gross and numerous mistakes," according to one report, in 1954. In 1956 Khrushchev stated that a system must be established so that new machines would be sent to the stations only on the application of the directors, and, in 1957, he complained that collective farms planned for the use of tractors on their fields without reference to MTS resources. Finally, in 1958, the Soviet press described still a third problem, though related to the first one:

Certain machines were allowed to pass into serial [mass] production with serious construction defects and, arriving at the MTS and sovkhozy, proved unfit for work. The leaders of the ministry cannot be ignorant of the idle time and the damage of hundreds of valuable machines, unused for years in Kalinin and other provinces.[9]

Though the stations were assigned to coordinate agricultural activity, they themselves often were uncoordinated. Even Party controls were not always effective. As early as 1934, standard contracts between the stations and kolkhozy were decreed. This standard contract also served to increase MTS control over the kolkhozy. In 1939 even stricter controls were necessary, as Leonard E. Hubbard described in *The Economics of Soviet Agriculture*:

The new contract differed from its predecessor in laying down more rigid rules and enforcing a greater degree of responsibility on both parties in the punctual and accurate performance of their respective obligations. This same problem of coordination appeared with regard to the use and distribution of spare parts, the situation being so bad that tractor stoppages, as a result of technical disrepair, exceeded 4,000,000 tractor hours in one province.[10]

The attempt to introduce cost accounting, in 1956, was of particular significance in revealing administrative problems because of (ac-

cording to *Kommunist*) "the negligent attitude of the directors of
some MTS toward financial and economic aspects of MTS work,
toward rational utilization of collective farm land and toward operating economically."[11] Stated differently by Khrushchev to the
Twentieth Party Congress:

The presently existing order of financing MTS through the state budget
begets irresponsibility and lack of control. Many workers of the MTS
do not study deeply the economic indices of the work of the machine-
tractor stations and do not display proper interest in the rational use of
machines. MTS are financed independently from the results of [their]
economic achievement; payment for the labor of MTS workers is not
dependent on the effective use of machines [or] on the yield of agricultural products and the productiveness of animal-husbandry on the kolkhozy.[12]

There is some evidence that at least three factors were responsible for this state of affairs:

    1. a shortage of trained personnel at the local level to report
rapidly and accurately,
    2. a desire by the central authorities to maintain control over
kolkhozy even at the price of poor allocation of resources, and
    3. a friction between the kolkhozy and tractor stations.

Whatever the cause, the Soviet leadership increasingly reflected a
recognition that the MTS had become a costly, inefficient operation
that was no longer needed since other means of control over the
peasant and his produce were now available. As implied, the demise
of the MTS was a major move in the direction of eliminating the
separation of the Party and state administration, thus an important
move in the direction of monohierarchical polity.

The End of   Quite abruptly, in 1958, Khrushchev *sug-*
the MTS   *gested* the sale of all MTS equipment to the
                        kolkhozy, a startling proposal that would re-
sult in a basic change in economic relationships. Plowing and sowing of grain crops, cotton, sugarbeets, and certain other crops on
the kolkhozy were almost completely mechanized at this time
through MTS. Moreover, the MTS administrative device was nearly
thirty years old, and even in an authoritarian setting "the way it
has always been done" cannot easily be brushed aside.

Several factors explain the radical change. Abandoning the MTS served to end the national subsidy to the collectives through central financing of the MTS and to cut down the central government's share of what apparently had come to be regarded (in 1958) as an overinvestment in agriculture since Stalin's death; after all, every added ruble invested in agriculture would be a ruble less for industrial expansion. On the political side, the MTS monopoly over collective farms was no longer necessary; other controls had been developed. As noted earlier, after 1950 the trend toward reducing the differences between the Party and the state was on, and an all-out effort was made to choose Party members as chairmen. As a result, by 1958 the Party was fully entrenched in the farms' administrations. Moreover, indoctrinated agricultural technicians and administrative and mechanical specialists now tightly held in the closed bureaucratic ring were present on nearly every farm. Finally, by 1958 there was no longer an acute shortage of agricultural equipment as there had been when the stations were first created, so that central allocation of scarce resources was not as important as it had been earlier.

In short, Khrushchev apparently concluded that efficiency now was on the side of decentralized auxiliary services, and that the Party's new presence on the farms assured avenues of direct control over agriculture at the lowest level. Possibly, the centralized power of the MTS had grown to be a threat, and their abandonment was viewed as diminishing the state organization and at the same time increasing the role of the Party. Certainly, under the new situation there was no loss of effective control, and the action gave substance to Khrushchev's claim that already the state was beginning to wither away, though the Party, of course, was not.

Soviet Institutions: Artificially or Socially Defined Most contemporary students of government might agree that a fundamental difference between democracies and dictatorships is that the governors in the former must depend upon popular authority to carry out their rule, whereas the latter depend more upon power, force, or threat of force. Thus important differences can be found in an examination of the institutions used by the two systems as instruments of rule. The important institutions of democratic rule are those that come to life and are accepted by society as essential for the promotion of the needs and desires of the citizenry. Although these vital parts of government in an open society must, and do, change, no politician nor political group in its right mind would dare to abolish them overnight. For example, under Franklin Delano Roosevelt, the New Deal WPA that provided hundreds of thousands of jobs was not killed by a politician; rather it died a natural death due to increased economic activity that ended the problem of unemployment. However, the demise of that institution was an exception. Once created, the vast majority of such governmental agencies in democratic systems became a vital part of the political, social, and economic fabric; longevity is virtually assured.

The MTS in the USSR was not an institution isolated from the people. It employed millions, and it dealt daily and directly with nearly one-half of the Soviet population. When one compares it with Western democratic institutions, however, one is immediately struck by the relative artificiality of both its beginning and its ending. In its inception, the MTS was created by decree. Its officials held a monopoly over the agricultural machinery which provided the MTS managers with the power to impose their will upon the collective farmers. Furthermore, one speech by the first secretary of the Party was all that was necessary to decree the end of the MTS. Artifically created, the particular Soviet institutions of today may mostly be gone tomorrow; the MTS has not been an isolated phenomenon in this regard. Agencies, indeed ministries, have whirled by at such a speed that one doubts that the average citizen has even attemped to keep track of them. Continued administrative reorganization is a major means whereby the top leadership attempts to maximize response to the central will.

PART IV The Adjuncts:
Citizens and
Indirect Controls

CHAPTER 10

Ostracism and Other-Direction*

*The New
Soviet Man*

THERE is no diffusion (separation) of powers among the central agencies of government in the Soviet Union and no such separation between Moscow and the fifteen republics, and in a very real sense there is also no separation between the state's interest and that of the citizen. (Here, the term *state* is meant to encompass both government and Party agencies of rule.) True, in Western democratic systems, private organizations (e.g., the Boy Scouts and the Chamber of Commerce) do become actively interested in government, but both constitutional principle and public attitude have provided effective opposition to state intrusion into the activities of such private organizations. As far as the individual's private life is concerned, the British claim that "a man's home is his castle" is a

* *Other-Direction* is borrowed from David Riesman and colleagues "other-directed society."[1]

vital precept of all open societies. But society in the USSR is not open, and invasions of privacy are not uncommon.

Building on the view that man is a communal animal and buttressed by the dictatorship's belief in the need to root out all possible sources of opposition and the conviction that all economically related matters must be centrally coordinated, the Soviet system has quite effectively circumscribed the private as well as the public sectors of life. We have asserted that the mainstay of the Soviet monohierarchical paradigm is the total administrative state supported by a single vision of truth. All economic and social activity is incorporated at some level of the bureaucratic hierarchy, but even with a bureaucracy in which the direction of virtually every economic and social activity is under the same administrative roof, maximum control is not achieved merely because all work for the same employer. The guiding philosophy of Marxist–Leninist "science" demands control over the whole man; therefore, even beyond the pervading Party and governmental apparatuses, various institutions and practices have been added, adjuncts to the administrative network, to assure that nothing is overlooked that might aid in creating "the new Soviet man," the absolute conformist.

The post-Stalin leadership has increasingly revealed an understanding that the guiding theory behind Soviet institutions—that man is a communal animal—demands important changes in man if Soviet society is to go further. Thus, as one Soviet writer has noted, in the Soviet world, "the people's vital energy is determined by the concurrence of the individual's interest with the interest of society . . . [Where] 'mine' and 'ours' merge . . ." is the place where the "seeds" of the future Communist society are germinating. Here, then, is the human soil that receives the attention of the Soviet political cultivator.[2]

Although it is now recognized that much of what was long regarded as fixed human nature is, in fact, quite mutable, Western social sciences tend to retain the premise that beyond helping those who are obviously mentally ill, the social scientist has no right to attempt to force a change in man. Aside from the motivational research of "Mad. Ave." hucksters, which is frowned upon, and sanctioned attempts to remake the criminal elements of society, social engineering is widely regarded as tampering with something sacred, an activity that might well destroy the "open society" itself.

Soviet society, however, is closed, and since the Party-designed institutions, created for a perfect and knowable future, must be fitted to a society still possessing some of the ills of generations of exposure to a rotten past environment (as we shall see in a subsequent chapter), Soviet social science is charged with aiding in the task of changing man, as they have it, promoting proletarian class consciousness to the point where all classes will be destroyed, and replaced by a society of "the new Soviet man" who will express his correct "Socialist" (i.e., communal) nature.

As seen by Marxist eyes, the march of the dialectic of history unfolds in stages. Thus, an integral part of Stalin's declaration that socialism within a single state had been created by 1936 was the asserted recognition that by that early date Soviet man had already attained a higher plateau of consciousness. Later, with Khrushchev's assertion that a middle level communism will be attained in the foreseeable future (1980, a date his successors have not repudiated) came the claim that Soviet society had already achieved an even higher level than that of Stalinist socialism.

What the Westerner would call social engineering, then, becomes for the Soviets, in Khrushchev's words, a vital "function of all the ideological work of our Party and state to develop new traits in Soviet people." Continuing further in his statement of what must be done to achieve the future, the former Party chief noted that the people must be trained "in collectivism and love of work, in Socialist internationalism and patriotism, in the lofty and ethical principles of the new society, in Marxism–Leninism." Communism will be "the most just and perfect society," and with the full bloom of the new Soviet man "all the finest moral traits of free men will unfold to the full. . . ." And then the first secretary charged "[W]e must bring up the man of the future today."[3] That the campaign to create a new man has been most earnest was solidly confirmed by a resolution of the Party Central Committee a year following the first secretary's remarks:

. . . as socialist democracy develops further and the socialist state system gradually evolves into communist public self-government, persuasion and education of the masses are becoming to an ever greater extent the chief method of regulating the activity of Soviet society. . . . The molding of a new man with communist traits, habits, and ethics, and the elimination of the survivals of capitalism in the minds of the people are at present among the main practical tasks.[4]

In 1968, Khrushchev's successor L. I. Brezhnev spoke of "Soviet man" in his address to the All-Union Congress of Teachers, stressing that Soviet "socialism differs from other social systems in that by its entire development, it consciously and purposely moulds and prepares its future," especially by "inculcating" a "Communist outlook" in the young.[5]

Marx, Engels, and Lenin had asserted that the state must eventually "wither away," but other than the cryptic assertion that the nonstate without anarchy would be an "administration of things" rather than men, their description of the future was most unclear. Whatever they had in mind, however, recent events in Soviet society and new pronouncements on the matter reveal what is planned for Soviet society after 1980—one is tempted to say 1984.

First of all, the Soviet leaders have made it quite clear that although most of the state institutions now in existence will be gone, the Party will still be there. Therefore, an outside observer is forced to conclude that, with the overall advance of the Party in administration, the present responsibilities of the hierarchy of state offices paralleling those of the Party will be taken over by the Party—"A rose by any other name would smell as sweet."

In the blush of victory during the early months of Soviet rule, the highly idealistic side of the new leadership was expressed in attempts to let the state wither away by allowing the workers to run the plants and by establishing a nearly complete equality of wages. However, this "honeymoon of communism" was shortlived, killed by the necessities of the civil war and by the hard-learned lesson that, at least at that early stage, the class consciousness assertedly necessary if an extreme egalitarian system were to work, had not sprung into being among the Soviet people.

Lenin and, even more emphatically, Stalin learned that monetary incentive was the most easily manipulated tool for getting production out of society. Thus, Stalin said that the Communist formula ("from each according to his abilities, to each according to his needs") was for the future and that the ruling principle of Socialist construction was ". . . to each according to his work."

Besides monetary awards, various psychic rewards, initiated during Stalin's day, were employed to involve the individual in the goals of the state. Mothers were awarded medals for breeding

numerous children. The *Stakhanovite* workers ("rate buster") received public acclaim as the most valuable of all Soviet citizens.

Rate-busting was all right during the forced-draft industrialization of the USSR, but as the economy became more complex,
workers whose production was way out of line from that of their
fellows disrupted the achievement of plan more than they helped
this goal. Moreover, such schemes encouraged individualism, whereas
industrial operations are inherently collectivist institutions that run
most efficiently when each worker operates as part of the team,
one cog on the gear fulfilling his assigned task in complete harmony
with all of the other cogs in the machine.

Even before Stalin's death, "Socialist discipline" and "Socialist
competition" came to be the means encouraged for future progress
toward the evolution of the "new Soviet man." Members of a
shop in a given factory or whole plants have been encouraged to
engage in competition with similar units in the same or a related
factory. Such practices to strengthen collectivism had started under
Stalin, but they have been carried much further under his successors, not only in terms of controlling the work situation but also
in terms of capturing the whole Soviet citizen in his off-work
hours. Yet, as seen in that important institution, the "voluntary
peoples' militia," roots for today's more sophisticated institutions of
social control can be found in early Soviet history.

From "Committees   During the period of "War–Communism,"
of the Poor"   1918–1921, perhaps the most serious prob-
to "Voluntary   lem was obtaining food from the peasantry
Militia Squads"   for the city workers and particularly for the
                       Red Army who were fighting with the
Whites. Most of the peasantry had little enough to feed themselves, but the more fortunate did have grain.

A stalemate existed in the exchange of goods between the
cities and villages. The peasants were unwilling to sell what little
farm food surpluses there were for grossly inflated rubles. However, without food, the wheels of industry could not even begin to
turn in order to produce those commodities for which the peasant
would be willing to bargain. Quite apparently, some drastic means
was needed to break this stalemate if the factories were to operate
and the army was to fight.

This was done by forced requisitioning of food surpluses. Ostensibly the so-called distributive quota was to be applied only to peasants who actually had surpluses, but in fact, it was often applied to homes which were without any surplus grain. In principle, the so-called *kulak* ("tight fist") segment of the peasantry should have been the ones most affected by this program, but actually, a large section of the "middle-peasantry," who were unquestionably neither exploiters nor hoarders, became victim of this plan. To implement the program the Party organized about "30 thousand committees of the poor."[6] These committee members were peasants who were organized and encouraged by urban Party zealots assigned to the countryside to help enforce the requisitions and charged by Lenin with collecting "every particle of surplus grain (for) the state reserves, because *the whole country must be swept clean* of concealed or ungarnished grain surpluses."[7]

A less astute leadership could easily have failed to discover the surpluses hidden by a peasantry long-practiced in concealing their small hoards from Tsarist officials. This problem was shrewdly solved, however, by harnessing the natural jealousy of the very poor and the shiftless to the cause. The hiding places and the tax dodging ruses of their more fortunate neighbors were well known to the hungry peasants. Therefore they became ideal tax gatherers when organized into the Committees of the Village Poor.

In an attempt to salvage the tsardom, Nicholas II's Prime Minister Peter Stolypin (1906–1911), having realized the importance of the peasantry, instigated plans for creating a peasant middle class, a Russian yeoman farmer. Stolypin had lost in his government's "wager on the sturdy and the strong." Now, Lenin placed the fate of Bolshevism in the hands of the "needy and the drunken" (Stolypin's words), and as a result the war was won. Interestingly, even though the peasants were obviously divided, the official line repeated in Soviet histories has been that nearly the whole peasant population was in favor of the requisitions. This view is seen in a work published in 1954 in which the Soviet historian Kraev asserted that "the poor organized and petitioned the urban proletariat to assist them in a combined effort to obtain bread."[8]

As for the peasant attitude, a policy which continued to recognize their private interests in the land tended to compensate for the distasteful requisitioning program. Had the level of the peasants' information been higher, the double-edge policy of forced requisitions and excessive pressure on them to join the communes might well have resulted in widespread peasant dissatisfaction with the new government. Instead, however, the vast majority of peasants who still regarded the Soviet government as the source of political support for the seizure of the land from the current Tsarist landlords did not connect the government with either the requisitions or the pressures to join the communes. This fact was clearly recognized by Lenin and was later recorded in a "Report Delivered at the Eighth Congress of the Russian Communist Party (Bolshevik)," March 23, 1919. In this report, Lenin argues that as a result of "careerists and adventurers" who had attached themselves to the ranks of the Communists "like leeches" and who were resorting to damaging "coercion" to join the communes, many of the peasants exclaim"

"Long live Soviet power, but *down with the communia*!" This is not an invention; these facts are taken from real life, from the reports of comrades in the localities. We must not forget what enormous damage is always caused by lack of moderation, by all rashness and haste.[9]

Although Lenin's committees had far from tapped the will of all the peasantry, sufficient numbers had voluntarily, and even eagerly, joined the move to win success for the Party goals.

Again in the early years of forced collectivization, Stalin sent new Party zealots out to the countryside, to organize the natural hatred for the rich by the poor, the downtrodden, and also the shiftless into "Committees of the Poor" to achieve the ends of the Party. Again the kulak was used as bait, this time described as the chief element barring the less fortunate from the creation of the collective farms, which created, would shortly guarantee security for all.

The British historian E. H. Carr has argued that perhaps even more important than getting the peasants' food, the early committees were designed as a political gesture "to split the peasantry," thereby diminishing the possibility of concerted peasant political action. He is probably right although one can also conclude that at least passive acquiescence by many of the peasants was necessary

for the scheme to work.[10] The principle of rule, successfully employed in the "Committees of the Poor," is still utilized today.

The ability to shape mass public opinion, within constitutional limits, is fundamental for the leadership in "open societies,"
and political studies stress that for large numbers of voters the
band wagon principle—the desire to be on the winning side—
is of great importance to the individual's decision as to what he
approves and disapproves. Nevertheless, in a constitutional democracy, there is considerable opportunity for dissent, particularly
since the citizen who wishes to differ from official policy can
usually anticipate finding fellow dissenters with whom he can
join in the expression of opinion. In the Soviet setting, however,
just to feel opposition is to place oneself in isolation as the outsider at the bottom of the heap who has dared to retain some
of the elements of the "inner-directed man." This is particularly
true in the contemporary Soviet situation in which virtually all
possibility of organized popular opposition has long since been
destroyed (not to be confused with the fight for power among the
elite at the top of the hierarchy at the time of a succession), and
in which nearly three generations of Soviet citizens have heard
nothing but the virtue of becoming what David Riesman and
colleagues called the "other-directed man."[11]

To date, the most dramatic exploitation of the old "committee" principles has been in the organization of "militia squads."
These "voluntary" organizations are reported to have been particularly effective in Khrushchev's campaign to develop the New
Lands area of Kazakhstan. In his report to the Tenth Party Congress of Kazakhstan, First Secretary of the Kazakhstan Communist
Party Central Committee, D. A. Kunayev admitted that the un-
settled situation in Kazakhstan had precipitated the creation of
some four thousand "militia units" composed of 132,000 individuals by the spring of 1960. The prime target of these vigilante
committees was the Kazakh natives. Their task was to root out
customs and religious survivals of the past that assertedly were
responsible for "private-ownership mentality, a disdainful attitude
to labor, theft of public property, and other antisocial phenomena."
Before the New Lands project could be truly successful such
"survivals" of the past must be rooted out, Kunayev declared.[12]

Although peasant class consciousness is regarded as being

the furthest from the ideal of "the new Soviet man," the new committees and the principles designed to increase social conformity have not been restricted to agriculture; they have been applied to the whole society. Reflecting on the guidelines established at the Twenty-First Party Congress, A. I. Denisov underscored the importance of such social pressures throughout Soviet society.

The growing role of public organizations is manifested by countless processes in the life of society, in particular by the transferring to the jurisdiction of public organizations of a number of functions exercised by state institutions. . . . The Congress expressed its profound belief that the public could play an exceptionally important role in combatting breaches of socialist law and order. "Our public organizations" N. S. Khrushchev said at the Congress, "have no less adequate capacities, means and forces for this than the militia, the courts, and the prosecutor's office."[13]

A series of Party resolutions, draft laws, and decrees of the Supreme Soviet, as well as speeches by dignitaries from the top leadership on down, and articles and editorials in the government-controlled newspapers have indicated the intention of the regime regarding the role of volunteer citizens' groups. Citizens have been urged to take measures to combat "violations of socialist order," but mainly through officially sanctioned forms of public participation in law enforcement. The individual, however, does act on occasion, as revealed in a letter to the editor of *Komsomolskaya Pravda*. "Our laws are aimed at combatting hooliganism. Society is rising up against it ever more widely and resolutely. . . . More and more often we see 'unorganized' people grab scoundrels by the arm and give them a real talking-to. . . ."[14] Nevertheless, the greatest official emphasis is on the formation of public organizations. In addition to the volunteer workers' militia detachments, there are also comrades' courts, public inspection services, and organizations to supervise paroled lawbreakers. Thus, as A. I. Denisov observed: "The 21st Party Congress emphasized that the withering away of the state means the development of the socialist state system into communist self-government."[15]

Not only in agriculture but in the urban centers as well, "voluntary workers' militia detachments" have been created. For example, a conference of trade union committees was held in the largest plants in Leningrad as early as November 21, 1958. "And everywhere," according to *Izvestia,* "the firm opinion was expressed: workers' militia detachments must be created." This initiative was approved by higher authority, and it was decided that the units would be created "from the best and most politically conscious among the workers and employees."[16] Of course, such a move is aimed at the overt criminal, but as in the old drive against the kulak, the major goal is that of capturing the will of the vast majority of the masses. Joining the mob in its concentration upon the recalcitrant, the individual citizen is given the satisfying sense of participating in something meaningful.

Guided by an all-pervasive, tightly disciplined Party leadership, if and when such "voluntary" organizations become fully entrenched in the Soviet social fabric, these organizations easily identifiable as state organizations (for example, the courts) probably can be allowed to wither away. In the USSR, these groups are not ordinary mobs, and although they tap human spontaneity, they are not unguided social missiles. This is "guided democracy" operating under the closest scrutiny and the tightest control of trusted local Party leadership. Therefore, the major goal is that of providing the mob-type media wherein, as in all mobs, individual consciousness, that is, individual will becomes completely submerged in the will of all. The social and political nonconformist (thus, the "inner-directed man") is the major target. Clearly, the Soviet dictatorship is deliberately attempting to exploit those undemocratic forces that De Tocqueville feared might accidentally destroy democracies.

Although the criminal is the subject under discussion in the following extracts from *Izvestia* and *Kommunist,* little reading between the lines is required to recognize that the noncriminal element is even more important.

Only the broad public can and must make the defendant's psychological change of heart permanent and help him to free himself from the influences that have led him to commit a crime.[17]

Often cases occur in which public condemnation or the fear of it has a stronger influence on those who have violated the standards of conduct than does punishment under law.[18]

There are a great many lawbreakers who stand trial only before their fellow men. The great preventive value of public opinion must here be recognized. It is one thing if a hoodlum has to answer only to a judge and a score of spectators. If, on the other hand, he is the target of hundreds of pairs of eyes belonging to his comrades and acquaintances, that is quite a different matter.[19]

What more effective means of assuring total conformity is there than arranging society so that each feels he is standing alone, but in the center of the crowd "the target of hundreds of pairs of eyes," each watching for the slightest unfamiliar, and thus unacceptable, move.

Since the great Stalinist purge of the 1930s, Soviet guilt has been not only that of the actual criminal but that of the Puritan as well. Even to have considered the possibility of commiting a crime or an antisocial act is just as deserving of punishment.

Reared in societies that stress individuality, the Westerner may tend to totally depreciate the possible effectiveness of such artificially created "voluntary" institutions. However, studies such as those conducted by Alex Inkeles and his colleagues have revealed attitudes and traits comparable to those commonly found in earlier Russian literature, especially that of Dostoevski. Dostoevski paints a picture of people brought up by their culture to be very sensitive to the approval or censure of their group, less inclined to independence and nonconformity than people brought up in the more individualistic Western tradition. Institutions, such as the "voluntary militia squads" can be an enormous mainstay for a mature totalitarian system—an authoritarian society not dependent upon terror to achieve high levels of conformity to the central will.

The Westerner whose culture has reinforced "inner-directed" attitudes should not be too quick to argue that the intrusions upon the individual in the USSR go against human nature. As noted earlier, beyond attitudes arising from basic needs common to all men, what is often called human nature is not really so similar from society to society. For example, personal privacy is very important to most Americans. Whenever possible, homes are designed or purchased to provide each member of the family with a private room. Children are repeatedly told that they cannot satisfactorily do their homework in a crowded kitchen or living room—they must go off by themselves if they are to have time to think. Yet, in many parts of the world, specifically in the USSR, housing shortages have been so great that large families have had to crowd into two or three rooms, often sharing cooking and toilet facilities with neighbors. True, Soviet authorities and the citizenry alike have long recognized the importance of expanded housing. Yet, in the USSR and related Eastern European cultures, one repeatedly hears of incidents in which individuals have had an opportunity to live in more spacious quarters, offering greater privacy, only to opt for the cramped togetherness of grandparents, parents, and children all living in one or two rooms. Certainly, this author's first-hand observations in Eastern Europe and the USSR have convinced him that large numbers of people in these societies gain an important sense of security from constant close contact with others, under conditions that would seem intolerable for many "inner-directed" Americans.

The employment of locally organized groups to impose conformist behavior on neighborhood deviants from the social (or political) norms probably seems natural to the "other-directed" Soviet citizen, whereas similar employment of social pressures in Great Britain or the United States would be considered unacceptable meddling in one's private affairs.

Voting Behavior   Whatever their particular functions, all Soviet institutions must serve the single purpose of maximizing the degree of popular conformity to the single central will. This is the role of the courts, the role of the various Soviets, and the role of elections.

The average vote in the average Soviet election consists of 98 to 99% of the voters, and only very few of these citizens cross out the name rather than vote for the single candidate offered. Government coercion has played a part in turning out these votes, but at election time the individual Soviet citizen's desire to act as a part of a single will, expressing a voice of approval for the leadership, is also important. The Soviets use the term *election,* but again one must remember that as with so many concepts, their definition of the term differs from ours. Soviet elections are not designed to pick government officers or to register disapproval of the in's. Soviet Election Day is a national holiday on which all are invited to cry,

"Hurrah for the USSR! Look what we have accomplished!" Putting one's "X" on the piece of paper provided is a matter not of voting but of saying, "I am proud of my country." This does not mean that if given the opportunity to express himself, the individual Soviet citizen would not say he does not like this or that law or official. However, the Soviet ballot is not designed for this purpose.

In one interesting way there is perhaps an important similarity between Soviet and Western elections. Studies of Western voters' habits have revealed that many voters are voting the past. A man votes for a party because it was the party of his parents; he votes for a candidate and his party because in his memory the party of the opposing candidate was less kind to his pocketbook. Whether voting in important elections or merely expressing approval of the in's, men's decisions are influenced much more by the past than they are by promises for the future. Therefore, Soviet politics must be viewed (if one is thinking of the opinions of its citizenry), not in terms of Western systems but in terms of Tsarist rule. Life in Russia had been more difficult under the tsars than it was under Lenin. In spite of forced collectivization, mass terror, and perhaps near revolt at times, Stalin did make the USSR powerful. Moreover, under Stalin many, perhaps most, lived a less tenuous existence than their fathers—certainly life expectancy increased greatly, education became universal, and employment was assured. Since Stalin, further noticeable improvements have been made. Therefore, when the Soviet citizen votes, it is not Election Day in the Western sense but rather a kind of Soviet "Fourth of July"; He is encouraged to think of how much better off he is than his father so that to cross off the name on the ballot would be to deny the tremendous progress made by his beloved country.

The observations made here on the nature and purpose of Soviet elections has been underscored by a most interesting analysis of "dissent" (i.e., crossing off the single name on a ballot) in Soviet elections. As Professor Jerome Gilison notes along with his statistical analysis of this phenomenon, Soviet writers agree with Western analysis that Soviet elections are essentially positive, participatory, legitimizing, demonstrative, educational, and patriotic. True, the 500,000 to 700,000 voters who do dissent in any given election do reflect a reality of opposition. Indeed, the 0.001% of all the candidates defeated in "any given election" must have been defeated by an organized opposition, but this opposition always has been against candidates at the very lowest levels, never against those running for higher offices. Moreover, Gilison's findings have led him to conclude that "most negative voting throughout the Soviet Union is probably based on economic and local issues rather than 'purely political' issues of national policy."[20]

Given the relative lack of secrecy in Soviet balloting, Prof. Gilison certainly is right to speak of the "brave souls" who still dare to cross out a name. Perhaps his conclusion that the decrease in voting dissent in recent years (which he documents) stems from "increased liberalization" and "improvement in living standards." This may be, but the casting of fewer negative votes also agrees with the present author's view that since Stalin, an increasingly more efficient use of the bureaucracy and a more adroit exploitation of adjunctual means of control has produced an ever higher level of "other-directed" citizens.[21]

CHAPTER 11

Unions and Collective Farms

CHANGES over the years, particularly changes in the rural USSR brought about by Khrushchev's agricultural administrative reforms, have placed both the collective farms and the trade unions in a position of being nearly totally subsumed under the bureaucratic hierarchy of rewards and punishments that extends from its center in Moscow to most local levels of economic activity. However, both the unions and the collective farms are more than just local economic administrative institutions. Both are utilized to intrude into the private and social affairs of the workers and peasants in ways that are not common in most other societies. Both are quasi-governmental institutions wherein virtually all of their economic activity has been neatly incorporated into the administrative monohierarchy. However, additional activities performed by these institutions place them also in the category of adjuncts to the system of rule. In theory, both the unions and the kolkhozy are independent non-governmental cooperatives. In practice, however, they serve as prime examples of intermeshed Party and state hierarchies which provide an unbroken chain of communications and controls from Moscow to the peasants' and workers' private lines. Here, the Party is the major link. Here also, one can see a basis for the genuine possibility of the state (i.e., its agencies) withering away in name, leaving the Party hierarchy to continue the rule much as before.

Company Unions   As Professor Alfred Meyer has pointed out, organization of activity in the USSR is very similar to that in a huge Western corporation.[1] Ironically, however, even though there is great accuracy in referring to the Soviet system as the "USSR Incorporated," whereas paternalistic company unions long since have passed from the scene in Western states, there is great similarity between Soviet unions and the company unions of an earlier era in the West. Leaving the legal distinctions involved in ownership to the side, the key Party members in the Soviet Union are comparable to the corporate owners in a non-Communist setting. Party members not only dominate the Soviet counterpart of the board of directors as well as other key managerial posts but also monopolize trade union leadership. Nevertheless, Western students of Soviet unions report that the various trade unions do serve the interests of the workers, collectively and individually.

Although the unions assertedly are organized democratically, in practice, at all levels union officials owe their positions to Party cooptation from above. Unlike elsewhere, where the right to strike is the independent union's key weapon, no such right is allowed the Soviet trade unions. Moreover, from the top to the bottom they are organized to work hand in glove with the Party and state officials to give top priority to the demands of the economy as determined by higher Party authority. Economic success of the enterprise, whether gauged by fulfillment and overfulfillment of plan or by showing a profit by cost accounting *(khozraschet)* procedures, is just as much the first duty and responsibility of Soviet trade union officials as it is the duty and responsibility of Soviet plant managers.

Throughout the country, Soviet unions are organized on the basis of industrial divisions. Even though dues are very nominal, by Western standards, one might assume that the nature of Soviet unions would discourage workers from belonging. In fact, however, there are indications that the vast majority of workers as well as the managers are willing members of the unions. Widespread membership is not just a reflection of pressures placed upon the industrial worker to join the union.

As Professor Alec Nove has pointed out, even though the worker has no choice as to whether or not he will work overtime or will devote his day off to extra work in order to assure plan fulfillment, neither at the highest nor at the lowest levels do the unions or their officials have any veto in such matters. For these reasons, Soviet unions do not constitute a "pressure group" of the kind that make union organizations so important in the political affairs of other countries.[2] Yet, unions do serve the interests of the Soviet workers at the factory level. Soviet unions sign agreements with Soviet plants, and although they have no bargaining role in the determination of wages as such, union locals do represent their workers on matters related to living conditions and the availability of cultural ammenities. For example, the unions work together with management to determine how wages will be paid, that is, whether they will be paid on the basis of piece-work rates or monthly salaries plus premiums for work of extra merit. Social security payments in the USSR are managed by the unions. Moreover, there are laws in the USSR relating to the working conditions. Managers are often overeager to cut corners in order to fulfill plan and, as a result, violate labor laws. In such cases, union locals are responsible for seeing that bad working conditions are corrected. Similarly, if a foreman or some other plant official is accused of abusing a worker's rights, investigations will be made, and whenever the worker is in the right, there seems to be a good chance that his grievance will be acted upon.

Most activities at the local level are handled by committees. Indeed, the grievance and production committees seem to be the most important. Thus, a grievance committee would investigate a case in which a worker or his comrades assert that unfair dismissal has occurred. Similarly, such committees work closely with management in the crucial matter of housing. Here again, unlike management in many other economic systems, Soviet industrial management is often deeply involved in working to assure that their employees have decent housing. Plans for housing developments often are drawn up jointly by trade union representatives and the managers of a particular industry or plant.

As stressed earlier, however, there is another side to the coin. Union production committees are responsible not only for participating in drafting production plans but also along with management they are responsible for seeing to plan fulfillment. If a new invention is developed by a worker in the plant, this becomes an interest of the union as well as management. The institutionalization of *kritika i samokritika* ("criticism and self-criticism") as important supports of the highly conformist political culture is promoted by the Soviet unions, and they are held responsible for criticizing management for its shortcomings. Here again, stress should be made that the Party serves as the unassailable leaven in a mix that produces conflict in other systems. Management-union production conferences involving workers are called. Unions organize "Socialist competition" between various segments in a plant or between working groups at one plant and those at another, and they initiate factory committees at the lowest level to encourage "mass participation" by the workers in the activities of their plant.[3]

One institution, the Comrades' Courts, which is supported by the unions was created within the factories to involve the Soviet worker even more in his society. These quasi-judicial institutions are below the People's Courts. In part, they manage the prosecution of petty crimes that fill the docket of the lowest courts in the United States. In addition, however, Comrades' Courts have the function of punishing or admonishing recalcitrants and other deviants from the "Socialist" norm for practices and attitudes (e.g., tardiness, drunkenness, etc.) which would not be regarded as outside the law, and relatively rarely would be brought into the civil courts in pluralistic political systems. Thus, they are similar to "kangaroo courts." Comrades' Courts have been established in virtually all plants with over fifty workers.[4]

The worker is a primary interest of Soviet unions, but as the above discussion has stressed, several responsibilities that would not be found in a noncompany union have been given to Soviet unions. Although they are described as non-Party agencies, their activities are under tight Party control. Indeed, locals of any size will support Party units. Soviet unions are a prime agent serving for the growth and the advancement of the economy. For the workers' good, but also for the good of the growth of the economy, Soviet unions engage in efforts to advance the education of the workers. However, not the least of the educational responsibilities is the teaching communism and thus helping to rear the "new Soviet man" from the ranks of the Soviet industrial worker. Thus, a slogan for the forty-eighth anniversary of the Bolshevik Revolution was "Hail to the Soviet trade unions, a school of communism."[5] Indeed, this responsibility was particularly stressed by Lenin who viewed the unions both as organs for education in communism and as tools for the advancement of the Party. The importance of inculcating the workers with a sense of patriotism has been stressed by the press and the leadership, and was a point often made by Nikita Khrushchev.

The unions provide an important bridge between Party goals and the workers' private interests and attitudes. Indeed, Brezhnev stressed in his report to the Twenty-third Party Congress that an "indispensable" condition for an increase in the activity of Soviet unions lies in an improvement in the Party's work in the selection and training of key union leaders.[6] Such is the stuff of mass mobilization in a closed political culture.

Kolkhoz Democracy   As a result of administration changes in recent years, the kolkhozy, like the unions, have become economic agencies at the local level which are tightly integrated into the monohierarchical structure. Yet the kolkhozy, like the unions, are theoretically independent cooperative activities. Even more than the unions, however, the kolkhozy (and the sovkhozy as well, being state agencies in the first place) encompass private and social activities that in most other societies would not be a part of a centrally directed apparatus.

However organized, farms are economic enterprises primarily engaged in producing the foods and fibers needed by society and the economy at large. However, what is often missed in looking at the rural setting, whether in Communist states or in other political cultures, is that in addition to engaging in production activities, farming is a way of life which encompasses basic social and political units. Even in the United States where the organizational pattern is that of individual farmsteads, the farm is at once an economic activity and at the same time a home for the farmer and his family. In the United States, social and political activities, such as school-centered 4-H programs, and local Grange, or Farmer's Union, activities, may be rural based or they may be centered in a nearby town or city. In Eastern Europe and the Soviet Union, agriculture predominantly has been a village affair. Thus, the village in addition to being the center for economic activity and the peasant farmer's family home, it is also the primary place of social and political activity, as well. Under the tsars, the church was the village church, the priest the village priest, and whatever political and social activity was not dominated by the landlords before 1917 was left for the mir and the village elders.

After the 1930s when the peasants were forced into collective farms, much was formally changed; yet from the average peasant's point of view, the pattern must seem to be very familiar. The village communities persist. The old landlords are gone but the new state landlord is there. The kolkhoz chairman and the sovkhoz director each play a role strikingly similar to that of the old landlord or, more precisely, a manager of the former landlord's holdings. During visits to collective and state farms in Eastern Europe and the Soviet Union, this author met farm chairmen who must seem to be remote, powerful figures in the eyes of the peasant membership. The enormous importance of the collective and state farms as an adjunct to the monohierarchical structure of rule can perhaps best be seen by reviewing the reasons why Soviet agriculture was collectivized in the first place. In spite of shortcomings to the point where agriculture has been, and remains, the major problem area of both the Soviet economy and the Soviet society, the leadership continues to promote the huge collective and state farms.

Nearly every Western review of Stalin's decision to forcefully collectivize agriculture carries the correct observation that the Soviet leadership saw in the farms a way of maximizing the extraction of the peasant's output for use as capital in rapid industrial construction. This economic rationale behind collectivization was enormously important, but just as important, if not more so, were certain political and social factors. Marx correctly observed that whoever controls the means of production has the base for dominating political and social affairs, as well. By forcing the peasants into collectives, Stalin transferred control over the means of production from the village to a Party–state combine. Whether due to the twenty-five years of the MTS or Party domination within the farms resulting from Khrushchev's administrative reforms, the central Party leadership has deliberately exploited its grasp upon the means of production to control or to influence all other aspects of rural life, ever since the beginning of collectivization. Thus, political and social control over the peasants in a way that the pre-collectivization village did not allow was a most important factor behind collectivization.

On the ideological side, how could the Soviet leadership have rationalized any advance toward socialism in the USSR if a Socialist form had not been introduced into the countryside? After all, in the early 1930s the vast majority of the population was rural, and nearly half of the population still resides in the countryside at the dawn of the 1970s. Ideological considerations played an important role in the original decision to establish the collective and state farms, and the new Soviet nationalism has been important in the continuation of these institutions in the countryside. Indeed, an important success of the Soviet experiment in creating a new form of rule has been the distinctive nature of the kolkhoz–sovkhoz institution. To a degree, the collective *ejido* in Mexico, the *kibbutzem* (many of which are Leninist) in Israel, and all of the collective and state farms of Eastern Europe reflect varying attempts to follow the Soviet model.

Local government and economic management are combined into one in the Soviet villages. Theoretically, the governing body of the kolkhoz is its general meeting at which basic policy assertedly is laid down under the principle of "kolkhoz democracy." Theoretically, the chairman and his administrative staff are elected at these meetings by the members of the farm. In recent years, the greatly increased size of the farms has resulted in a move to create representative bodies of the peasants—since few farms had auditoriums large enough to hold all of the membership at one time. In practice, however, with the exception of the lax central controls over the farms during the Second World War, from the beginning, the general meetings have only rubber-stamped the decisions already made by the chairman and his administrative board made up of chief agronomists, head zootechnicians, accountants, and other leading kolkhoz administrators. Although "kolkhoz democracy" is one of the most often stressed themes in the literature related to the rural USSR, the kolkhoz chairman is on the *oblast nomenklatura* ("appointments list"). Indeed, during the early 1950s when

Khrushchev moved to entrench Party members as farm chairmen, he called for and got some 20,000 Party-member volunteers to go out into the countryside and offer themselves as candidates for kolkhoz chairmanships where they were duly "elected" to the posts.[7]

To the degree that the peasant family is left to its own devices in cultivating the small household plot (averaging less than an acre) and in marketing their private produce in a nearby city, Soviet farms encompass the anathema of the system, independent activity. Over the years, the Soviet political leadership has left no doubt that one of their prime goals is to achieve a level of production efficiency on the collective fields that will allow the elimination of the private plots. Perhaps equal to the desire to remove private production from agriculture is a resolution to eliminate the city collective markets where the bulk of such produce that is not consumed by the peasant families is sold. Beyond the vexing existence of such private trade, the role that the kolkhoz markets play as communications media also must be a very sore point for the leadership. With the monopoly over the press and other communications media and the management of information presented in productions meetings, on-the-farm educational courses, and lectures on Party and cultural affairs, etc., information received by the great bulk of the peasants would be almost totally controlled if it were not for the gossip and news gleaned during weekly visits to the city markets to sell produce, while exchanging views with acquaintances from other farms and with city customers. As in the urban factories, devices such as Comrades' Courts and Socialist competition plus the exploitation of ambitious non-Party *active* are utilized to achieve the highest degree of conformity among the kolkhoz peasants.

As we have summarized elsewhere,[8] beyond the direct economic linkage with Moscow in the administrative hierarchy, which the kolkhoz and sovkhoz provide as an enterprise, the Soviet form of organizing the rural USSR has provided several distinct advantages for the system of rule:

1. In the past, the kolkhozy have prevented the outbreak of new peasant revolts, and the passing of each generation brings a reduction in the negative attitudes of the peasantry toward the

regime. Potential interest groups that would have evolved into farm unions or other political pressure groups in non-Communist societies have been effectively blocked in the USSR.

2. The relative isolation of the farm setting has provided a captive peasant audience for the Party's agitation and propaganda machines. The farms also serve as valuable "schools for communism."

3. However imperfect they may be, both the kolkhozy and the sovkhozy satisfy the doctrinal need to bring communism to the countryside.

4. Unlike the situation of the independent farmer in a nation such as the United States where the advice of government agricultural agents can be heeded or ignored according to the farmer's own judgment, the collectives assure the ready and widespread adoption of new techniques and practices championed by higher authority.

The kolkhoz and the sovkhoz play important roles as adjuncts to the system of rule. Given the Soviet political culture, one may assume that the average peasant's participation in the "kolkhoz democracy" of the general meetings does give him some sense of participation in the affairs of his farm. After all, whether it was the village elder and the Tsarist landlord before 1913, or the kolkhoz chairman and sovkhoz director after 1930, there is little in Soviet history or culture to encourage the relatively independent and individual economic and political decision-making practiced by the farmer in open pluralistic societies of Western Europe and North America. However exotic and unnatural the organization of union and farm activity in the USSR may seem to Western eyes, such activity must seem quite normal, perhaps even desirable, in the eyes of most Soviet citizens. Article IV, k of the original Model Charter for Agricultural Artels (the basic farm law issued in 1935) instructed the kolkhoz chairmen to enter the peasants' homes, to enlist the women not just as farm hands but particularly as participants in the social fabric, as well. The new charter, adopted in 1970, only reinforces this spirit, stressing the unique value of the contribution of the collective farms to the Soviet political culture.[9]

CHAPTER 12

Education and Youth

IN the USSR, the schools and youth organizations are closely interrelated entities. Taken together they are one of the most important adjuncts to the Soviet system of rule. Just as Western observers often miss the vital importance of beliefs to the Soviet polity, so there are incorrect impressions concerning the contribution of the Soviet educational scheme to the leadership's attempt to create a new and different social and political system. True, there is ample evidence that in the USSR, as elsewhere in the world, there are disenchanted youths who reject many of the society's values—young people who would rather tune out and/or tune in on the values of some culture other than their own. Clearly, a segment of Soviet youth is disenchanted and cynical. Nevertheless, an examination of the combined educational-indoctrinational effort suggests a conclusion that considerable success has been achieved. Indeed, Western students of Soviet affairs who specialize in analyzing Soviet education and Soviet youth programs have reached similar conclusions.

A Political Tool   As in any other society, a basic educational aim in the USSR is to prepare the upcoming generation for the day when it becomes responsible for carrying society forward. All societies attempt in their various ways to equip their young with the knowledge necessary for achieving personal security. All societies, even the most pluralistic, have been unable to refrain from trying to utilize the schools in indoctrinating their youth with the dominant values and goals of the society. However, while displaying the universal traits of educational systems on one hand, Soviet education, on the other hand, reveals important goals that differ from the educational aims of pluralistic systems.

As Nigel Grant has stressed, "Education in the USSR is primarily a political tool for the construction of a communist society."[1] Thus, although providing youth with the necessary knowledge and skills to carry forward the work of the society is a vitally important goal of Soviet education, this educational aim is secondary to the primary political aim. In his day at the helm of the Soviet leadership, Nikita Khrushchev repeated time and again that the efforts of society should be directed primarily at creating the "new Soviet man." The same futuristic charge to Soviet education was stressed by the general secretary of the CPSU, L. I. Brezhnev, in a 1968 speech to the All-Union Congress of Teachers. Brezhnev emphasized the importance of acquiring knowledge in order to carry on the business of society and the economy, but even more that "all the qualities determining the aspects of Soviet man (his communist consciousness, love of work, patriotism, humanness, and feeling of internationalism) are inculcated under the influence and with the active participation of schools and *this is something which one can say without exaggeration*." (Italics added.) Indeed, Brezhnev stressed the view that the fundamental difference between socialism in the USSR and all other systems is that "consciously and purposefully" the whole development of Soviet society is pointed to molding and preparing "its future."[2]

One fundamental difference between the philosophy of education held in the USSR and that held in "open societies" is the attitude toward the nature of truth. The view that truth is known, or knowable, in areas where doubt is the rule in nonauthoritarian systems is a part of the Marxist–Leninist doctrine, but furthermore, such views are carried over into classroom practice. Thus, all the way through the universities rote memorization of "laws" related to the social sciences and humanities is very prevalent. True, the social sciences now being developed in the USSR are being asked to add further details to the "laws" discovered by Marx and Lenin. Nevertheless, whereas social scientists in the West will leave a question mark indicating that a particular observation represents the best guess of the current specialists in the field, similar views are taught as fundamental "laws of social development" in the Soviet schools.[3]

Closely related to the Marxist–Leninist scientific underpinning of Soviet education is the attitude toward the individual in the educational process. As the minister of higher education has noted, because "education is to assist in the building of a communist society," teachers are trained and curricula are organized to produce fighters for communism.[4] Unlike pluralistic societies in which there have been strong tendencies to place the development of the individual first, no attempts whatsoever are made to justify or conceal the fact that Soviet educational psychology rests upon the Marxist–Leninist doctrine that the individual is "developed for the benefit of society and not actually for the individual himself."[5] Here then, even more than the elements of "mysticism" present in Freud, are the roots of the Soviet rejection of that pioneer psychologist. Freud's work stressed independent personality traits, traits which are in opposition to the communal personality projected for the new Soviet man.[6]

Although Western social science investigators are not allowed to conduct their questionnaires in the USSR, in recent years, a few Soviet sociologists have used survey instruments designed to measure student attitude. The few published results support the observation made earlier that although indoctrination has been far from totally successful, important gains have been achieved. However, beyond the limited existence of such measures, there is impressive evidence to indicate that the Soviet educators and Party leaders have achieved considerable success with their psychology of education.

In the time of the tsars, the vast majority of the Soviet population was illiterate. Today, the USSR has one of the highest literacy rates in the world. Although when compared with the United States, the USSR has not nearly as large a percentage of its youth attending universities, the vast majority of the youth at least have completed their eight-year schools. In recent years, many, if not most, of the lower schools have been transformed into ten-year schools. In addition, an impressive array of special technical, correspondence, and night schools have been created for those who will not have the opportunity to go to the universities. Indeed, although Soviet educational purposes do not provide the liberal educational programs that are characteristic of American and many Western educational systems, as Professor Nicholas DeWitt has stated, "There has not been a single study in the United States or Western Europe which could challenge the proposition that in qualitative terms Soviet science and engineering education is not inferior to the West."[7]

Pioneers and Komsomols   In the West, although the Boy Scouts, the Girl Scouts, and other youth organizations often work closely with the schools, they are still quite separate from the schools; this is not the case in the USSR where the seven- to nine-year-old youths belong to the Octoberists, the ten- to fourteen-year-old group to the Young Pioneers, and the fifteen- to twenty-seven-year-olds may join the Komsomols (i.e., Young Communist League). In the schools collectivity is stressed, and circles are created around every conceivable activity and centered on the youth groups. More than this, every faculty of higher education has a Komsomol branch representative who sits on the administrative body of the school.[8] Indeed, of the 2.5 million teachers in the USSR, some 630,000 are members of the Communist party and another 450,000 are Komsomols.[9] Throughout the USSR, there are said to be 348,000 primary Komsomol groups, which encompass one-third of the eligible youth.[10]

Nearly all, that is, 80 to 90%, of the students in institutions of higher education are members of the Komsomol.[11] Apparently, some young people get into institutions of higher education who are not members of the Young Communist League, although recommendation by the Komsomols is required for entry into these institutions.[12]

Members of the youth groups each work as "an immensely valuable ally of the teacher"; thus, the youth groups and particularly the Komsomols are charged with instructing the youth in what is good and what is bad.[13] In this connection, inculcating into the youth Communist, thus atheistic, philosophical attitudes is a very important activity of the youth groups. All schools are said to have antireligious circles.[14] Beyond the stress given to Soviet patriotism and Marxism–Leninism in all subjects, special courses on scientific communism are taught. Unlike school systems elsewhere, which will encourage experimentation with various methods and in which the teachers, or at least the particular schools, often determine the curricula and select their own texts, the Soviet school system expends enormous effort to achieve rigid uniformity in courses, texts, and the whole range of educational activities.[15]

With the Soviet stress on an established future and the necessity for the individual to conform to what is deemed necessary for the construction of communism rather than the desires of self, not only is great stress put upon indoctrination in the earliest school years but also there tends to be specialization from the very start.[16] Moreover, enrollment in institutions of higher learning is not determined by the number of students who are interested in, and qualified to carry out, a particular course of study, but rather it is dependent upon class quotas based upon the projected needs of the society.

There are, of course, important flaws in the Soviet educational system, and in the effort to indoctrinate the youth. Whereas virtually every youth eligible for the Pioneers is a member, as noted earlier, far from all of the youths who are eligible join the Komsomol. Futhermore, the turnover among membership is high. Visitors to the USSR do meet genuinely disenchanted youths. Occasionally, articles in the youth press reveal a widespread feeling that many of the Komsomol activities need improvement. Many of the meetings are said to be sterile and unexciting. Nevertheless, some 60% of the military are Komsomol members, and another 22% are Party members.[17] Moreover, as noted earlier, membership in the Komsomol is virtually a *sine qua non* for achieving higher education. Reported incidents of expelling youths from higher schools because they exhibit religious affiliations provides evidence of deviation, and also indicates that if success is to be achieved, conformity is essential.[18] Along with grades, a good Komsomol record is important in obtaining better jobs,[19] and revised Party rules now require that no one under twenty-three may become a member of the Party unless he has been a member of the Komsomol.[20]

Three Generations Some degree of cynicism and apathy toward
of Indoctrination the Soviet regime must exist among the
youth. But one may ask if the segment of Soviet youth that shares such views is any greater than the relatively small minority of American youth who classify themselves as hippies or young militants engaged in total rejection of, or revolt against, society. Recently, in a course on Soviet government and politics given by this author, one of the students was an older person who had only recently emigrated to the United States. This man had spent twelve years of his career teaching in the Soviet secondary schools. The limited available evidence leads us to agree with his observation that "in fulfillment of the political goals the schools have had considerable success in evoking a committment to communism. Many groups in the West underestimate the Russian people's enthusiasm for their own system. Soviet citizens are as loyal to their government as serious citizens everywhere."[21]

If the citizen is deprived of all avenues of political opposition and of all group membership except in wholly dependent social groups, and there is only one employer for which he may work what are the possibilities for achieving personal security or fulfilling his ambitions outside of the rigidly determined sociopolitical structure? In the era of boss-run cities in America, few individuals were so desirous of self-destruction as to fight City Hall. Ambitious men joined forces with the boss, by far the easiest path to success, or they moved to another non-boss-ridden city. In the Soviet Union, there is no place to move, and only the most foolhardy deign to fight the only system they have known for fifty years.

As in an army, material security for the contemporary citizen in the Soviet Union is relatively easy to obtain. The bureaucracy provides free medical care, housing (poor as it is) is most inexpensive, and everyone is guaranteed work. A few of the ambitious still try to act independently by breaking the strictly enforced economic laws in an attempt to amass small independent fortunes through clandestine private-enterprise operations. For those who are more sensible, however, by far the easiest way to fortune and the only way to personal fame, outside of the arts (which are tightly controlled), is through the ranks of the bureaucratic hierarchy. Hard work, persistence, and loyalty to higher officials are rewarded in bureaucracies, and they are particularly well rewarded in the Soviet total administrative state. Social mobility, in terms of the opportunity for the peasant's or worker's son to become a top-ranking administrator, is high, although perhaps not as high as in the United States. Such mobility has been deliberately maintained in order to maximize the efficient use of the talents of the Soviet people.

Bureaucracies in the East as in the West do, of course, tend to take care of their own, and incidents of nepotism are not uncommon. Because of his superior background, the child of an upper middle-class Soviet bureaucrat has a headstart both in school and on the job. Nevertheless, assertions that the Soviets have evolved a rigid, hereditary class society miss the point that the leadership has long recognized that for their own good and that of the system, they should seek out and train the best brains in the whole population. Although places in the universities most comparable to our own institutions of higher learning are difficult to get, good technical schools equivalent to the engineering colleges within America's universities are numerous, and on the whole there seems to be much less waste of potential technical talent (as defined by the needs of the state and not individual wants) than in the United States. Measured in terms of satisfying the needs of society as determined by the state, and in terms of removing anxieties over economic security, Soviet personnel and educational policies have been highly successful.

Prior to the nuclear age with its ugly implications, American fathers assumed that many of the profits of their labors would be left behind to improve the lives of their progeny. "My son will have it better than I did," expresses the American dream of increased life expectancy and greater economic security for their children. Similarly, since the 1917 Russian Revolution, Soviet parents have found hope for the fulfillment of the same dream. While the vast majority of the world's peoples still have little hope for material advance, and thus for succeeding generations to have an easier life, the USSR has turned the trick, and the post-1917 transformation has brought nationwide educational opportunity, a rising standard of living, and an increased life expectancy. However harsh the sacrifices demanded by Stalin of the adult generations, Soviet citizens surely are aware that these important advances represent the desirable fruits of Communist rule.

Although the social historian will remind us of the cooperation so essential to the building of America (such as harvestings and barn raisings on the frontier), the lonely struggles of Willa Cather's American pioneers were far from fantasy. One was ultimately dependent upon his neighbors and the town, however far away, but the contest with nature was very much a lonely battle by "inner-directed" fathers of individual families. As in so many things wherein the Soviets have looked elsewhere for examples, the concept of the pioneer has been distorted in its adaptation to such things as the opening of the lands in the Siberian wastes and capturing the imagination of impressionable youth. For the spirit is not that of the self-sustaining individual, but rather of "other-directed" collectivism. The struggle for building a better, more secure future is there, but the future is total allegiance to the Communist vision. Mass pioneering, mass education, and mass indoctrination through regimented schools and youth organizations rather than encouragement of individual adventure and enterprise is the investment in the future of communism.

Stalin felt the need to exploit youthful patriotism by organizing the young to spy upon their parents. Surely the fact that most of today's parents have been educated in Soviet schools and spent at least part of their youth in one or more of the youth organizations is one important factor behind the lack of a felt need to push the present generation to spy on its parents. Soviet motivations are probably as complex as those of any society, but enrollment in the legions begins very early and the lessons of "not to question why," of having a secure existence as a result of doing just what is expected, must be deeply engraved in the Soviet citizen's conscience. The Westerner who has spent his time in the armed forces has experienced the opiatelike feeling of security that comes from knowing his roof and food are guaranteed and from being told when to go to bed and when to brush his teeth. Life is more secure if one learns that Mother (or the State) always has the right answers and that she will punish or praise as the circumstances warrant.

On the job and after hours, in school and during play, every opportunity is exploited to regiment each Soviet citizen. Mother Russia's resources guarantee all material security; and Father, the Party leadership, is a most stern disciplinarian in a system that must be credited with having developed a highly conformist citizenry. Three generations of Soviet youth have known nothing other than the carefully designed system of indoctrination briefly outlined here.

CHAPTER 13

Communications Media

AN INSTRUMENT OF INDIRECT CONTROL

INTENSE indoctrination in the schools, workers' and peasants' institutions that maximize the control potential of the employment situation, voluntary organizations that capture the sense of civic responsibility, and monopoly over all communications media provide the major means of capturing the minds of the Soviet citizenry in all areas of activity. Together they provide an imposing array of instruments of indirect rule that have been a vital part of the Soviet experiment in political controls.

Civitas Dei and
Civitas Terrena   A major root of modern Western guarantees of the fundamental freedoms—press, association, and religious belief—was planted by Christ (see Gospel according to St. Luke, Chap. 20, V. 19–25). St. Augustine defined and clarified the establishment of two jurisdictions. In his time there was no press, and most of what was

written was transcribed by the clergy and concerned matters of the soul. Thus, Augustine described two worlds: the realm of God and the realm of man (or, *Civitas Dei*, the City of God, and *Civitas Terrena*, the Earthly City). Thus, he clearly showed the division between the material and the abstract; the Caesars could rule the material world, including having control over the bodies of their subjects to the point of determining life and death, but the explanation of life and death were matters that belonged to the Church and her teachings.

With the tradition of freedom from the state in matters of belief established after Augustine's work (but, of course, dictated by the Church), in recent times freedom of the press was able to follow this precedent because it too dealt primarily with matters of belief. If, however, there are no Caesars, and the rulers all are members of the priesthood, then no jurisdictional problem exists and there is no need to claim freedom for the press. In the USSR, where the Party is somewhat similar to the Church hierarchy directed by the belief—all that is written must be truth—nothing is outside the realm of *Civitas Dei.*

According to the Marxist–Leninist view, outside the Soviet orbit there is no free press, since all such systems are dominated by exploiting classes, and no ruling class would be so stupid as to allow anything as mighty as the pen to be used against it. True, an occasional book and a few periodicals will be allowed to print criticism of the system, but just enough to permit the rulers to counter claims of press monopolies, never enough, however, to pose any real threat to the exploiting classes. In Yugoslavia, one intelligent young man of our acquaintance was not prepared to give his opinion on the 1967 Arab–Israeli War the day after it began because, as he explained, the official line had not yet been published in the Belgrade newspapers. In his view, the Government had access to much more information than the ordinary citizen and it would distinguish the truth from misrepresentation and shortly explain it all to the populace. When the concept of free press was mentioned, he was shocked. Disbelief covered his countenance. Surely, we were mistaken, surely even in America the government provided some control over the lies that would be promulgated by private news media if they were permitted free rein.

Socialist Realism   Andrei Vyshinsky's *The Law of the Soviet State* was for a long time the guide to Soviet legality, and in this work he explained, through Lenin's words, the inherent "counterrevolutionary" nature of the bourgeois press as well as the need for complete Soviet control.

Only in this way (Lenin said) is it possible and our boundless duty to knock out of the hands of the bourgeoisie a mighty instrument for lying and defaming with impunity, for deceiving the people, for leading the peasantry into error, for preparing counterrevolution.[1]

With the coming of the post-Stalin "thaw," Pasternak sent his *Doctor Zhivago* to an Italian publisher, but he was to suffer great condemnation for his act. The Soviet censors erred and published Vladimir Dudintsev's *Not By Bread Alone* in *Novy Mir* before the error was caught. The error of both writers, of course, was engaging in unapproved criticism. The press monopoly had failed temporarily. Dudintsev's major mistake was in clearly exposing the rigidity of the bureaucracy, a rigidity he pictured as extending almost, but not quite, to the very top of the system. As Khrushchev himself was subsequently quoted, Dudintsev had "mended his ways." Khrushchev's successors also have labored to retain tight reins over the publications field.

An American student once noted in a research paper analyzing the Soviet press, "As I read various passages from articles which had appeared in Soviet publications such as *Pravda* and *Izvestia*, I realized that the Soviet press is dedicated to the purpose of presenting an optimistic view of the existing situation in the Soviet Union."* Indeed, whatever the communications media, be it painting, music, the press, or a textbook in economics at the university level, this is the dedication, this is the meaning of "Socialist realism," the presentation of the overwhelming correctness of the Communist system.

The Soviet writers, in the words of Khrushchev at the Twenty-First Party Congress, are "engineers of human souls," and, as he

---

* Professor John Swanson. Several years ago, as my student he researched several of the quotations cited here.

was to emphasize, the engineering is for one purpose only, "building communism."

Soviet literature and art, which play an important role in building communism and bringing up the new man, should in present day conditions, strengthen their ties with the life of the people even more and reflect more fully the Soviet people's struggle to build a communist society.

Workers in literature, motion pictures, the theater, music, sculpture and painting are called upon to raise the ideological and artistic level of their work and to continue to be active helpers of the Party and state in the communist up-bringing of the working people, in developing multinational socialist culture, in forming high aesthetic taste and in propagating the principles of the communist ethic.[2]

Since only the imperfect stage of socialism has been achieved, individual error will still occur in the USSR and these errors must be acknowledged. A fundamental principle of Soviet life is that of *kritika i samokritika* ("criticism and self-criticism"). Individuals err, and not only is there the duty of others to criticize them but also there is the duty of the wrongdoer to admit his mistakes and publicly criticize himself. Much space in the Soviet press is devoted to such activity, an important part of which is the letter to the editor. But, as we have seen, "socialist realism" dictates that it is the individual citizen or the individual administrator that is wrong, not the policy or the Party, and *never the system.* Praise for the system, criticism of the individual who has failed, and damnation of the non-Soviet way constitute the major themes of Soviet publications—even the most technical journal will usually carry at least one of these elements.

The Soviet lexicon makes no distinction between propaganda and objectivity; as with everything else there has to be the preceding modifier, that is, "Socialist objectivity," if not written, then at least always understood. More than half a century (nearly three generations) have passed under the iron-rigid contours of the Soviet press. In the days when newspapers had a near monopoly on the communication of news in the United States, Will Rogers said, "I only know what I read in the papers." Almost from the beginning of Soviet rule, all communications media have spoken only that which the Party leadership has willed and that leadership has become increasingly astute in the means of controlling even word-of-mouth exchanges among the citizenry. Everywhere the "other-directed" men are but reflections of what their environment asks of them, and in the Soviet Union there is little that is not part of a carefully created Socialist environment.

Through   Convinced of the superiority of Western
the Soviet   ways, well-meaning Americans often assert
Looking Glass   that Soviet citizens allowed to visit the United
                     States cannot resist being impressed by the
superiority of our system. This view, however, fails to account for at least two important realities. In the first place, all who travel to the West are screened. In the second place, considering the totality of their past environment, Soviet eyes that view the American scene cannot see what American eyes see.

Although Britain is an "open society" and the closest friend the United States has, past literature has so impressed the importance of British social classes upon American minds that many who journey to modern England still see only lords and commoners and fail to see how relatively unimportant title and class are in the twentieth-century United Kingdom. Yet, the American at least has a chance to learn of changes and to grasp the whole perspective in a way nearly totally denied the Soviet citizen. Moreover, the United States has its serious faults and when these, and only these, are carefully selected and presented to the Soviet citizen, year after year, an impressive negative image is created. What the American sees as typical prosperity, the Soviet sees as a carefully designed facade to hide the fundamental ills, the poverty, the insecurity, and the misery in the United States.

Western self-criticism, in spite of the pleading of Norman Vincent Peale for "positive thinking," is not always favorable. Therefore, in practicing what is regarded as a major source of strength within a free society, the Western press provides the Soviet *agitprop* mills (the agitation and propaganda sections of the Party) with more than ample material for making its condemnations convincing. In the following material taken from the Soviet press, the United States is the major target, but similar judgments are made of the entire Western world, indeed, perhaps to a lesser degree, the entire non-Soviet world.

The Draft Program of the Communist Party, published in August, 1961, noted the "general crisis of capitalism" and presented the following evidence for this conclusion:

". . . the mounting struggle between labor and capital; an acute intensification of the contradictions within the world capitalist economy; . . . repudiation of bourgeois freedoms and the establishment of fascist and despotic regimes in a number of countries . . . all these are manifestations of the general crisis of capitalism." Furthermore, "oppression by finance capital keeps growing. Giant monopolies . . . dominate the life of the nation. . . ."[3]

All this while unemployment continues to rise and the standard of living keeps falling. Obviously, the Marxian laws are continuing to work their havoc on Western systems.

The wealth of America is widely known, and no attempt is made to deny this truth, but wealth is only part of the picture. In the words of a Soviet visitor to the USA:

. . . indeed, in no other place are there represented in such a concentrated view all the contradictions of bourgeois society, as on this little piece of our planet: the dazzling sparkle of wealth and the terrible faces of beggars, grieved by sores, by the unseen possibilities of darkness, lack of culture, decline of manners. . . .[4]

The very real problem of unemployment in the United States is one that a Marxist–Leninist critic can really attack, and nothing is allowed to escape the propaganda mill. Records of American unemployment even found its way into the 1961 *Party Program.* "A considerable part of the productive capacity lies idle, while millions of unemployed stand at the factory gates,"[5] and the Party journal *Kommunist* cited official United States statistics to make its points:

According to official (US) data, the work load of 17 fundamental branches of the manufacturing industries fell in 1960–1961 to 69 percent, and in smelting, the increase of the work load to 58 percent in April, 1961, was considered an "achievement." Millions of workers are doomed to full or partial unemployment. . . .[6]

When thinking about their country, many Americans engage in a form of positive thinking that blinds them to its imperfections.

America is the richest nation in the world and the standard of living is among the highest. However, as the recent uprisings in the cities have demonstrated, there is imperfection and blight. Soviet citizens who visit the USA may see strength and health, but if dirt is what they are looking for, dirt is what they will find. Certainly, to date, the vast majority of Soviet visitors to the United States have seen mostly dirt. Few eyewitness reports, printed in the Soviet press, on American·visits contain lies, but all present only part of the truth because this is what impressed their viewers. Here, for example, is what impressed a Soviet visitor to New York, in 1961. The region is one of large factories, but because of the recession 15 to 20 percent were underworked, "In the automobile industry the deficiency reached 40 percent, in oil refineries 30, in steel foundries to 60 percent."[7]

The same visitor traveled to Los Angeles where he visited a Kaiser metallurgical factory and saw that "out of ten divisions only six were working. The number of workers was recently cut down by almost three thousand persons." Moreover, his hostess at a Los Angeles reception cited a newspaper account carrying a prediction that within three or four years the United States would have 10 million unemployed.[8] This writer has served as host and temporary local tourguide for Soviet visitors. The visitors were well behaved, but it was clear both from what they wanted to see and from our discussion that their thoughts tended to concentrate on the negative aspects of the United States, which they had been schooled to expect.

Another Soviet visitor to America reported in the labor paper *Trud* on work layoffs in a cannery in Chicago and a steelmill in Los Angeles.[9] *Kommunist* doesn't miss stressing the sharp contrast between full employment in the USSR and the assertedly deteriorating situation in the USA. Problems that have arisen through the advance of automation are seen not as a rough period that can be traversed, but as a portent of worse to come.

In smelting in the U.S.A. 250 thousand now carry on the same work which 500 thousand men did twelve years ago; in conjunction with automation in Detroit 160 workers will never return to the automobile plants; 200 thousand miners now produce the coal, and 400 thousand miners have been supplanted by machines; the railroads, by means of mechanization, have decreased their needs in working strength by 1 million men; in the offices during the past 40 years new electronic machines have cut down the need for workers by one-fourth, and in the next half century the number of displaced office workers may amount to 4 million. . . .[10]

The Soviet press is filled with such accounts, and no bit of evidence is neglected which seems to prove the validity of Marxist–Leninist prediction. How can the Soviet citizen help being convinced that the USA is indeed seriously ill when he never experiences unemployment and reads that in May of 1961 in the United States, there were "4.8 million fully unemployed and 2.8 million partially unemployed"? He must be deeply impressed when he learns that in 1960 in the USA, there were 37 areas considered "depressed areas"—population points where the number of unemployed was 6% or more of the working force. In 1961, there were 88 such areas.

The Soviet reader can only conclude that such a situation inevitably must worsen, and such a conclusion is documented by statistical records and emphasized by quotations from authorities such as Professor Paul Samuelson, past president of the American Economic Association, who served as special advisor to President Kennedy. Samuelson is cited, "We should not hold any illusions in respect to the scale of proposed measures. Even if you allow the middle of the year (1961) as the aim of an upswing . . . , there will not be a great basis for supposing that by the end of the year unemployment will be much less than at present."

If dirt is what one expects, dirt is what one will find, for it is there in more than ample quantities, and Prof. Samuelson's colleagues provide a clincher in their conclusion:

One-third of the families of the U.S.A. has inadequate lodging, is poorly fed, and poorly dressed. The situation of housing in the country, as the American writers V. Perlo and K. Marzani have pointed out, "appears as a real national scandal."[11]

Through the Soviet looking glass, American workers' incomes in terms of real wages are woefully inadequate. The ruling classes eat well, but the "white collar" worker has his problems, and the "blue collar" worker is in serious straits. Thus a report of a conversation with a woman textile worker painted the assertedly true picture. In her words:

> I will tell you about the budget of worker's families—textile workers, whom I know very well. Their average income is $60 a week. Here is how they distribute it: $9.80—federal taxes, $1.80—social security, $1.25—state sales tax, rent—$30 to $35 (a two-room apartment costs $120 to $150). Figure it up; it leaves $15 to $20 a week to live on.
>
> I've given you an example of a family which receives three thousand dollars a year, but here there are five million families which do not have more than a thousand. What can you say about the unemployed? Here they live in corners, in old buses. Necessities are always getting more expensive. A few years ago bread cost 15 cents a pound . . . , but now—27. Add to that the wholly unbelievable cost of medical care: births are $500; three visits to the doctor for examination —$145. Women have to give birth at home. . . .[12]

Parallel to the above, Soviet press reports repeatedly stress that a few score entrepreneurs have annual incomes of more than 1 million dollars, and the assets of families such as the Rockefellers, Mellons, DuPonts, and Fords are measured in billions.

Since most of the Soviet government's revenue comes from profits made by the state enterprises, this is asserted not to be a tax, and the claim is made that the USSR citizen is virtually without a tax burden. Not so the American who, according to data quoted from the *Christian Science Monitor,* pays not only his regular taxes but "notable sums" in hidden taxes, as well. "The Tax Foundation set forth that there are at least 100 taxes on eggs, 116 taxes on men's suits, 150 taxes on women's hats, 151 taxes on a loaf of bread, and 600 taxes on a house."[13] As far as the total tax bill is concerned, the average American's burden is frightening indeed:

> What awaits the "average American" in the future? Will the tax burden be greater or lighter? To this question the magazine *Reader's Digest* answers negatively. By way of an example, the magazine cites an "average" American family of four persons. Its income is $5,183 per year. The head of the family is 29 years old. In the next 36 years until the head of the family reaches age 65 . . . , he will have to pay $47,221 in the form of taxes. . . .[14]

Based upon this evidence, there must seem to be a considerable ring of truth in the conclusion stated in the 1961 *Draft Program of the Communist Party* that "the monopolists deprive the masses of people of the possibility of expressing their will and of electing true champions of their interests."[15]

Such is the Soviet view, not only of income, housing, and taxes but of the whole American scene. The citations here have concentrated on the economic problems of lower-income workers, but similarly convincing presentations of America are made in regard to the plight of the small farmer, ethnic minorities, and many other problem areas of life in the United States. Indeed, a student did a study of the Soviet coverage of the 1967 race riots and counted 104 of these articles in *Pravda* and *Izvestia* between July 10 and September 3, 1967.

Zhdanovism   The previous glimpse at the nature and content of what the Soviet citizen reads (and also hears) about the United States illustrates the leadership's use of its monopoly over the communications media in all areas as an instrument of rule. Politburo member Andrey Zhdanov was one of Stalin's key lieutenants, and his ideas shaped much of the practice of employing the written word as a key political tool of the Party, thus Zhdanovism. Clearly, there have been changes since the death of Stalin. For a time there seemed to be a liberalizing trend reflected in the title of Ilya Ehrenberg's book *The Thaw*. Ironically, however, this author vividly remembers reading (I believe it was in an issue of *Moscow News*) some lines written by Ehrenberg a few days after Stalin's death. As usual, the picture drawn by this clever writer was vivid. The scene was a pass in the Andes. Two illiterate Latin American peasants met. Since they were from different tribes, they did not share a common language. Each was engaged in the bitter struggle for survival that is the lot of the worker in the non-Communist world. According to Ehrenberg only one word passed between them. A word that bridged all boundaries and said everything. It was "Stalin!" Ilya Ehrenberg was a clever and talented writer. True to his past performance, however, given the literary crackdown that has occurred since his death, if he were still living, he would probably be writing passages expounding the necessity for a literary refreeze.

The crackdown on literary freedom in the late 1960s had many complex ramifications. Western specialists on Soviet affairs have presented several logical reasons to justify Soviet leadership's decision to invade Czechoslovakia in August 1968. However, by far the most persuasive of the reasons was the Soviet leadership's fear of the creeping liberalism that was seeping into the USSR from Czechoslovakia. "If the Czechs can have a free press, why not the Soviet Union," must have been a thought in the minds of many Soviet intellectuals. Nevertheless, there is also evidence that, as in the West, Soviet writers are not all of one mind. As noted earlier, most of the Soviet writers who have been applauded in the West for their criticism of the Soviet system have insisted both by their words and their deeds that they too are Leninists. Zhdanovism and the Soviet political culture have made their marks. Pasternak, after all, was an exception. The vast majority of the Soviet writers imply agreement with the reality that their strength lies in their tie to the Party. The powerful Union of Soviet Writers is a creature of the Party. Self-censorship within the Union along with the three more formal means of censorship continue to assure tight control over the printed word in the USSR. The clear implication of the sections of the Soviet criminal court code which deal with the printed word is that Soviet law cannot and will not tolerate any anti-Soviet material. In achieving this end, there is *Agitprop,* the Department of Propaganda and Agitation, *Glavlit,* the Office of Literature Publication and the external filter that the Soviet news agency *Tass* provides, since this is the channel through which all foreign news enters the Soviet Union. Moreover, as suggested previously, one has virtually no chance for achievement in the Soviet writing field unless he is a member of the writer's union. This Party-dominated organization takes great care to admit only those whose politics will serve Party ends. Even these controls, however, are not enough. The editor of *Pravda* is officially appointed by the Central Committee of the CPSU, thus in practice, the Politburo. Local newspapers are organs of the district Party committees and "operate under their direct guidance."[16] The chief task of all newspapers, whether technically Party organs (e.g., *Pravda*), or State organs (e.g., *Izvestia*), is giving "active assistance to the Party and the people" in the construction of communism as spelled out by the editors of *Pravda.*[17]

Clearly, there is discontent among Soviet writers, and it is at least expressed more openly today than it was a decade or so earlier, certainly more openly than during the time of Stalin. Yet, the Party has had important success among the writers. As Katherine Hunter Blair has pointed out, there are at least three vitally important cultural threads related to the present role of the communications media in the USSR. There is a long history of censorship in Russia. Under the tsars, many writers looked to history to provide answers in a way very similar to the "historical synthesis" or "critical realism" that is the modern Soviet theme. Most important of all, perhaps, is that the positive hero was a major theme of the literary greats in the past, including Gogol, Tolstoy, and Dostoevsky, and little effort was needed to adapt this attitude to the modern emphasis on the development of "the new Soviet man."[18] Obviously, there are weaknesses in the Soviet attempt to use the communications media as a major adjunct of rule. Nevertheless, Leonid Brezhnev touched on part of the truth when he spoke on the occasion of *Izvestia's* fiftieth anniversary, and stressed the importance of the role of the press in advocating the general line of "Leninist policy." In his view, the press serves as a major means of inspiring the Soviet masses "to achieve new heights."

The level of sophistication in presenting the Party line has risen significantly since Stalin's death. Here then is a regime dedicated to its view of truth, manipulating human communication in a way and to a degree previously unknown in history. Seen in this light, Bertrand Russell's observation of nearly two decades ago takes on an even more serious meaning. He said: "The discovery that man can be scientifically manipulated and that governments can turn large masses this way or that as they choose is one of the causes of our misfortunes."[19] Certainly, such manipulation of public information has provided a means of major support for the evolving monohierarchical system of Soviet rule.

CHAPTER 14

Soviet Social Sciences

A Substitute for Terror THE single most important factor motivating the recent trend to develop social sciences in the Soviet Union may well be the leadership's felt need to create new instruments of control to fill the void left when, under Khrushchev, Stalinist terror was removed. As noted earlier, under Stalin, terror served as the "linchpin" of the Soviet system.[1] Since terror was a key instrument of Stalinist rule, perhaps something new must be provided to preserve old levels of control.

There is ample historical evidence indicating that manipulation of threats to individual security can be a primary instrument in holding a society together. All societies use both the carrot and the stick to one degree or another. Presumably Western constitutional systems have stressed the carrot aspect with the assumption that commonly held beliefs and self-generated incentives are the most desirable web to hold a society together and to allow its economy to advance. True, the motorist in a constitutional democracy will not speed for fear of being fined, if caught. Similarly, one reason he will tend not to cheat on the payment of his income tax is that the stick also is used in "open societies." In the Soviet Union, even under Stalin, there must have been positive elements. Certainly, his appeal to traditional nationalism was an important factor in the impressive struggle of the Soviet people against Hitler's invasion during the Second World War. Nevertheless, the stick of Stalin's terror was much more effective than the police systems in the West. The negative aspects of rule were stressed to such a point that after Stalin's death the nature of changing social and political sanctions, for example, the abrupt reduction of the threat to personal security, left a number of citizens reared in the Soviet environment with a sense of insecurity. True, to a fair degree, the promise and the realization of increased economic reward and a greater emphasis on the production of consumer goods worked to fill part of the gap. Nevertheless, "man does not live by bread alone," and evidence of new unrest rose to a disturbing level in a society lacking in constitutional tradition. Specifically, there is reason to believe that the publication and distribution of the underground manuscript press became more widespread. In addition, young poets and writers, and even the not so young such as the late Ilya Ehrenburg, produced social commentary of a nature that would have been unthinkable in the days of Stalin. Similarly, Prof. Liberman championed changes in the economic system that, however overstated in the West, suggest a trend in the economic realm that must have caused Stalin to writhe in his grave. In other Communist states, even more overt evidence of change and unrest was present in the form of uprisings in several eastern European states and a further evolution of Western liberalism in Yugoslavia. Prior to the August 1968 invasion, Czech journalists carried out widespread uncensored criticism of the system and its past faults. What might have resulted in the Soviet Union in 1969? Under Stalin, the answer would be clear, a severe crackdown and an increase in the use of terror.

Paradoxically, the liberalization on the economic front asked by Liberman, and the scores of articles and discussions calling for the development of social sciences that started as early as the Twentieth Party Congress, has been paralleled by possibly the most severe crackdown on the literary profession since Stalin's death. Perhaps this is not so paradoxical, however, in that a review of the literature encouraging the development of social sciences reveals repeated stress that their development holds the key to improved controls over Soviet economy and society. Indeed, A. M. Rumyantsev, vice president of the USSR Academy of Sciences, stated this point most succinctly when he noted that "sociology yields what in cybernetics is called the feedback mechanism and the result is a rise in the efficacy of the control of society and of political and ideological work."[2] Although few of the commentators on the need for the development of social sciences are as candidly explicit on this point as Rumyantsev, a rough analysis of the points made concerning the need for social sciences in scores of articles indicates that in one form or another, explicitly or implicitly, the need for enhanced controls over political and ideological affairs is by far the most common theme. For example, some writers stress the need to "set up special research institutes on problems of the administration of society,"[3] whereas others concern themselves with the assertion that it is "difficult to overestimate the role of social research in raising the standard of ideological work."[4] Nearly all of the social sciences are given a charge in this direction. Thus, "social psychology is called upon to resolve the rather complex problem of the 'content' of speech which will influence man (instructions, teaching, agitation, and propaganda), along with example and demonstration, and finally punishment and encouragement," as a means of enhancing ideological understanding and discipline.[5] Similarly, social science is considered to be a key to "raise the level of the party leadership." Indeed, examples are cited of social science studies that have already been done in areas of research into improving the effectiveness of ideological work in the villages.[6] Under the Stalinist system, threats of force were used to hold society in line whenever shortcomings were obvious and to sweep under the rug less obvious ills. Today, shortcomings cannot be hidden so easily, and the Party has called "upon the workers of the social sciences not to avoid the acute questions of reality, such as, for instance, the causes of various shortcomings in the economic development, the sources of antisocial views and actions (egoism, nationalistic survivals, philistinism, money-grubbing, alcoholism, crime, and others), but to pose these questions boldly, make a thorough study of them and point out means of eliminating the negative phenomena."[7]

Closely related, in fact, an integral part of the whole concern over the problem of control, is a growing worry over the loss of influence of ideology on society, especially on young people. Public-opinion polls have become the "in" instrument of the burgeoning Soviet social sciences and some of the published results show specific areas for concern over ideology. For example, one group of students was asked the question, "To whom do you turn in order to clarify questions of a political nature?" Among those examined thirty-four said they sought the answers in themselves, fourteen said they turned to the teacher, but *not one* indicated that he turned to Young Communist League personnel. The Soviet observer's comment is surely an understatement when he notes that "both the Young Communist League Aktive and the instructors have something to think about."[8] As many Western observers have noticed previously, the dogmatic approach to social and economic criticism under Stalin meant that in examinations students were merely expected to regurgitate verbatim the accepted doctrines. Now, however, this practice is recognized as having been most harmful. As one key Soviet official has observed, the "widespread phenomenon in universities" of a mere mechanical parroting of lecture material is "a great evil." Such memorization will not "heighten his political awareness or conviction nor does it enrich his ideological level."[9] The formation of students' social and political views and ideological training is one of the most acute current philosophical and political problems.[10] The new civics that should be taught in Soviet educational institutions seems to be dependent upon the development of the social sciences.

Extending   In the last part of this chapter the fact that
Marxism–Leninism   more stress is given to problem-solving by
                     Soviet social sciences than by Western social
sciences is discussed in greater detail. Hopefully, problems related to economic choice will be alleviated, and the flowering of the new disciplines will remove the cause for concern over wrong youthful opinions. Soviet writers, then, see social science as the major means of developing the desirable "civic conscience," since, "in the socialist society the comprehensive development of the personality of each is an objective, vital necessity that raises a question of exceptional practical importance."[11]

Virtually every Soviet participant in the discussion stresses the conviction that historical materialism, that is, the science of Marxism–Leninism, is *the base* on which the evolving social sciences must rest. More than one participant in the discussion has gone so far as to say that under the situation in the past, "stagnation" in social development is the result of the old doctrinaire, dogmatic approach. The fundamental laws of historical materialism are not to be challenged, yet Soviet writers note that "a lag is observed in research on the fundamental theoretical problems comprehensively disclosing the mechanism of the laws governing social development."[12] Therefore, to deny the right "of the specialist in the social sciences to advance scientific hypothesis is to doom these sciences to stagnate and vegetate."[13] Perhaps, the implication of possible change resulting from the introduction of the new social sciences is no more profound than the implicit, often nearly explicit, admission of a challenge to Marxism–Leninism in the discussions. During Stalin's time, who could have written the observation found in a Soviet publication in 1967 that "of course, certain tenets of Marxist–Leninist science can prove insufficiently accurate or applicable in a new condition"? Thus, this writer continues, "Marx and Engels in their mature period, after establishing the basis of their teachings, found it necessary to make public mention of the immaturity of certain conclusions in their earlier works." Lenin, it is observed, often changes his point of view on both strategy and tactics, and thus "every honest scholar should have a similar attitude toward his work, and toward science."[14] As indicated, the basic laws of historical materialism are to go unchallenged, but these admittedly are "a comparatively limited arsenal of known economic laws," such as "The law of the planned proportional development of the national economy, and the law of steady growth of labor productivity and distribution according to labor, the socialist law of accumulations, the law of value, the law of preponderant growth of production of means of productions, and certain others."[15] Thus, these "laws" are recognized as far too few and too vague for the operation and further development of a complex modern society.

Closely related to the argument that the development of social sciences will enhance the level of controls over Soviet society is the repeated assertion that developing the new disciplines will enormously strengthen the weapons for defending Marxism–Leninism both against revisionism within the Communist world and against the falsehoods of Western bourgeois social sciences, including attacks by Western specialists on the Soviet society. Thus, social science workers are said to have a responsible role in the struggle against revisionism and nationalism, "against the big power anti-Soviet ideology, Mao Tse Tungism"[16] on the left, and on the right, the revisionism arising from the "agents of the union of Communists of Yugoslavia."[17] This responsibility of the new disciplines was particularly stressed in the 1967 resolution of the CPSU central committee "On Measures for Further Developing Social Sciences and Heightening Their Role in Communist Construction."[18] The resolution read in part:

One of the most important tasks of the social sciences is to wage a systematic militant struggle against antiCommunism, to give a thorough criticism of contemporary bourgeois philosophy, sociology, historiography, law and economic theories of apologists of capitalism: to expose falsifiers of ideas of Marxism–Leninism, the history of development of society, the Communist and workers' movement; decisively to repulse manifestations of right and "left" revisionism and national narrowness both in theory and in politics.[19]

One channel through which the objectives of this resolution may be advanced is the international conference, and indeed, past absence of Soviet social scientists from these conferences has been criticized as having been harmful to the USSR. For example, an editorial in *Kommunist* expressed concern over damage to the Soviet cause by poor representation to the 1954 International Demographic Congress at which among the 600 delegates there were only three from the USSR in contrast to 90 delegates from the USA. Assertedly, "we are going to have not only literary battles but also face-to-face disputes at international conferences with those whom we must win over to our side."[20] In this connection, although there probably is no one as yet in the Soviet Union who can be said to possess the credentials of a Western political scientist, when this writer was in Eastern Europe during 1967, he was informed that at that time the Soviet political science association consisted largely, if not entirely, of a president who would then qualify as a Soviet representative to attend International Political Science Association meetings.

An Empirical   Besides concern over lagging political con-
Necessity   trols and stagnation on the ideological front,
                         there are other important and less negative
reasons behind the campaign to develop Soviet social sciences. Indeed, so much stress is given to the practical benefits that can be realized by developing new disciplines that another reviewer of this material might well argue that the present writer's interest in political affairs has misled him, or that even more important than political and ideological control factors is the promise that political, social, and economic studies might give to the further development and advancement of the society and the economy. Implicitly, recognition is given in the Soviet literature that application of the Liberman reforms in the consumer goods area still will leave many of the problems of production and distribution unsolved. Thus, a Soviet social scientist argues that "without demographic research it is impossible to solve such an economically important question as the assortment of clothing and shoes in connection with the constantly changing age and position of the population."[21] Indeed, some practical research has already been done on this problem. Thus, the Novosibirsk University laboratory of economic and mathematical studies is cited as having conducted a study to determine "how many and what kinds of apartments" should be built in Novosibirsk in order to "make the most rational use of the housing fund and to satisfy the housing needs of the population."[22] New work in the geography field is being called for, particularly to solve problems of the location of new plants and industries,[23] and research in the agricultural area is being used to help determine the volume of output of products, the need for new machinery, mineral fertilizers, and other material resources.[24]

In a very real sense, the promises of benefits to come from the development of social sciences have given new heart to the conviction that the problems blocking the full development of communism can and will be solved. Little is left out of the catalog of tasks being assigned to the social sciences. They have been admonished by the Party leaders to discover the most rational uses of natural resources, to solve the problems of the distribution of production forces in view of technical progress as well as those of investment and labor productivity, and to perfect "planning and administration on the scale of the whole national economy as well as the individual branch and individual enterprise."[25] Although shortcomings and distortions of Western social sciences are continually stressed, their asserted achievements are also cited for emulation. For example, one writer observes that the US has 3,600 firms and social agencies to study the market, and he concludes that a planned Socialist economy needs such agencies even more than capitalist systems.[26]

For the most part, Western social sciences have the advantage of many decades of continuous development, and although one ought to stress that within the disciplines, various schools of thought still exist early in the 1970s, important common trends are present that bring a new unity to the disciplines. Descriptive and historical studies are still being done in all social sciences. Nevertheless, a strong turn to empiricism, involving the creation of models, reliance on mathematical measures, and concentration on so-called behavioral approaches does seem to dominate most Western social sciences, particularly those in the United States. In comparison, what might one say about the new disciplines being developed in the Soviet Union? First of all, although there is an increasing number of studies in the social sciences, with the major exception of economic studies, which more or less survived during Stalin's reign, what would be called social science in the West is still mostly talk in the USSR. True, as one author observed, there are at least "2,000 researchers working on various sociological problems" in the USSR.[27] Yet, as another observer noted, geography had been "dropped" from the list of earth sciences in the USSR Academy of Sciences.[28] Furthermore, although there is a Soviet Sociological Association, "There is no scientific center. There are insufficient cadres. There is no training of cadres. No journal. No textbook. No popular literature. No this, no that." Indeed, "There is not a single institute or department of sociology in our country."[29] As still another Soviet writer concludes, there is not "a single field in the social sciences deeply engaged in the study of the questions of management."[30] In short, therefore, a comparison of Soviet social sciences with Western social sciences must rest largely on analysis of what the political leaders and people working in the field say ought to be at some future time.

Beyond expressing a felt need to increase political and ideological controls and emphasizing hope for practical results, commentators are expressing many oughts that involve a wide variety of points of view. Surely few Western social scientists would quarrel with the assertion that "investigation of our sociological problems should be based first of all on objective scientific lessons, covering large groups of people (being representative) and utilizing mathematical and statistical methods for processing the material obtained."[31] Similarly, an assertion that "sociology is the science of optimal solutions" and that perhaps the major practical value of these studies is that of "destroying wrong, preconceived stereotypes and overthrowing common truisms,"[32] represents a view widely shared in the West. Nevertheless, as implied previously a survey of the literature indicates that there will be some important differences between Soviet and Western social sciences.

Great stress is given to the asserted advantage that exists in the USSR environment for the development of social sciences. Repeatedly, the point is made that the existence of Marxist–Leninist science rooted in historical materialism provides a base which Western social science in its pragmatism and empiricism seriously lacks. Indeed, although a great new stress is being placed on social "science" in the West, Soviet social science seems even more endangered by the pitfalls of scientism. Soviet investigators involved in the field refer again and again to "laws" in ways that Western social scientists tend to avoid. In their knowledge of what the ultimate future will be, Soviet social science writers express a confidence that is largely absent in the West. Therefore, much stress is laid upon filling in the gaps in the "laws" left by earlier Marxist–Leninist discoveries.

"1984" or Liberalization? Although it is far too early to come to any confident conclusion concerning the final impact of the development of social sciences on the Soviet system and Soviet society, several interesting speculations do come to mind. Clearly, a new dialectical tension has been introduced. Surely the possibilities for creating more effective controls

for the mature totalitarian system should not be dismissed lightly. Widespread, sophisticated social engineering would be the major key to the creation of a "1984." Those who dismiss this possibility lightly can logically be accused of believing that the American advertising agencies waste millions of their clients' dollars every year since motivational research can have no important influence on public opinion and choice.

In the United States, such social engineering is confined largely to selling products, and there is competition among corporations such as Ford, General Motors, and Chrysler. In the USSR such competition not only does not exist but, in addition, there has been a continuing effort to use all the means of persuasion to sell the public on a single interpretation, a monolithic view of truth. Now we see a major effort being made to develop social sciences in order to increase ideological and political controls. Yet, there is a reverse side to the coin, and a Pandora's box of discovery may well have been opened.

Not only have public opinion polls become the "in" thing but also many students in the field obviously have been influenced by Western social science literature. Surely, unless new, very tight controls are used, opinion-polling will increasingly reveal a disparity between popular beliefs and public desires and what has been asserted to be the doctrinaire truth. For example, the discovery that probably a majority of the working peasants still have icon corners in their homes seems to conflict with repeated claims of a great increase in atheism in the USSR.*[33] The very fact that public opinion is being given attention indicates that beyond the now-recognized importance of consumers' needs, the more abstract human needs and desires of the population are demanding attention. Will not the polls discover that there is no single public opinion but rather there are public opinions? As indicated from the icon count, studies already published bring to light the existence of gaps between past claims and reality, such as differences between conditions in the town and those in the villages and the differences between available leisure time in the USSR and elsewhere. Thus,

---

* This is not in contradiction to the point made earlier in this work, that popular acceptance of religion is far below the level it was prior to the 1917 Russian Revolution.

for example, although one published study stresses that the Soviet people seem to devote much more time to cultural improvement than Americans, it also compares the time that women in a Soviet city have to devote to housework with the time that women in a comparable American city have, giving the indication that the Soviet women must devote nearly one hour more per day to such chores than her American counterpart.[34]

Unless closely censored, Soviet social science studies very likely will challenge the infallibility of the official pamphlet and, indeed, the infallibility of authoritarian leaders. Again and again the point is made that although the social sciences had a good start under Lenin, as a result of "the cult of the individual" under Stalin, great harm was done to the society due to the lack of a scientific approach to solving problems. No less a figure than Politburo member Suslov himself has emphatically stressed that Stalin's personality cult "left not a few harmful consequences in the field of the development of the social sciences." He asks, "Why is this task so important still?" His answer is

Unless there is accomplished an elimination of dogmatic thinking in some professors and scientific personnel, unless there is a complete exposure and liquidation of the harmful consequences of the personality cult, then there will be in substance no possibility either of creative boldness or of a swing of scientific researches to the urgent theoretical and practical problems of the construction of communism and the training of the new man.[35]

What may we conclude? As suggested above, the social sciences may well become a major lever for the achievement of a "1984," or they may be the greatest organized force yet (much more than the push for the Liberman proposals) for political and social liberalization. In our opinion, in spite of the primary stress on the element of controls, the forces pushing for pluralism may be the strongest in the long run, but the movement must be carefully watched for several years before any definite trend can be identified. We personally agree with the Soviet writer's implication that the primary task of social sciences has been, and will continue to be, a critic of a society, smashing old shibboleths and "overthrowing common truisms" that block attempts to approach social truth. In this role, Western social sciences have been an important mainstay for the preservation and advancement of the "open society." There could have been no *Brown* v. *The Board of Education* in the United States if overwhelming social science evidence had not demonstrated that separate schools cannot be equal. The evidence so far indicates that as in the West, the interests of many of those calling for Soviet social sciences also are deeply rooted in concern over problems of human equality and freedom. Even if those who call for more sophisticated instruments of control are in a majority, as an attempt is made to indicate, the evidence they deal with can become an important weapon in the hands of the opposition.

PART V

The
USSR
Today
and Tomorrow

CHAPTER 15

The Balance Sheet

*Tensions in
the Paradigm:
Liberalization*
THE claim made in the foregoing pages is that although the Soviet model is far from perfect, a unique and relatively successful monohierarchical polity has evolved, a bureaucracy completely carried through and buttressed by the environment (including the tsarist past), a "new Soviet nationalism," and "adjuncts" that serve to encompass the citizens in the system more completely than the controls of the administrative hierarchy.

The system seems stable, yet the pace of change probably is more rapid than during most of the years of Stalin's rule. As stressed earlier, particularly in the Introduction, a number of Western observers seem to have concluded that the balance of the forces for change are in the direction of liberalization. Arguments are made that there are universal forces operative in political modernization and that as elsewhere (e.g., Japan), Soviet authoritarianism is destined to be eliminated, allowing for a convergence of the Soviet

205

and Western democratic systems. Such a change must include the evolution of politicadl interest groups and an opening up of public debate, two of the key aspects of pluralistic political systems. Perhaps such innovations will occur some day, but the evidence offered in this study indicates that that day is not in the forseeable future. When forces which might be said to operate in the direction of liberalization are compared with forces that tend to work in the direction of enhanced controls, the balance seems to be clearly against liberalization. Figure 4 illustrates this conclusion, both by indicating roughly in the order of importance (in this author's judgment) the forces for enhancement of controls and those forces which may be said to work in the direction of liberalization.

Figure 4, through the use of "greater than" (>) and "less than" (<) symbols, assigns relative weight to the various forces for change (i.e., on the left the forces are on the side of controls and on the right forces seem to be for liberalization). Moreover, as the ranking in Fig. 4 suggests, some relative value also has been assigned to the forces in each of the columns. Unfortunately, the present state of the science of comparative politics is not far enough advanced to pretend much by way of precision in such an exercise. Therefore, although we may be right in the judgment that to date the abandonment of terror (ranked No. 1 on the positive side of the ledger) has been a much more important force for liberalization than the asserted pluralistic element inherent in the move to develop Soviet social sciences (ranked No. 10)*, there really seems to be no satisfactory way to weigh these comparatively with the other eight liberalizing forces. Beyond this shortcoming in the analysis, probably no two social scientists (however empirical their individual approaches) would agree exactly upon just what items should be included in the list attempted here, much less on the relative value of the various forces for change that are included. Recognizing all this, the comparisons set forth in Fig. 4 were presented with a deliberate attempt to err in favor of liberalization. Assuming this exercise has been relatively successful, we must conclude reluctantly that in such an attempt at quantitative comparison,

---

* This ranking of the social sciences at the beginning of the 1970s is not considered to be contradictory to the *potential* importance of the social sciences for enhanced controls. Soviet social sciences may work both ways; this was stressed earlier. If they are developed along Western lines, they could become a most important force for liberalization.

Enhanced Controls (or retention of present levels)	Greater than**	Liberalizing
Rank*		Rank*
1 Bureaucracy completely carried through in an all-encompassing monohierarchial administrative scheme	C > L	3 Decentralization moves—e.g., Liberman and other reforms
2 Highly disciplined Party monopoly over all key leadership posts	C > L	6 Evidence of factions within the Party—e.g., the "anti-Party" group under Khrushchev
3 Near total nationalization of the economy and socialization of society with decreasing distinction remaining among the social, economic and political realms	C > L	4 Persistence of private economic activity in the peasant's garden plots
4 The successful transformation of the USSR into the world's second major industrial power under Communist rule resulting in widespread acceptance of the superiority of the Soviet system	C > L	5 Underdevelopment and cultural lag in the rural USSR, buttressed by dissatisfaction with the highly authoritarian collectivized system
5 Indoctrination of youth through the tightly controlled monopoly over education and youth programs	C >< L	8 Apathy and disenchantment among a segment of the youth
6 Informational control through rigid editorial control over all communications and artistic media	C >< L ***	7 Evidence of dissidence among the intellectuals, particularly the writers—e.g., the circulation of umpublishable manuscripts
7 Evolution of the new Soviet nationalism wedding Marxism-Leninism with traditional nationalism and lessons gleaned from practice	C > L	2 Persistence of nationalism among the various ethnic groups, persistence of religion among a segment of the population
8 Exploitation of popular forces for social conformity—e.g., the "voluntary" militia squads and the people's courts	C > L	9 Popular resistance (however slight) to such intrusion upon private affairs
9 1,000 years of an authoritarian political culture	C < L	1 Abandonment of terror as a major instrument of rule
10 The promise of enhanced social engineering by the development of Soviet social sciences	C < L	10 The strong pluralistic element inherent in the social sciences as developed in the West

*The author's judgment as to the relative importance of the items in each of the columns.
**C > L   Probable balance of forces on the side of retaining, or increasing, present levels of control.
 C < L   Probable balance of forces on the side of greater liberalization.
 C >< L   Balance of forces in doubt.
***Although writers clearly have had greater freedom than under Stalin, under the post-Khrushchev leadership, there has been an obvious reversal of the earlier liberalization trend.

Figure 4: Forces for change (the trend since Stalin)

the implication is that the forces for enhanced controls are probably more than three times greater than those for liberalization. Thus, excluding the two comparisons adjudged as approximately equal $(C>-<L)$, there are six comparisons wherein the weight seems to be strongly on the side of enhanced controls $(C>L)$ as compared with only two instances where the weight seems to be in the direction of greater liberalization $(C<L)$. Beyond the intrinsic value of an attempt to assay the overall trend for change in the USSR, such an exercise seemed necessary in light of our attempt to view the Soviet system of rule as an operative political model. This is to say that although few Western observers any longer imply that the Soviet political experiment is on the verge of collapse (as in the early decades of the USSR), a similar kind of wishful thinking on the part of individuals who strongly disapprove of Soviet communism may be partially responsible for a new prognosis implying that forces for convergence are evolving toward a liberal Soviet political system similar to the welfare state systems that have evolved in the West. Perhaps an assay of similar forces for change near the end of Stalin's rule would have reflected a weighting, let us speculate, of five or six against liberalization. Whatever the possible lessening of the odds, however, they still remain formidably against a fundamental change in the Soviet political system in any foreseeable future. In sum, although we emphatically agree that the major change in the USSR since 1953 has been the use of less oppressive means of rule, the rough comparison attempted here supports the following observation: Although the freedom to choose among options is greater, the use of more subtle and pervasive means of control may mean that the average Soviet citizen has even fewer options for exercising individual initiative at the beginning of the 1970s than his counterpart had at the height of Stalin's power. Surely, the new methods of control are more efficient than terror and, as a result, the USSR may be a more tightly structured society than previously.

Collectivization   The several key characteristics of the model
versus Fragments   are summarized in detail in the Introduction
                      (see *The Essences of the Paradigm*). Assuming that the description there is a valid picture of a USSR that has evolved a successful paradigm of monohierarchical rule, we

certainly must recognize that Soviet society reflects neither the social tranquility of utopian communism in Marx's vision nor the degree of control that the more pragmatic central dictatorship would like to maintain. Even if our judgment is correct that the balance of forces at work are against any significant trend to liberalize, a central question remains: Can the Soviet Union, or any Communist society, for that matter, advance beyond the levels of conformity achieved in the USSR by the onset of the 1970s?

Perhaps not; perhaps Soviet communism is incompatible with man's nature. Perhaps the present stage in the evolution of the model represents an apex, and factors unaccounted for here will produce liberalization at an accelerating rate. As noted in the discussion of Soviet ideology, Marx's view of the nature of man was that he is in essence a communal being. Does such a view fit the actuality of human behavior? Certainly much of what, at one time or another, has been regarded as immutable human nature has, in fact, proved to be subject to change. Nevertheless, there are some static limits and unchangeable desires. None will question that, in one form or another, men have always required and always will require food, shelter, satisfaction of sexual drives, and some degree of personal security. *Ergo,* successful systems of rule must, at a minimum, allow the mass of society to fulfill these inherent needs. Beyond forces emanating from such basics, however, there are fundamental disputes among social scientists over tendencies in sociopolitical behavior, which reflect basic differences both within Western societies and between the social and political fabrics of the Western and Soviet systems. For example, within the West what are the elements that are peculiar to the German political culture that have influenced a turn to strong authoritarian rule in times of stress when the opposite seems to be happening in Britain? Beyond basic needs common to all systems, what kind and what degree of interest articulation is necessary for the maintenance of a viable sociopolitical system? Do men naturally tend more toward collectives than to pluralistic political systems? Morgan's study of the American Indians led him to conclude that natural man is a communal being, able to dispense with strong leadership arrangements to hold divisive social elements together. Modern anthropology rejects Morgan's extreme conclusions. Nevertheless, it is still possible that both he and Marx came to the right conclusion, even if their evidence was questionable. From Plato and Aristotle onward, observers of human behavior have concluded overwhelmingly that man is a social being. Many, including Plato and Marx, went even further, to the point of asserting that the close bonds of a communal relationship reflect man's true nature.

Khrushchev's prediction at the Twenty-Second Congress that when, by 1980, the USSR will have demonstrated its economic superiority, the whole world will rapidly join the Communist fold, was nothing new in the statement of Soviet goals. However, had Khrushchev taken the time, he would have argued (as he and other Soviet leaders have argued at other times) that his optimistic prognosis rests on the Marxian "scientific" fact that the Soviet psychology of rule is correct, whereas Western rule based upon individualism is incorrect. If we are to advance the science of political behavior, the key point, or perhaps better, the key question that remains unresolved is, "How mutable is what is often loosely labeled 'human nature'?" Perhaps sophisticated means of conditioning behavior are capable of producing communal attitudes that would be reflected in a society wherein "all would live as one." Perhaps a society similar to the communist society envisaged by Marx can be created by social engineering.

A fundamental difference between the Soviet and Western systems rests upon a basic difference between Western and Soviet views of the nature of man. According to the Soviet view, man's will is determined by society and its relationship to the means of production. Therefore, freedom is defined by Soviet philosophers as the "perception of necessity." In short, the steam roller of history can go in only the correct direction, and the closest an individual can come to enjoying freedom is to recognize the scientifically determined direction of change and join in the movement. Those pathetic fools who fail to perceive this truth must, unfortunately, be crushed as the *kulaks* were in their resistance to forced collectivization.

Is what has been called human nature so mutable that the dream of creating a "new Soviet man," whose behavior at all times will be collectively motivated, realizable? Here, undoubtedly, is the most important question concerning the future of the Soviet political experiment. Although often modified by the demands of the moment, Soviet institutions of rule are designed with the communal man in mind. Recognizing that the Soviet peasants form the largest single segment of society and that the peasants and their agricultural problems constitute the major demestic problem area, both economically and politically, Sir John Maynard summarized the situation most succinctly in the late 1940s in his *Russia in Flux.* "[If] the rulers have discovered in collectivization a way of life which can be made to harmonize with his [the peasant's] instincts [needs], the system will survive." On the other hand, if the Soviet peasant "is submitting uneasily to a compulsion which irks him, the skipper must veer off upon another course, or Russia will again become the land of fragments depicted in Mayakovsky's play."[1]

Unfortunately (since this author's personal prejudices cry for a counter conclusion), our judgment is that the Soviet citizenry, including the peasantry, find the system less irksome today than they did more than two decades ago. Indeed, an important point of this volume has been that most studies of Soviet politics give too little attention to evidence indicating that there is an increasing acceptance of common beliefs by Soviet society, and that this "new Soviet nationalism" is an important strength of the system. Many factors are involved in this change, but our suspicion is that the turning point came in the USSR at the time of the Second World War.

At first, Hitler's generals approached the peasants in captured areas as liberators from the collective farms. In many instances, such overtures were accepted, and the peasants met their liberators with the traditional bread and salt. However, the German invaders needed the peasants' food and discovered that the kolkhozy had been valuable collecting agencies. The policy was reversed. The collective farms were re-created, and the peasants responded by opening guerrilla warfare against the Nazi invader. At least the former collectives had been dominated by fellow Slavs.

True, the evidence offered here leading to the conclusion that "there is an increasing acceptance of common beliefs" is not as conclusive as it would be if social scientists were able to carry out extensive attitudinal studies in the USSR. However, unless one is prepared to reject the assumption that every viable political system (even one ruled by terror) must possess a minimal level of com-

monly accepted beliefs, the question is not whether such beliefs
exist in the USSR (and existed under Stalin), but rather how they
have changed since Stalin's death. As recorded here, the reduction
in the number of peasant homes with icon corners, the decline in
voter dissent, the judgment by Western students of Soviet youth
and education that the educational system has achieved important
successes, and the existence of a common theme among the most
lucid of the Soviet critics (i.e., the writers and poets) of accepting
the faith while damning the failure to fulfill its promises is evidence
supporting our conclusion. Thus, Yevgeniy Yevtushenko's clear cry
that he does not reject the goals, while sharply criticizing what has
been done in the name of Marxism–Leninism, is in important contrast to Boris Pasternak's rejection of both the new beliefs and
what was done. The difference between the two men is a difference
between generations that emphasizes the point. Pasternak (1890–
1960) was a pre-Revolutionary man, a child of the hopes of another era who rejected the experiment to remake society. Yevtushenko (1933–   ) was born with the hopes of a new era.
Although the Party leadership hardly regards him as an example
of "the new Soviet man," he is a new Soviet man in that much
of his anger is directed at the failure to live up to the promises of
the new beliefs.

One of the most difficult problems encountered by observers
of other societies is to avoid imposing one's own values, his own
"human nature," the political behavior observed in his system, on a
foreign people. Thus, as a student of Southeast Asia, my colleague
Carl Landé stresses the need to understand the importance of "deal
making," as opposed to "following the rules" (in the Western
manner) to the political culture of that part of the world. In short,
our suspicion is that the most serious errors in understanding Soviet
affairs probably arise out of Western European and American observers finding Soviet institutions, beliefs, and behavior incredible
after their immersion in the political culture of constitutional democracies.

The attempt here has been to evaluate the Soviet political scene
primarily in its own terms, and therefore we must conclude that
as believing beings the present-day citizens of the USSR are not
Britishers, Americans, or Frenchmen—or even Russians, Ukrainians,
etc., as they were under the tsar. Aspects of earlier beliefs and

practices remain, yet a new Soviet nationalism has evolved which is marked by a peculiar set of social and political attitudes, producing behavioral patterns of its own. In sum, a distinct Soviet political culture has emerged, one that seems to articulate relatively comfortably with the monohierarchical paradigm fostered by the Party leadership.

Bibliography

SELECTED BOOKS (IN ENGLISH)

ON SOVIET POLITICS AND RELATED AFFAIRS*

Arendt, Hannah, *The Origins of Totalitarianism*. London: G. Allen and Unwin, 1958; New York: Meridian Books, 1960.

Armstrong, John A., *Ideology, Politics and Government in the Soviet Union*. New York: Frederick A. Praeger, 1962.

———, *The Politics of Totalitarianism: The Communist Party of the Soviet Union from 1934 to the Present*. New York: Random House, 1961.

———, *The Soviet Bureaucratic Elite: A Case Study of the Ukrainian Apparatus*. New York: Frederick A. Praeger, 1959.

Barghoorn, Frederick C., *Politics in the USSR*. Boston: Little, Brown and Co., 1966.

———, *The Soviet Cultural Offensive*. Princeton, New Jersey: Princeton University Press, 1960.

Bauer, Raymond A., Inkeles, Alex, and Kluckhohn, Clyde, *How the Soviet System Works: Cultural, Psychological and Social Themes*. Cambridge, Mass.: Harvard University Press, 1956.

* Excluding books primarily devoted to foreign affairs.

————, *The New Man in Soviet Psychology*. Cambridge, Mass.: Harvard University Press, 1952.

————, and Wasiolek, Edward, *Nine Soviet Portraits*. Cambridge, Mass.: Mass. Institute of Technology Press and New York: John Wiley and Sons, Inc., 1955.

Baykov, Alexander, *The Development of the Soviet Economic System, An Essay on the Experience of Planning in the USSR*. Cambridge, England: The University Press, 1946.

Belov, Fedor, *The History of a Soviet Collective Farm*. New York: Frederick A. Praeger, 1955.

Berdiaev, Nikolai A., *The Russian Revolution*. Ann Arbor, Mich.: University of Michigan Press, 1961.

Berdiaev, Nicolas (trans. from Russian by R. M. French), *The Origin of Russian Communism*. Ann Arbor, Mich.: University of Michigan Press, 1937, 1948, and 1960.

Bergson, Abram (ed.), *Soviet Economic Growth*. Evanston, Ill.: Row, Peterson & Co., 1953.

Berman, Harold J., *Justice in Russia: An Interpretation of Soviet Law*. Cambridge, Mass.: Harvard University Press, 1950.

Bienstock, Gregory, Schwartz, Solomon M., and Yugow, Aaron, *Management in Russian Industry and Agriculture*. London–New York: Oxford University Press, 1944.

Bober, Mandell Morton, *Karl Marx's Interpretation of History*. Cambridge, Mass.: Harvard University Press, 1948.

Bochenski, I. M., *Soviet Russian Dialectical Materialism*. Dordrecht, Holland: D. Reidel Publishing Co., 1963.

Brumberg, Abraham (ed.), *Russia Under Khrushchev—An Anthology from Problems of Communism*. New York: Frederick A. Praeger, 1962.

Brzezinski, Zbigniew K., *Ideology and Power in Soviet Politics*. New York: Frederick A. Praeger, 1962.

————, *The Permanent Purge: Politics in Soviet Authoritarianism*. Cambridge, Mass.: Harvard University Press, 1956.

Campbell, Robert W., *Soviet Economic Power: Its Organization, Growth and Challenge*. Boston: Houghton Mifflin Co., 1960.

Cantril, Hadley, *Soviet Leaders and Mastery over Man*. New Brunswick, New Jersey: Rutgers University Press, 1960.

Carr, Edward Hallett, *A History of Soviet Russia* (9 vols). London and New York: Macmillan Co., 1950–1960.

Chamberlin, William H., *The Russian Revolution, 1917–1921* (2 vols.). New York: Macmillan Co., 1952.

Conquest, Robert, *Power and Policy in the USSR: The Study of Soviet Dynastics.* New York: St. Martin's Press, 1961.

———, *Russia After Khrushchev.* New York–Washington–London: Frederick A. Praeger, 1965.

Crankshaw, Edward, *Khrushchev's Russia.* Baltimore, Md.; Penguin Books, Inc., 1959.

Curtiss, John Shelton, *The Russian Church and the Soviet State, 1917–1950.* Boston: Little, Brown and Co., 1953.

Daniels, Robert Vincent, *The Conscience of the Revolution: Communist Opposition in Soviet Russia.* Cambridge, Mass.: Harvard University Press, 1960.

——— (ed.), *A Documentary History of Communism.* New York: Random House, 1960.

Degras, Jane T., *Soviet Planning: Essays in Honour of Naum Jasny.* Oxford: Basil Blackwell, 1964.

Deutscher, Isaac, *Stalin, A Political Biography.* New York: Oxford University Press, 1949.

DeWitt, Nicholas, *Education and Professional Employment in the U.S.S.R.* Washington, D.C.: National Science Foundation, 1961.

Dirscherl, S. J. (ed.), *The New Russia.* Dayton, Ohio: Pflaum Press, 1968.

Djilas, Milovan, *The New Class: An Analysis of the Communist System.* New York: Frederick A. Praeger, 1957.

Dobb, Maurice Herbert, *Soviet Economic Development Since 1917.* London: Routledge and Kegan Paul, Ltd., 1958.

Dudintsev, Vladimir, *Not By Bread Alone.* New York: E. P. Dutton and Co., 1957.

Engels, Friedrich, *Socialism, Utopian and Scientific.* New York: International Publishers, 1935.

Fainsod, Merle, *How Russia Is Ruled* (2nd ed.). Cambridge, Mass.: Harvard University Press, 1963.

———, *Smolensk Under Soviet Rule.* Cambridge, Mass.: Harvard University Press, 1958; and London: Macmillan and Co., 1959.

Feifer, George, *Justice in Moscow.* New York: Dell Publishing Co., 1965.

Fisher, Ralph Talcott, *Pattern for Soviet Youth: A Study of the Congresses of the Komsomol, 1918–1954.* New York: Columbia University Press, 1959.

Fundamentals of Marxism–Leninism, Manual. Moscow: Foreign Languages Publishing House (n.d.).

Granick, David, *Management of the Industrial Firm in the USSR: A Study in Soviet Economic Planning.* New York: Columbia University Press, 1954.

————, *The Red Executive: A Study of the Organizational Man in Russian Industry.* Garden City, N.Y.: Doubleday and Co., Inc., 1961.

Grant, Nigel, *Soviet Education.* Baltimore: Penguin Books, 1964.

Gripp, Richard C., *Patterns of Soviet Politics.* Homewood, Ill.: Dorsey Press, 1963.

Gyorgy, Andrew, *Communism in Perspective.* Boston: Allyn and Bacon, Inc., 1964.

Harper, Samuel N., and Thompson, Ronald, *The Government of the Soviet Union.* New York: D. Van Nostrand Co., Inc., 1949.

Hazard, John *Law and Social Change in the USSR.* Toronto: Carswell Co., 1953.

————, *The Soviet System of Government.* Chicago: University of Chicago Press, 1960.

Hendel, Samuel (ed.), *The Soviet Crucible: Soviet Government in Theory and Practice.* Princeton, New Jersey: D. Van Nostrand Co., Inc., 1959.

Hubbard, Leonard, *The Economics of Soviet Agriculture.* London: Macmillan Co., 1939.

Hulicka, Karel, and Hulicka, Irene M., *Soviet Institutions, The Individual and Society.* Boston: The Christopher Publishing House, 1967.

Hunt, Robert Nigel C., *A Guide To Communist Jargon.* New York: Macmillan Co., 1957.

Inkeles, Alex, *Public Opinion in Soviet Russia, a Study in Mass Persuasion.* Cambridge, Mass.: Harvard University Press, 1950.

Jacobs, Daniel Norman, *The New Communist Manifesto and Related Documents.* Evanston, Ill.: Row, Peterson and Co., 1961–1962.

Jasny, Naum, *The Socialized Agriculture of the USSR.* Stanford, Calif.: Stanford University Press, 1951.

Juviler, Peter H. and Morton, Henry W. (eds.), *Soviet Policy-Making.* New York: Praeger, 1967.

Kassof, Allen, *The Soviet Youth Program.* Cambridge, Mass.: Russian Research Center Studies, 49, Harvard University Press, 1965.

Kulski, Wladyslaw W., *The Soviet Regime: Communism in Practice* (4th ed.). Syracuse, New York: Syracuse University Press, 1963.

Labedz, Leopold (ed.), *Revisionism: Essays on the History of Marxist Ideas.* New York: Frederick A. Praeger, 1962.

Laird, Roy D., *Collective Farming in Russia: A Political Study of the Soviet Kolkhozy.* Lawrence, Kansas: University of Kansas Publications, Social Science Studies, 1958.

————, and Laird, Betty A., *Soviet Communism and Agrarian Revolution*. Middlesex, England: Penguin, 1970.

————, Sharp, D. E., and Sturtevant, R., *The Rise and Fall of the M.T.S. as an Instrument of Soviet Rule*. Lawrence, Kansas: G.R.S. No. 22, The University of Kansas, 1960.

———— (ed.), *Soviet Agricultural and Peasant Affairs*. Lawrence, Kansas: University of Kansas Press, 1963.

————, and Crowley, Edward L. (eds.), *Soviet Agriculture: The Permanent Crisis*. New York: Frederick A. Praeger, 1965.

Lamont, Corliss, *The Peoples of the USSR*. New York: Harcourt, Brace and World, Inc., 1946.

Laski, Harold Joseph, *Communism*. New York: H. Holt & Co., 1927.

Lenin, *Collected Works* (38 vols.). Moscow: Foreign Languages Publishing House, 1960.

Leonhard, Wolfgang, *The Kremlin Since Stalin*. New York: Frederick A. Praeger, 1962.

Lichtheim, George, *Marxism: An Historical and Critical Study*. New York: Frederick A. Praeger, 1961.

Lorimer, Frank, *The Population of the Soviet Union*. Geneva: League of Nations, 1946.

Luxemburg, Rosa, *The Russian Revolution and Leninism or Marxism?* Ann Arbor, Mich.: University of Michigan Press, 1961.

McClosky, Herbert, and Turner, John E., *The Soviet Dictatorship*. New York: McGraw-Hill Book Co., Inc., 1960.

Marx, Karl, *Capital* (3 vols.). Moscow: Foreign Languages Publishing House, 1958.

Maynard, Sir John, *Russia in Flux*. New York: Macmillan Co., 1948.

Meyer, Alfred G., *Communism*. New York: Random House, 1960.

————, *Leninism*. Cambridge, Mass.: Harvard University Press, 1956.

————, *Marxism*. Cambridge, Mass.: Harvard University Press, 1954.

————, *The Soviet Political System, An Interpretation*. New York: Random House, 1965.

Mitrany, David, *Marx Against the Peasant*. New York: Collier, 1961.

Monnerot, Jules, *Sociology and Psychology of Communism*. Boston: Beacon Press, 1960.

Moore, Barrington, Jr., *Soviet Politics—The Dilemma of Power*. Cambridge, Mass.: Harvard University Press, 1950.

————, *Terror and Progress, USSR*. Cambridge, Mass.: Harvard University Press, 1954.

Morgan, Glenn G., *Soviet Administrative Legality: The Rule of the Attorney General's Office*. Stanford, Calif.: Stanford University Press, 1962.

Nove, Alec, *The Soviet Economy*. New York: Frederick A. Praeger, 1961.

Ploss, Sidney I., *Conflict and Decision Making in Soviet Russia: A Case Study of Agricultural Policy 1953–1963*. Princeton, New Jersey: Princeton University Press, 1965.

Rauch, Georg von (trans. by Peter and Annette Jacobsohn), *A History of Soviet Russia*. New York: Frederick A. Praeger, 1957.

Reed, John, *Ten Days That Shook the World*. New York: Modern Library, 1935.

Reshetar, John S., Jr., *A Concise History of the Communist Party of the Soviet Union*. New York: Frederick A. Praeger, 1960.

Ritvo, Herbert (ed.), *The New Soviet Society*. New York: The New Leader, 1964.

Rosenberg, Arthur, *A History of Bolshevism*. London–New York: Oxford University Press, 1934.

Rostow, Walt W., Levin, Alfred, and Daniels, Robert, *The Dynamics of Soviet Society*. New York: W. W. Norton and Co., Inc., 1953.

Rush, Myron, *Political Succession in the USSR*. New York: Frederick A. Praeger, 1955.

Sabine, George H., *Marxism*. Ithaca, New York: Cornell University Press, 1958.

Schapiro, Leonard B., *The Communist Party of the Soviet Union*. New York: Random House, 1960; London: Eyre and Spottiswoode, 1960.

———, *The Government and Politics of the Soviet Union*. New York: Random House, 1965.

Schlesinger, Rudolf, *Marx, His Time and Ours*. London: Routledge and Kegan Paul, Ltd., 1950.

———, *Soviet Legal Theory, Its Social Background and Development*. London: Oxford University Press, 1945.

Schuman, Frederick L., *Government in the Soviet Union*. New York: Thomas Y. Crowell Co., 1961.

———, *Russia Since 1917*. New York: Alfred A. Knopf, 1957.

———, *Soviet Politics, at Home and Abroad*. New York: Alfred A. Knopf, 1946.

Schwartz, Harry, *The Red Phoenix: Russia Since World War II*. New York: Frederick A. Praeger, 1961.

———, *Russia's Soviet Economy*. Englewood Cliffs, New Jersey: Prentice-Hall, 1958.

Schwarz, Solomon M., *Labor in the Soviet Union*. New York: Frederick A. Praeger, 1952.

Scott, Derek J. R., *Russian Political Institutions*. New York: Frederick A. Praeger, 1961.

Seton-Watson, Hugh, *From Lenin to Khrushchev, The History of World Communism.* New York: Frederick A. Praeger, 1960.

Shabad, Theodore, *Geography of the USSR: A Regional Survey.* New York: Columbia University Press, 1958.

Shaffer, Harry G. (ed.), *The Soviet Economy: A Collection of Western and Soviet Views.* New York: Appleton–Century–Crofts, 1963.

——— (ed.), *The Soviet System in Theory and Practice—Selected Western and Soviet Views.* New York: Appleton–Century–Crofts, 1965.

Shub, David, *Lenin.* New York: Doubleday, 1948.

Souvarine, Boris, *Stalin: A Critical Survey of Bolshevism.* London: Secker and Warburg, 1940.

Spulber, Nicholas, *The Soviet Economy.* New York: W. W. Norton and Co., 1962.

Stalin, Joseph, *Economic Problems of Socialism in the USSR.* New York: International Publishers, 1952.

———, *Leninism: Selected Writings.* New York: International Publishers, 1942.

Stewart, Philip D., *Political Power in the Soviet Union.* Indianapolis and New York: The Bobbs-Merrill Company, Inc., 1958.

Swearer, Howard R., and Longaker, Richard P. (eds.), *Contemporary Communism: Theory and Practice.* Belmont, Calif.: Wadsworth Publishing Co., 1963.

———, *The Politics of Succession in the USSR—Materials on Khrushchev's Rise to Leadership.* Boston: Little, Brown and Co., 1964.

Timasheff, Nicholas S., *Religion in Soviet Russia: 1917–1942.* New York: Sheed and Ward, Inc., 1942.

Towster, Julian, *Political Power in the USSR, 1917–1947: The Theory and Structure of Government in the Soviet State.* New York: Oxford University Press, 1948.

Treadgold, Donald W., *Lenin and His Rivals: The Struggle for Russia's Future, 1898–1906.* New York: Frederick A. Praeger, 1955.

———, *Twentieth-Century Russia.* Chicago: Rand McNally and Co., 1959.

Triska, Jan F. (ed.), *Soviet Communism: Programs and Rules.* San Francisco: Chandler Publishing Co., 1962.

Trotsky, Leon, *The History of the Russian Revolution.* Ann Arbor, Michigan: University of Michigan Press, 1957.

———, *My Life.* New York: Charles Scribner's Sons, 1930.

———, *Stalin.* New York: Harper and Row, 1941.

Tucker, Robert, *Philosophy and Myth in Karl Marx.* Cambridge, England: Cambridge University Press, 1961.

Ulam, Adam B., *The New Face of Soviet Totalitarianism*. Cambridge, Mass.: Harvard University Press, 1963.

Utechin, S. V., *Russian Political Thought: A Concise History*. New York: Frederick A. Praeger, 1964.

Volin, Lazar, *A Survey of Soviet Russian Agriculture*. Washington, D.C.: U.S. Government Printing Office, 1951.

Von Laue, Theodore H., *Why Lenin? Why Stalin: A Reappraisal of the Russian Revolution*. Philadelphia–New York: J. B. Lippincott, 1964.

Vucinich, Alexander, *Soviet Economic Institutions*. Stanford, Calif.: Stanford University Press, 1952.

Vyshinsky, Andrei Y., *The Law of the Soviet State*. New York: Macmillan Co., 1948.

Walsh, Warren B., *Russia and the Soviet Union. A Modern History*. Ann Arbor, Michigan: University of Michigan Press, 1958.

Webb, Sidney, and Webb, Beatrice, *Soviet Communism: A New Civilization?* (2 vols.). New York: Charles Scribner's Sons, 1936.

Wetter, Gustavo A., *Dialectical Materialism: A Historical and Systematic Survey of Philosophy in the Soviet Union*. New York: Frederick A. Praeger, 1959.

Wilson, Edmund, *To the Finland Station: A Study in the Writing and Acting of History*. Garden City, New York: Doubleday and Co., 1955.

Wolfe, Bertram D., *Khrushchev and Stalin's Ghost*. New York: Frederick A. Praeger, 1957.

———, *Three Men Who Made a Revolution*. New York: Dial Press, Inc., 1948.

Notes*

Introduction

1 See, for example, the discussion of modernization in Richard E. Dawson and Kenneth Prewitt, *Political Socialization,* Little, Brown and Company, Boston, 1969.

2. R. M. McIver, *The Web of Government,* The Macmillan Company, New York, 1948, pp. 4 and 5.

Chapter 1. The Land and the People

1. Carl Zoerb, "The Virgin Land Territory: Plans, Performance, Prospects," Roy D. Laird and Edward L. Crowley (eds.). Frederick A. Praeger, New York, 1965, pp. 29–43.

---

* Unless otherwise designated, titles of Soviet articles in English imply the authors' use of such excellent translation sources as the Joint Publications Research Service and The Current Digest of the Soviet Press. Often however, the translation was checked against the original if this seemed desirable.

2. Lazar Volin, *A Survey of Soviet Russian Agriculture,* Agricultural Monograph No. 5, 1951, United States Department of Agriculture.
3. *Strana Sovetov za 50 let,* Sbornik statisticheskikh materialov, Moskva, 1967, p. 15, *Narodnoe, khozyaistvo SSSR v 1968 godu,* tsentral'noe' statisticheskoe upravlenie, Moskva, 1969, p. 7.
4. *Ibid.,* pp. 16 and 17.

Chapter 2. A Capsule Summary of Russian History

1. George Vernadsky, *A History of Russia,* Yale University Press, New Haven, 1954, p. 80.
2. *Ibid.,* p. 2.
3. Maynard, Sir John, *Russia in Flux,* The Macmillan Company, New York, 1945, p. 24.
4. Gerard Tanquary Robinson, *Rural Russia Under the Old Regime,* The Macmillan Company, New York, 1949, p. 35.
5. *Ibid.,* p. 194.
6. Naum Jasny, *The Socialized Agriculture of the USSR: Plans and Performance,* Stanford University Press, California, 1949, pp. 141 and 142.
7. *Forty Years of Soviet Power in Facts and Figures,* Foreign Languages Publishing House, Moscow, 1958, p. 234.

Chapter 3. Marxism

1. Karl Marx, *Capital: A Critical Analysis of Capitalist Production* Vol. 1, Foreign Languages Publishing House, Moscow, 1958, pp. 244 and 245.
2. *Ibid.,* pp. 254 and 255.
3. *Ibid.,* p. 641.
4. Alfred G. Meyer, *Marxism: The Unity of Theory and Practice,* The University of Michigan Press, Ann Arbor, 1963, pp. 74–90.
5. Max Eastman (ed.), *Capital: The Communist Manifesto and Other Writings,* The Modern Library, 1932, p. 318.
6. *Ibid.,* p. 381.
7. *Ibid.,* p. viii.
8. V. I. Lenin, *Collected Works* Vol. 19, Foreign Languages Publishing House, Moscow, 1963, p. 26.
9. *Ibid.*
10. Marx, *op. cit.,* p. 171.
11. *Ibid.,* p. 325 ff.
12. *Ibid.,* p. 355.
13. *Ibid.,* p. 360.

14. Murray Yanowitch, "Alienation and the Young Marx in Soviet Thought," *Slavic Review* Vol. XXVI, No. 1 (March 1967), pp. 29–53.
15. Lenin, *op. cit.*, p. 574.
16. Meyer, *Marxism:* ... *op. cit.*, p. 78.
17. Lenin, Vol. 19, *op. cit.*, p. 26.
18. Eastman, *op. cit.*, pp. 342 and 343.
19. *Ibid.*, pp. xii–xv.
20. J. Plamenetz, "The Communist Ideology," *The Political Quarterly* Vol. XX, No. 1 (January–March 1951), pp. 16–26.
21. Eastman, *op. cit.*, p. xi.

Chapter 4. Leninism

1. George H. Sabine, *A History of Political Theory,* Henry Holt and Company, New York, 1950, p. 847.
2. Alfred G. Meyer, *Leninism,* Frederick A. Praeger, New York, 1962, pp. 19 and 31.
3. *Ibid.*, pp. 37–56.
4. *Ibid.*, see especially Chapters 7 and 11.
5. See Lenin's writings on "The Agrarian Question" and "The Agrarian Program," *Collected Works* Vol. 13, *op. cit.*
6. P. N. Fedoseyev, "Great Threshold in the History of Mankind," *Izvestia* (April 30, 1967), p. 2.
7. Roger E. Kanet, *The Soviet Union and Sub-Saharan Africa: Communist Policy Toward Africa, 1917–1965,* Princeton, Unpublished Doctoral Thesis, 1966, pp. 48–49.
8. A. A. Galkin, et al., *The Building of Communism and World Revolutionary Process,* Nauk, Moscow, 1966, 533 pp., *JPRS* translation (June 22, 1967), p. 40.
9. *Ibid.*
10. "The National Liberation Movement: An Integral Part of the World Revolutionary Process," *Kommunist,* No. 2 (January 1962), pp. 15–20.
11. Galkin, *op. cit.*
12. V. I. Lenin, *Polnoye Sobraniye Sochineniy* Vol. 32, p. 99, as cited by Galkin, *op. cit.*, p. 375. On this point, also see L. I. Brezhnev, "Fifty Years of Great Victories of Socialism," *Pravda* (November 4, 1967), pp. 2–6, and M. S. Ozhunusov, ". . . The Nation as a Social-Ethnic Community," *Voprosy istorii,* No. 4 (April 1966), pp. 16–30.
13. Galkin, *op. cit.*, p. 430.

14. A. Chernyayev, "Socialism is the Main Force of World Revolutionary Development," *Pravda* (August 3, 1963), pp. 5–6 and Ye. Zhukov, "The National Liberation Movement in a New State," *Kommunist*, No. 12 (August 1963), pp. 23–32.

15. Chernyayev, *op. cit.*

16. Fedoseyev, *op. cit.*, and "The Supreme International Duty of a Socialist Country," *Pravda* (October 27, 1966), pp. 3–4.

17. Kanet, *op. cit.*, pp. 46 and 47, and V. A. Fanasyev, *Marxist Philosophy*, Foreign Languages Publishing House, Moscow, n.d.

18. Ozhunusov, *op. cit.*

19. "100th Anniversary of the First International: 1864–1964 (theses)," *Pravda* (September 11, 1964), pp. 1–3.

20. Kanet, *op. cit.*, p. 33.

21. "The National Liberation Movement . . ." *op. cit.* and Galkin, *op. cit.*, p. 86.

22. *Ibid.*

23. *Ibid.*

24. Fanosyev, *op. cit.*, p. 104.

25. N. A. Simoniia, "On the Character of National Liberation Revolutions," *Peoples of Asia and Africa, Narody Azii i Afriki*, No. 6, 1966, pp. 14–21.

26. Nikolai Rozanov, "From Feudalism to Socialism, Bypassing Capitalism," *Moscow News*, Supplement to Issue No. 7, 1967, pp. 22, 23, and 32.

27. "Replies of N. S. Khrushchev to Questions of Editors of Ghanian Times, Alger Republican, Le Peuple ad Botatieng," *Pravda* (December 22, 1963), pp. 1 and 2.

28. Galkin, *op. cit.*, p. 84.

29. G. Starushenko, "Fiction and Truth about Wars of Liberation," *Kommunist*, No. 12 (August 1965), pp. 94–97.

30. "The USSR and the National Liberation Struggle," *Pravda* (June 28, 1965), pp. 2 and 3.

31. Fedoseyev, *op. cit.*

32. Yu. Krasin, "Questions of Theory: Experiences of Lasting Significance," *Pravda* (January 11, 1967), pp. 2 and 3.

33. A. Iskenderov, "The Army, Politics, and the People," *Izvestia* (January 17, 1967), pp. 9 and 10.

34. Krupskaya, N. K., *Memories of Lenin* (translated by E. Varney), Vols. I and II, International Publishers, New York, 1930, p. 189.

35. *Complete Works*, Vol. 28, *op cit.*, p. 289.

36. *Ibid.*, Vol. 25, pp. 381–492.

Chapter 5. Soviet Nationalism

1. J. Stalin, *Leninism: Selected Writings,* International Publishers, New York, 1942, pp. 169–174.
2. M. F. Puzrina, "Novie manery burzhuanznikh sovetologovagrarni-kov," *Istoriya SSR,* No. 1, 1969, pp. 175–188.
3. Arthur Koestler, *Darkness at Noon,* The Modern Library, New York, 1941, p. 14.
4. Roy D. Laird, "The New Soviet Myth: Marx is Dead, Long Live Communism!" *Soviet Studies* Vol. XVIII, No. 4 (April 1967), pp. 511–518.
5. Alec Nove, "Was Stalin Really Necessary?" *Encounter* (April 1962), pp. 86–92.
6. Y. V. Arutyunyan, "Sotsial'naya struktura sel'skogo naseleniya," *Voprosy filosofii,* 1966, No. 6, pp. 51–61.
7. Alec Nove, "Ideology and Agriculture," *Soviet Studies* Vol. XVII, No. 4 (April 1966), pp. 397–406.

Chapter 6. The Hierarchy and the Political Elite

1. James Burnham, *The Machiavellians,* Putnam and Co., London, 1943, p. 202.
2. Robert C. Tucker, "Towards a Comparative Politics of Movement Regime," *The American Political Science Review* Vol. LV, No. 2 (June 1961), p. 283.
3. Hannah Arendt, *The Origins of Totalitarianism,* Meridian Books Inc., New York, 1959, p. 520.
4. See the "Symposium," *Slavic Review* Vol. XVI, No. 1 (March 1967), pp. 1–28.
5. *Ibid.*
6. N. S. Khrushchev, *Report on the Program of the Communist Party of the Soviet Union: Documents of the 22nd Congress of the CPSU* Vol. 2, Crosscurrents Press, New York, 1961, p. 150.
7. "Report Delivered by F. R. Kozlov, Secretary of the Central Committee of the Communist Party of the Soviet Union, to the Twenty-Second Congress of the CPSU" (October 28, 1961), *Amendments to the Rules of the Communist Party of the Soviet Union,* Press Department, Embassy of the Union of Soviet Socialist Republics, Washington, D.C. (November 9, 1961), p. 9.
8. Milton Lodge, "Soviet Elite Participatory Attitudes in the Post-Stalin Period," and John Schwartz and William R. Keech, "Group Influence and the Policy Process in the Soviet Union," *The American Political Science Review* Vol. LXII, No. 3 (September 1968), pp. 827–839 and 840–851.

9. Milovan Djilas, *The New Class,* New York, Frederick A. Praeger, 1957, p. 214.
10. "CPSU in Figures," *Partiinaya zhizn,* No. 19 (October 1967), pp. 8–20, and *Narodnoe khozyaistvo SSSR v 1968 godu,* tsentral'noe' statisticheskoe upravlenie, Moskva, 1969, p. 7.
11. *Ibid.*
12. *Ibid.*
13. *Ibid.*
14. *Ibid.*
15. *Strana Soveta 3a 50 let, op. cit.,* p. 15, *Narodnoe khozyaistvo SSSR v 1963 godu,* tsentral'noe' statisticheskoe upravlenie, Moskva, 1963, p. 7, and *Current Economic Indicators for the U.S.S.R.,* Materials Prepared for the Joint Economic Committee Congress of the United States, US Government Printing Office, Washington, 1965, p. 25.

Chapter 7. Leadership: Some Characteristics of the Model

1. See Glen G. Morgan, *Soviet Administrative Legality: The Role of the Attorney General's Office,* Stanford, California, Stanford University Press, 1962, 281 pp.
2. Max Weber, *Essays on Sociology* (translation and editing by Gerth and Mills), Oxford University Press, New York, 1961, pp. 196–244.
3. Merle Fainsod, *How Russia Is Ruled,* Harvard University Press, 1953, p. 354.
4. Weber, *op. cit.* (present author's italics). The argument made by Alec Nove in his article "Was Stalin Really Necessary?" *Encounter* Vol. XVIII, No. 4 (April 1962), pp. 86–92, seems to be in line with this claim.
5. Here again, agriculture, which was much further behind than the urban part of the economy, was the area of major advance. Thus according to Khrushchev, whereas there were only 114,000 specialists working on the farms in 1953, by 1963 the figure had risen to 414,000. See *Pravda* (February 14, 1964), pp. 1–6.
6. Arendt, *op. cit.,* pp. 391–392.
7. Although there seems little doubt about Khrushchev's desire to have been *primus inter pares* in any Presidium, the examples he cited in his "secret speech" of the abuses of Stalin were too real. Moreover, as E. H. Carr has indicated, the myth of "collective leadership" is deeply ingrained in Soviet thought (if not practice). See *The Bolshevik Revolution* Vol. II, New York, Macmillan, pp. 187–188.
8. *Sel'skoe khozyaistvo* (April 10, 1957), pp. 1 and 2.

9. *Pravda* (December 25, 1961), pp. 1–4, as translated in *The Current Digest of the Soviet Press* Vol. XIII, No. 52 (January 24, 1962), pp. 7–10 and 25.

Chapter 8.   Bureaucracy "Completely Carried Through"

1. Tucker, *op. cit.*
2. Lenin, *op. cit.*, Vol. 25, p. 407.
3. Smith and Lurcher, *A Dictionary of American Politics*, Barnes and Noble, Inc., New York, 1947, p. 39.
4. Weber, *op. cit.*, p. 228.
5. *Ibid.*
6. *Strana sovetov za 50 let*, *op. cit.*, p. 116.
7. *History of the Communist Party of the Soviet Union*, Foreign Languages Publishing House, Moscow, 1960, p. 661.
8. N. S. Khrushchev, *The World Situation, The Construction of Communism in the USSR, The Role of the Communist Party: Documents of the 22nd Congress of the CPSU* Vol. 1, Crosscurrents Press, New York, 1961, p. 161.
9. *The CPSU in Figures, op. cit.*
10. Gregory Beinstock, Solomon M. Schwarz and Aaron Yugow, *Management in Russian Industry and Agriculture*, Oxford Univ. Press, New York, 1944, p. 30. As cited from Central Statistics Office, USSR, *The Country of Socialism*, Moscow, 1936, p. 94.
11. *Narodnoe khozyaistvo SSSR v. 1959 godu, gostatizdat*, Moskva, 1960, p. 452 and *Sel'skoe khozyaïstvo SSSR, gostatizdat*, Moskva, 1960, p. 474.
12. Lenin, *op. cit.*, Vol. 27, p. 339.
13. *Pravda* (January 28, 1959).

Chapter 9.   Policy Control: A Study of One Institution

1. "O dalneishem uvelichenii proizvodstva zerna v strane i ob osvoenii tselinnykh i zalezhnykh zemel'," Postanovlenie Plenume TSK KPSS, prinyatoe (2 marta 1954) g. po dokladu tov. N. S. Khrushcheva; *Pravda* (March 6, 1954), p. 1.
2. "V Soveta Ministrov SSSR i Tsentral'nom Komitete KPSS: O merakh po dal'neishem uluchsheniyu raboty mashinno-traktornykh stantsii," *Pravda* (October 1, 1953), pp. 1 and 3.
3. "For Further Improvement of Crop and Livestock Servicing of Collective Farms," *Sel'skoye Khozyaistvo* (September 1955), as condensed in *C.D.S.P.* Vol. VII, No. 35, 1955, p. 21.

4. "V Soveta Ministrov SSSR i Tsentralnom Komitete KPSS: O merakh po dalneishemu uluchsheniyu raboty mashinno-traktornykh Stantsii," *Pravda* (October 1, 1953), p. 1.

5. "Aims and Tasks of the Political Departments of the Machine and Tractor Stations and the Soviet Farms," (Resolution of the Joint Plenum of the C. C. and C. C. C. of the C. P. S. U. on the Report of Comrade Kaganovich, passed January 11, 1933) in *From the First to the Second Five Year Plan*, New York, n.d., p. 453.

6. *Ibid.*, pp. 464, 465, and 484.

7. Ivan Vinnichenko, "Time Doesn't Wait," *Oktyabr*, No. 11 (November 1957), pp. 205–223 (as translated in *C.D.S.P.*), Vol. X, No. 5, 1958, pp. 3–10 and 42.

8. "Ob Uvelichenii Proizvodstva Produktov Zhivotnovodstva" Doklad tovarishcha N. S. Khrushcheva na Plenume Tsentral'novo Komiteta KPSS 24 Yanvarya 1955 goda, *Pravda* (February 3, 1955), p. 2.

9. "Poteryannye Milliony" (M. Zamyatin), *Pravda* (January 17, 1958), p. 2.

10. Leonard E. Hubbard, *The Economics of Soviet Agriculture*, London, 1939, p. 150.

11. V. Dolzhnykh, "Kommunist on Transferring MTS to Cost Accounting" from *Kommunist*, No. 4 (March 1956), pp. 44–57, Translated in *C.D.S.P.* Vol. VIII, No. 25, 1956, p. 8.

12. "Otch'stny Doklad Tsentral' novo Komiteta Kommunisticheskoi partii Sovetskovo Soyuza xx s'ezdu partii; Doklad Pervoyu sekretarya TSK KPSS tovarishcha N. S. Khrushcheva," *Pravda* (February 15, 1956), p. 6.

Chapter 10. Ostracism and Other Direction

1. David Riesman, Nathan Glazier, and Raul Denney, *The Lonely Crowd*, Doubleday Anchor Books, Garden City, 1953, p. 32 ff.

2. B. Shuchkov, "The Chief Five," *Pravda* (July 26, 1959), p. 4.

3. N. S. Khrushchev, "O control'nikh tsifrakh sovetia narodnovo khozyaistvo SSSR na 1959–1965 godi," *Pravda* (January 25, 1959), p. 5.

4. "O zadachakh partinoy propagandi v sovremennikh usteviyakh," *Pravda* (January 10, 1969), p. 1.

5. "Speech by L. I. Brezhnev, General Secretary of the CPSU All-Union Congress of Teachers in Moscow on July 4, 1968, *Moscow News*, Supplement to Issue No. 28, 1968.

6. M. A. Kraev, *Kolkhoznevo stroya v SSSR*, Moskva, 1954, p. 126.

7. V. I. Lenin, *Selected Works* Vol. VIII, New York, International Publishers, 1943, pp. 14–21.
8. Kraev, *op. cit.*, p. 175.
9. Lenin, *Collected Works, op. cit.* Vol. 29, p. 210.
10. E. H. Carr, *The Bolshevik Revolution, 1917–1923* Vol. II, Macmillan and Co. Ltd., 1953, p. 157.
11. *Op. cit.*
12. *Kazhakhstanskaya Pravda* (March 11, 1960), pp. 2–7.
13. A. I. Denisov, "On the Relationship of State and Society in the Period of Transition from Capitalism to Communism," *Sovietskoye gosudarstvo i pravo,* No. 4 (April 1960), pp. 29–40.
14. *Konsomolskaya Pravda* (October 5, 1958), p. 6.
15. Denisov, *op. cit.*
16. "Rabochnaya militsia," *Izvestia* (November 22, 1958), p. 4.
17. E. Perlov, "Vsilit vospitatelnuyu volsuda," *Izvestia* (September 10, 1958), p. 3.
18. E. Turbai, "Na strazhe obshchestiannoyo poryadka," *Izvestia* (September 29, 1955), p. 3.
19. A. Kharchev, "Sem'ya i kommunism," *Kommunist,* No. 7 (May 1960), pp. 62–63.
20. Jerome M. Gilison, "Soviet Elections as a Measure of Dissent: The Missing One Percent," *The American Political Science Review* Vol. 62, No. 3 (September 1968), pp. 814–826.
21. *Ibid.*

Chapter 11. Unions and Collective Farms

1. Alfred Meyer, *The Soviet Political System, op. cit.*
2. Alec Nove, *The Soviet Economy,* Praeger, New York (revised ed.), 1966, p. 134.
3. Joseph Berliner, *Factory and Manager in the USSR,* Cambridge, Harvard University Press, 1957, pp. 271–272.
4. Merle Fainsod, *How Russia is Ruled,* Harvard University Press, Cambridge (revised ed.), 1963, p. 521.
5. *Pravda* (October 23, 1965), p. 1.
6. *Pravda* (March 30, 1969), pp. 2–9.
7. N. S. Khrushchev, *Pravda* (February 15, 1956), pp. 1–11.
8. See in particular, Roy D. Laird and Edward L. Crowley (eds.), *Soviet Agriculture: The Permanent Crisis,* Praeger, New York, 1965, pp. 147–158.
9. *Sel'skaya zhizn'* (April 24, 1969), pp. 1 and 2.

Chapter 12. Education and Youth

1. Nigel Grant, *Soviet Education,* Penguin Books, Baltimore, 1964, p. 23.
2. "Speech by L. I. Brezhnev, . . ." July 4, 1968, *op. cit.*
3. L. K. Petrova, "On Ways of Improving the Ideological-Moral Upbringing of Pupils," *Soviet Education* Vol. IX (April 1967), pp. 24–35.
4. V. P. Yelyutin, *Higher Education in the USSR,* International Arts and Science Press, New York, n.d., p. 41.
5. D. A. Epshteen, "The Content of Labor Polytechnical Instruction in the Secondary School," *Soviet Education* Vol. VIII (December 1965), p. 51.
6. B. L. Vul'fsun, "Freudianism and Bourgeois Pedagogy," *Soviet Education* Vol. VIII (January 1966), pp. 3–14.
7. Nicholas DeWitt, "Science Education and the School Reform," *School and Society* (Summer 1960), pp. 5 and 6.
8. Grant, *op. cit.,* p. 72.
9. *Uchitelskaya Gazeta* (July 3, 1958).
10. "Address by Comrade S. P. Pavlov, First Secretary of the Y.C.L. Central Committee, at the Eighth Plenary Session of the Y.C.L. Central Committee," *Komsomolskaya Pravda* (December 29, 1965), p. 3, and Grant, *op. cit.,* p. 33.
11. Jaan Pennar, "Party Control Over Soviet Schools," *The Politics of Soviet Education* (George Z. F. Bereday and Jaan Pennar, eds.), New York, 1969, p. 52.
12. Allen Kassof, *The Soviet Youth Program,* Harvard, Cambridge, 1965, p. 124.
13. Grant, *op. cit.,* p. 156.
14. A. Zhdanov, "Pressing Problems of University Education," *Soviet Education* Vol. III (September 1961), pp. 52–54.
15. Peter Vogel, *A Study of Soviet Education: Soviet Education in Action.* Unpublished M.A. Thesis, University of Missouri, Kansas City (May 1967), p. 8.
16. A. P. Usova, "Draft Program of Education in the Kindergarten," *Soviet Education* Vol. I (December 1963), pp. 163–168.
17. "On the Draft Law on Universal Military Service," Report by Deputy A. A. Grechko, USSR Minister of Defense. *Pravda* (October 13, 1967), pp. 5–6.
18. Joshua Rothenberg, "The Status of Cults," *Problems of Communism* Vol. XVI, No. 5 (September–October 1967), p. 122.

19. Grant, *op. cit.,* p. 34.
20. Perlov, *op. cit.*
21. Vogel, *op. cit.,* p. 5.

Chapter 13. Communications Media

1. Andrei Y. Vyshinsky, *The Law of the Soviet State,* The Macmillan Co., New York, 1940, p. 614.
2. *Pravda* (February 8, 1959), pp. 1–9.
3. "Draft: Program of the Communist Party of the Soviet Union," *Pravda* (July 30, 1961), pp. 1–9.
4. "American Acquaintances," *Izvestia* (June 7, 1961), p. 3.
5. "Draft: Program," *op. cit.*
6. L. Leontiev, "The Crisis of World Capitalism," *Kommunist* (October 1961), p. 117.
7. "American Acquaintances," *op. cit.*
8. *Ibid.*
9. A. Greshukin, "In America: Don't Look Through the Keyhole," *Trud* (June 11, 1961), p. 3.
10. L. Leontiev, *op. cit.,* p. 116.
11. "Peaceful Print About the Projected Program of the CPSU," *Kommunist* (August 1961), p. 114.
12. "American Acquaintances," *op. cit.*
13. *Christian Science Monitor:* "Taxes Gnaw Bigger Holes in Pockets," *Literaturnaya Gazeta* (June 14, 1960), p. 4.
14. *Ibid.*
15. "Draft Program . . .," *op. cit.*
16. "Criticism under Tutelage," *Pravda* (April 26, 1966), p. 2.
17. "To Our Readers," *Pravda* (January 17, 1969), p. 6.
18. Katherine Hunter Blair, *Review of Soviet Literature,* Ambersad Press, London, 1966, pp. 8–10.
19. Bertrand Russell, "An Outline of Intellectual Rubbish," *Unpopular Essays,* Simon and Schuster, New York, 1950, p. 95.

Chapter 14. Soviet Social Sciences

1. Merle Fainsod, *op. cit.,* p. 354.
2. A. M. Rumyantsev, "To Those Entering Science," *Komsomolskaya Pravda* (June 8, 1967), pp. 2 and 3.
3. "On Working out Problems of the Political Sciences . . .," *Pravda* (June 13, 1965), p. 4.
4. V. Shubkin, "Concrete Research into Social Processes," *Kommunist,* No. 3 (February 1965), pp. 48–57.

5. B. Pershnev, "Social Psychology and the Shaping of the New Man," *Kommunist*, No. 8 (May 1963), pp. 94–102.

6. E. Lisavtsev, V. Maslen, and N. Ovchennikov, "On a Scientific Basis: . . .," *Pravda* (May 11, 1965), p. 2.

7. S. Murashov and V. Orel, "The Student and Teaching Social Sciences," *Komsomolskaya Pravda* (April 20, 1965), pp. 1 and 2.

8. *Ibid.*

9. M. A. Suslov, "The Twenty-Second Congress of the CPSU and the Tasks of the Departments of Social Sciences," *Kommunist*, No. 3 (February 5, 1962), pp. 15–46.

10. Murashov and Orel, *op. cit.*

11. Rumyantsev, *op. cit.*

12. "On Measures for Further Developing Social Sciences and Heightening Their Role in Communist Construction," *Pravda* (August 22, 1967), pp. 1 and 2.

13. F. Konstantinov and V. Kelle, *Kommunist*, No. 1 (January 1968), pp. 9–23.

14. Rumyantsev, *op. cit.*

15. I. Kuzminov, "Objective Character of Economic Laws of Socialism," *Pravda* (November 11, 1966), pp. 2 and 3.

16. "On Measures . . .," *op. cit.*

17. Suslov, *op. cit.*

18. "On Measures . . .," *op. cit.*

19. *Ibid.*

20. "On Two Neglected Fields of Sociological Research," *Kommunist*, No. 17 (November 1963), pp. 81–87.

21. *Ibid.*

22. Shubkin, *op. cit.*

23. D. Armand, "The Dispute Continues . . .," *Literaturnaya Gazeta* (March 25, 19), p. 2.

24. V. V. Matskevich, "Tasks Posed by Life," *Trud* (April 4, 1965), p. 2.

25. "Ideological Weapon of the Party," *Kommunist*, No. 4 (March 1965), pp. 3–14.

26. V. Shubkin, *op. cit.*

27. "Meeting of the Soviet Sociological Association," *Voprosy filosofii*, No. 6 (June 1966), pp. 157–159.

28. V. Anuchin, "What Has Happened to Geography," *Literaturnaya Gazeta* (February 18, 1965), p. 2.

29. A. Yanov, "Time to Mature," *Komsomolskaya Pravda* (June 2, 1967), p. 2.

30. F. Burlatsky, "Politics and Science," *Pravda* (June 10, 1965), pp. 7 and 8.

31. I. Iovchuk and G. V. Osipov, "On Some Theoretical Principles, Problems and Methods of Sociological Research," *Voprosy filosofii*, No. 12, 1963, pp. 23 and 24.

32. "Meeting of the Soviet Sociological Association," *op. cit.*

33. Yu. V. Arutyunyan, "Social Structure of Rural Soviets, *Voprosy filosofii*, No. 6, 1966, pp. 51–61.

34. P. Fedoseyev, "Marxist Sociology and Concrete Sociological Research," *Partinaya Zhizn*, No. 20 (October 1967), pp. 34–41.

35. Suslov, *op. cit.*

Chapter 15. The Balance Sheet

1. Maynard, *op. cit.*, p. 389.

A
Soviet
Lexicon

Just as the student of chemistry must learn a new vocabulary—e.g., Cl is the symbol for chlorine or a precipitant is a product of chemical reaction—so one needs a new vocabulary in order to study Soviet affairs. Some of the terms encountered are familiar—e.g., "advocate" is a lawyer or attorney. Many terms seem familiar, but their Soviet usage is quite special—e.g., "criticism" is a key aspect of democratic centralism. Still other terms are wholly new and totally unfamiliar—e.g., *"drushiny"* are people's militia. The lexicon is not offered as a substitute for more thorough reference sources, but it is supplied as a tool that will allow the reader to comprehend quickly the common meaning of words or phrases found in the Soviet press or in this and other works on Soviet affairs by Western writers. Those who need more biographical material are urged to consult the *Who's Who in the USSR* produced by the Munich Institute for the Study of the USSR. Those who require more historical depth are urged to turn to Professor Sergei Utechin's *Everyman's Concise Encyclopedia of Russia.* Indeed, although much of our own time and research went into creating the present lexicon, the effort expended would have been much greater had it not been for the help of these works.

Appendix

A SOVIET LEXICON*

Able-bodied workers Full-time kolkhoz ("collective farm") workers as distinguished from their dependents who also live on the farms but devote, at most, only part of their time to work on the kolkhozy ("collective farms").

Active (Activists) Constant and eager participants in Party affairs.

Advanced farms That small percentage of kolkhozy ("collective farms") and sovkhozy ("state farms") that are markedly economically superior to the great bulk of Soviet farms.

Advokat Lawyer, attorney.

Agitator Dispenser of political information to the public and collector of political intelligence for the Party. A propaganda agent who senses public mood and concern and conveys this vital information (for which he is usually paid) to the leadership.

* The author would appreciate receiving suggestions for either additions or corrections to the Lexicon with the thought that these would be used in future editions.

237

Agitprop The Agitation and Propaganda Department of the Central Committee Secretariat. It has the general responsibility for mass agitation and Party propaganda; under Khrushchev it was allowed to control the assignment of key personnel in all major agencies under its supervision. It dispenses official information through lectures, books, pamphlets, broadcasts, posters, and exhibits; it embraces the arts, literature, and science; and it reaches the schools, the press, Party educational and research institutions, and cultural-enlightenment agencies.

Agitpunkt (Agitation Point) A local office which dispenses official propaganda and information to the citizens.

Agrogorod An agricultural town with the cultural and physical amenities of the city. (Krushchev's first speeches on the amalgamation campaign [1949] carried the promise that unifying the kolkhozy ("collective farms") would result in the creation of these farm-cities for the peasantry.)

All-union central council of trade unions The central controlling unit of all industrial unions. These unions do not permit strikes nor do they decide wages, hours, etc. They are largely creatures of the Party used for control and propaganda.

All-union farm machinery association An organization formed in 1961, replacing the MTS and the RTS, in charge of farm machinery, fertilizer sales, and spare parts for machinery repair.

Andropov, Yuri Vladimirovich (1914–   ) Trained in a water-transport technicum, he has been active in security and foreign affairs. He first joined the Party in 1936 and has been a candidate member of the Politburo since 1967.

Antiparty group A group of Communists, including Malenkov, Molotov, Bulganin, and Kaganovich, who opposed Khrushchev's position of power and in 1957 tried to oust him from his post of Party secretary. Through a direct appeal to the Central Committee, Khrushchev managed to defeat his opponents and had them expelled from the Presidium.

Apparat The highly efficient, centralized, working-class movement (Communist party) controlled by the principle of democratic centralism and all it entails.

Apparatchiki (Men of the Apparatus) The "practical" workmen of the Communist party organization, the men who often worked up through the ranks from a lowly origin—as opposed to the *literati* who were the intellectuals, the "old leaders." Stalin gathered the *apparatchiki* around him.

Artel A producers' cooperative. Originally applied to industrial cooperatives among itinerant workers but now expanded to include collective farms and artisans' groups.

Assessors Citizens elected to sit in court with the judges and decide both criminal and civil cases. Two of these untrained individuals and one judge hear each case in the People's Courts, and then hand down a majority decision.

Autonomous republic An administrative territorial area based upon nationality. It is similar to the Union Republic but lacks one or more elements of the latter (e.g., the right to recognize their own language as official). There are at present 19 of these republics in the USSR.

Barn yields The actual amount of grain supposedly harvested and safely stored or consumed. Western specialists claim that since 1953 when the Soviets turned to reporting crop statistics as "barn yields," new causes of statistical inflation (10–15%) have crept into official Soviet grain figures.

Beria, Lavrentiy Pavlovich (1899–1953) Member of the Party Presidium (Politburo) and long-time head of the secret police. (There is strong evidence that Khrushchev and his colleagues had Beria executed shortly after Stalin's death.)

Biological yields Reports of yields based upon estimates of potential harvest while the grain is still growing in the fields. (In Stalin's day, such reports resulted in greatly inflated, official Soviet crop statistics.)

Black earth (chernozem) The band of rich, black soil stretching across the southwestern region of the USSR.

Blat Illegal string pulling. Deriving favors or goods through bribery, gifts, entertainment, return favors, under-the-counter exchange, and so forth. The method which enables the *tolkachi* ("expediters") to obtain supplies or raw materials not easily acquired because of the bottlenecks in the Soviet economy. Necessary as this process may be to a Soviet economic enterprise, it must conceal such dealings to avoid prosecution.

Boarding schools *(Internady)* Schools which were central to Khrushchev's educational policy which sought to counteract the growth of "New Class" bourgeois mentality by training students in accordance with the ideal of the "new soviet man."

Bolsheviks (Majority) A radical group within the Social Democratic Labor party which, under Lenin's leadership, gained supremacy and called themselves the Communist party. They staged the 1917 Revolution and formed the Soviet Union.

Bonuses Special money awards paid to workers for service and extra effort. These are heavily relied upon for creating incentive in the USSR.

Bourgeoisie The relatively wealthy segment of a "capitalist society" which lives by exploiting the proletariat and profits from the surplus value of its labor.

Bourgeois objectivism An accusation leveled at many Russian intellectuals, in all branches of learning, who do not follow the Party line in the "ideological rearmament" of the Soviet peoples. Such intellectuals are accused of being apolitical or harmfully objective about the Russian past and the Western world.

Brest–Litovsk, Treaty of A demeaning treaty signed in 1918 giving Germany considerable Russian territory in the west, and demobilizing the Russian army.

Brezhnev, Leonid Il'ich (1906–) Metallurgical engineer by profession and long time leading figure of the Party which he joined in 1931. Currently, he is the general secretary of the Central Committee and the leading Party figure in the Politburo, in which he has been a member of since 1957.

Brigade A work unit in either industry or agriculture, often consisting of as many as a hundred members.

Bureaucracy According to the Soviets, an evil of bourgeois society, largely eliminated from the USSR. (Actually, the Soviet Union is involved in the biggest, most all-encompassing bureaucracy the world has ever known.)

Cadets See Kadets.

Cadre The key line personnel of an organization. Stalin said, "Cadres decide everything."

Capitalist encirclement (1) A term first coined by Stalin to refer to the geographic encirclement of countries with capitalistic economic systems. It represented the dimming hope of world revolution with Russia as the springboard and Russia's subsequent industrialization and ideal of an impregnable front. (2) An ideological construct by whose invocation mobilization of the country or various sectors of the economy or society could be demanded. Perhaps, it had roots in traditional Russian experience of insecurity and inferiority and the Allied intervention during the Civil War. Today the capitalist encirclement is said to be broken.

CCTU The Central Council of Trade Unions.

CEMA Council of Economic Mutual Assistance (COMECON). This council was formed in 1949 for the declared purpose of enhancing Socialist international cooperation; it originally included the USSR and the East European countries of the Socialist bloc. Yugoslavia did not belong to CEMA, and Albania was expelled in October 1961. Mongolia joined in 1962.

Centner A metric unit of weight (100 kilograms or 220.46 lbs.) used in measuring farm yields.

Central Committee (of the Communist party) Theoretically, the highest organ of the Party when a congress is not meeting. Actually, its power has fluctuated all the way from existing in name only under Stalin to being decisive in choosing Khrushchev over the anti-Party element in 1957. The Politburo is the Executive Committee of the Central Committee.

Cheka Soviet secret police from 1917 to 1922. Carried out a policy of terror. Replaced by GPU.

Chernozem See **Black earth.**

Chistka (cleansing or purge) See **Purge.**

Coexistence, peaceful A relationship with capitalist nations which decries a major nuclear conflict, applauds peaceful economic competition, but assumes the eventual collapse of capitalism, and therefore encourages in every way, short of all-out war, friction and strife within and among capitalist countries. Small "wars of liberation" in underdeveloped nations are to be encouraged and supported actively provided that support doesn't provoke a major conflict with the strongholds of capitalism. Assertedly, the idea originated with Lenin, thus Leninist peaceful coexistence.

Collective farm The Soviet kolkhoz. Theoretically, a Soviet co-operative of peasant farm workers. (In practice, it is under the direct control of the Party bureaucracy.) Personal income is dependent on farm income. See **Kolkhoz.**

Collective leadership A political situation in which the supreme decision-making authority is shared by and distributed among a few men (usually prominent members of the Politburo of the CPSU) rather than being held by one man, such as Stalin.

Collectivization This is the process by which the state owns and controls the agricultural means of production which are theoretically run by the peasants. This process is an ideological *sine qua non* of communism. It may be further interpreted as a method of grain collection for accumulation of capital.

Comintern This is the first worldwide organization set up in 1919 by the Bolsheviks with the purpose of spreading communism by a world proletariat revolution.

Commissar An early political title for certain high ranking officials. It is no longer used.

Committees of the Poor Groups of poor peasants (some of questionable character) organized by Party zealots to requisition grain from the kulaks by any means necessary, and to stir up resentment toward these relatively well-to-do peasants. The Committees were first used by Lenin during the period of War Communism, and again by Stalin to achieve forced collectivization in the late 1920s and early 1930s.

Commune (1) a group of people living and working together, holding all goods in common, and owning no private property. Theoretically, to the Communist, this is the most perfect human relationship, although in recent years the Soviets have rejected its use in China, as being reactionary. (2) The village organization under the tsars.

Communist Manifesto A document published in 1848, written by Karl Marx and Friedrich Engels explaining their theory of communism and predicting its future takeover. It was translated into Russian in the 1860s.

Comrades' Courts Courts composed of workers and/or peasants (ostensibly elected by the people themselves) whose purpose is to aid management in enforcing production discipline. Since 1959, these courts have been established in all plants and enterprises employing more than 50 workers. They are supposed to punish tardiness, drunkenness, neglect of safety regulations, and so forth, with fines up to a hundred rubles, and recommendations for demotion, dismissal, or prosecution. The courts play an important "shock-absorber role in relieving managers of the onus of directly asserting their disciplinary authority." They are established within factories, apartment houses and on farms to develop moral behavior of the new Soviet man.

Council of Ministers According to the Soviet Constitution, the "highest executive and administrative organ" of the USSR. Appointed by the Supreme Soviet, the Council of Ministers is theoretically responsible to that body; actually, its activities are always automatically approved. The president of the Council of Ministers is the premier or prime minister.

CPSU Communist Party, Soviet Union.

Credo, the The statement of the leading doctrines of "Economism," drafted by Madame Kuskoma in the late 1890s. It encouraged the workers to fight for economic improvement and urged the Marxian intellectuals to support the liberals in attempting to reform the state.

Criticism Constructive in nature by definition. Criticism is aimed at the execution of policies (how) rather than policies themselves (what). This is a principle of democratic centralism. See **Kritika i samokritika** (self-criticism).

Cult of personality A huge, subservient following gathered through personality or force by a top leader. A term used to describe Stalin's absolute control over the Party.

Cultural Revolution An effort in the late 1920s and early 1930s to raise the educational level and the cultural interests of the workers and peasants.

Dacha A summer cottage in the country.

Dekulakization Stalin's plan of "emergency measures" against the kulaks (well-to-do peasants) and middle peasants to place them in collective farms; part of his industrialization plan.

Demichev, Petr Nilovich (1918–   ) Trained as a chemical technologist, he has worked in that field as well as in Party affairs. He was first enrolled in the Party in 1939 and became a candidate member of the Politburo in 1964.

Democracy A term describing "representative government," which may be either good or bad depending upon its antecedent. "Proletarian democracy" (i.e., dictatorship of the proletariat), according to the Soviets, is composed of the "toilers" of the nation and therefore is the most representative form of government a state can have. (Withering away of the state in complete communism is, of course, better.) "Bourgeois democracy" is not truly representative; it is entirely hypocritical, "a paradise for the rich and a snare . . . for the poor." According to Lenin, "Proletarian democracy is *a million times* more democratic than any bourgeois democracy; Soviet power is a million times more democratic than the most democratic bourgeois republic." (See Lenin's essay, "The Proletarian Revolution and the Renegade Kautsky.")

Democratic Centralism Free discussion and deliberation of all issues by the Party congresses until a decision is actually made. Once the decision is made, it becomes law and every member follows it. After the decision is made, no discussion is tolerated except on the means of carrying out the plan. This is what Lenin called "freedom to criticize and unity in action."

Deputies Representatives to the various soviets (councils).

Deviation Departure from current Party policy or official line.

Dialectical Materialism Materialistic adaptation of Hegel's idealistic dialectics by Marx and Engels. Hegel believed ideas developed from a thesis acted upon by an antithesis, producing a synthesis—a new thesis from which to begin again. Marx and Engels stretched this concept to cover all development, i.e., material, human, social, and so forth. The struggle of two opposing forces produces a new and better form to be improved upon again by another struggle.

Doctors' plot Alleged plot among the Kremlin doctors (mostly Jewish) to "cut short" the lives of Zhdanov and Shcherbakov and to undermine the health of the military. Construed as a threat on Stalin's life. Exposed by Stalin in 1952 and rejected as untrue after his death.

Drushiny   Voluntary people's detachments; people's militia. An agency of the government revived by Khrushchev and entrusted with the task of enlisting public support in preserving labor discipline and public order.

Duma   Pre-Soviet representative assemblies. Four state dumas met between 1906 and 1917, finally becoming established as a workable parliamentary body though limited in its effectiveness because its makeup was clearly right wing.

Economism   The view held by an influential group of Social Democrats in the late 1800s that the proletariat should stay out of political affairs, which tended to divide them, and concentrate all efforts on trade union organization and strike activities. Lenin strongly opposed this attitude.

Election   A national holiday when Soviet citizens may demonstrate their support for their government and their enthusiasm for the progress their country has made by voting *Yes* for the entire ballot of Party-selected candidates.

Emancipation Edict of 1861   Emancipation of the serfs, but without the land which they considered theirs and which was necessary for their support.

Engels, Friedrich (1820–1895)   The son of a wealthy English manufacturer who helped finance Marx's research, and who collaborated in writing *Capital* and other studies.

Factionalism   The formation of dissenting groups whether minority discussion groups, written reports expressing the minority view, or a rival platform. Factionalism was outlawed by the Tenth Party Congress in 1921 as a breach of Party discipline.

Ferma   The livestock section on a collective farm.

Feuilleton   A brief commentary on, or criticism of, some aspect of Soviet life, carried in the central newspapers.

Five-Year Plan, the First   Stalin's plan ending the NEP, giving top priority to heavy industry, and initiating forced collectivization in agriculture.

Formalism   Originally a school of literary theory originating in the early 1900s which focused on technique and device. The school was outlawed in 1930, and since that time the word *formalism* has been applied to art forms—especially Western trends in music—which do not meet with Party-prescribed qualifications. See **Socialist realism.**

Freedom   The "perception of necessity." The understanding of the laws of human society, making it possible to use them to improve man's condition in that society. According to the Marxist–Leninist, freedom is impossible unless and until all members of society stand in equal relationship to the means of production, i.e., the state of integral communism.

General Meeting The central concept of "Kolkhoz Democracy." The Collective Farm Charter of 1935 specifically authorized the General Meeting of working members over sixteen years old to elect a chairman, a board of managers, and an auditing commission to check kolkhoz accounts. This theoretical procedure is rarely observed since Democratic Centralism is the operative principle. Thus, the General Meeting is a major instrument of propaganda and attempts to enlist peasant support. Although the agenda is prepared beforehand, the membership may discuss and decide upon the policy on labor days and approval of a plan on crop rotation, and so forth.

Gigantomania The Russian feeling of expansiveness that seems to arise out of an awe for the great stretches of land, and now probably incorporates the Communist tendency to regard the large (industrial) enterprise as inherently superior to small enterprises.

Glavk Abbreviation for Chief Administration.

"Going to the people" A movement, started by Peter Lavrov in his *Historical Letters*, which continued from summer 1872 to summer 1874. Lavrov emphasized the duty of the "critically thinking individual" to devote himself to the welfare of the masses. The masses did not understand or trust the flood of altruists—the movement died of disillusionment.

Gorkom The city committee of the Party which oversees the guidance of industry in cities; these city committees report to the regional committees. However, if an enterprise has more than five hundred Communists located outside urban centers, the enterprise will have its own Party committee directly responsible to the oblast (regional administrative unit). (Industrial enterprises located in the territory of agricultural production administrations are supervised by zonal, industrial-production Party committees responsible to the oblast.)

Gorod City.

Gosarbitrazh The state arbitration court which encompasses all government enterprises and institutions and resolves disputes between such organizations. These disagreements may have to do with prices, property lines, quality of goods, late delivery, failure to deliver, refusal to accept, and any other of the many disputes that might arise between enterprises. Gosarbitrazh hears the case, decides it, orders the execution of whatever decision it reaches, and assesses a penalty when appropriate. It may not arrest law breakers, but it can refer them to those who can.

Gosplan The State Planning Commission in the Soviet Union. It is responsible for creating the Five-Year Plans.

Gosstroi The USSR State Committee for Construction.

GPU State Political Administration, the security service created in 1922 to replace CHEKA. In 1934 it, in turn, became the NKVD.

Great Purge See **Yezhovshchina.**

Grishin, Victor Vasilevich (1914–   ) Trained as a mechanical engineer, he has been active in international affairs. He first joined the Party in 1939 and became a candidate member of the Politburo in 1961.

Hectare The common unit of measure of land in the metric system equal to 2.471 acres, or to 10,000 m².

Hooliganism The antisocial actions of youthful individuals or groups who are regarded as undesirable delinquents in Soviet society.

Icon corner A corner in an Eastern Orthodox believer's home containing an icon and candles on a small table. This corner, like an altar, is reserved for prayer and worship.

Icons Paintings, usually on wood, of holy figures, used for worship in the Eastern Orthodox Church and in the homes of believers.

Imperialism According to Lenin, the last, all-encompassing stage of capitalism just before its collapse. Having encircled as many small, underdeveloped nations as it can reach, it is ready to topple, and small wars of national liberation can provide the push that will send capitalism sprawling.

Incentives Rewards or goods for which one will exert himself. Theoretically, everyone under communism is eager to do his finest, most efficient work for the common good. Unfortunately, human beings need more tangible incentives than "the common good," and so the Soviets often have worked out a complicated piece-work system to provide tangible rewards for their workers.

Inspector-Organizers Officials in local agencies (formerly in the MTS, later attached to the TPA) held personally responsible for the production achievements of three or more of the kolkhozy ("collective farms") and sovkhozy ("state farms") in the territory.

Intelligentsia The Russian and Soviet term denoting all those people who are not peasants or workers. The term includes white collar workers and professional people.

Internady See **Boarding schools.**

Internationalism The commitent of Communists to eventual world communism, the obligation to do everything possible to facilitate its coming about.

Intourist The official Soviet travel agency.

Iskra The spark. A journal expounding Lenin's ideas. The term was later adopted by the faction of Lenin supporters at the Second

Congress. The idea of *iskra* was that a Russian revolution would provide the "spark" to set off a worldwide proletarian revolution.

Izvestia The Russian word for "news" and the name of the Soviet government's leading daily newspaper.

Kadets (also **Cadets**) Nickname given to the Constitutional Democratic party taken from the Party's initials K.D. Formed in 1905, this moderately left-wing group gained peasant support for their desire to establish a constitutional monarchy. They played an important role in Kerensky's government, but were outlawed after the Bolsheviks gained power.

Kandidat An individual who has completed university degree requirements and three additional years of study as well as a thesis. *Kandidat* status is very prestigious in the Soviet Union.

KGB Committee for State Security. The security police unit, which separated from the MVD (internal police) in 1954. Still active. Responsibilities include protection of high officials, conduct of espionage abroad, counterintelligence within Soviet territory, and supervision of a network of informers to detect disloyalty or political instability.

Khozraschet (economic or cost accounting) Precise economic accounting, especially used during NEP. It was hoped that this form of accounting, along with commercial principles and substantial freedom to buy and sell on the open market would be an adequate basis for expansion of enterprise under NEP. Today, *khozraschet* is again stressed, particularly in the consumers' goods industry.

Khrushchev, Nikita Sergeevich (1894–   ) A long-time key official in Soviet politics who reached the pinnacle of power as leader of the Party and chairman of the Council of Ministers in 1958. Failures during his period of rule, particularly in agriculture, resulted in his being deposed in 1964.

Kirilenko, Andy Pavlovich (1906–   ) Trained as an aeronautical engineer, he was long active in this field. Currently he is a member of the Politburo, having attained full membership in 1961. He first joined the Communist party in 1931.

Kolkhoz The collective farm, which is something of a concession on the part of the Party as far as preferred modes of production go. Generally smaller than the *sovkhoz* ("state farm"), *kolkhozy* still make up the majority of agricultural producers in the country. It is here that the Party must contend with the "petty-bourgeois propensities" of the former peasants who want to till their small vegetable gardens rather than work for the good of the whole. Wage depends on crop production. See **Collective farm.**

Kolkhoznik A member of a collective farm.

Komitetchiki The committeemen of the Communist underground (Stalin was one) who were the first prototypes of the *apparatchiki* ("men of the apparatus," e.g., Khrushchev) with whom Stalin was to forge his Party machine.

Komsomol The Communist youth organization; also, known as Y.C.L. or the Young Communist League; a Party-sponsored organization for young people generally from 15–27 years of age, and a training ground for future Party members.

Korenizatsia The policy under Stalin which used people of the "native populations" of the minority nationalities for the area's courts and administrative organs of direct government. Its primary purpose was to help the sovietization of minority peoples through their own native language, culture, and educational system.

Kosygin, Aleksey Nikolayevich (1904–   ) A member of the Politburo since 1960 who succeeded to the post of chairman of the Council of Ministers in 1964. He was educated in a textile institute. He first joined the Party in 1927.

Krai Territorial administrative unit subordinate to the republic Party organization. Region sometime used instead of Oblast.

KR's Counter-revolutionaries, a group of people looked upon with disfavor, especially during the NEP period. Included the one-time Kadets who supported rightist parties in the revolutionary period, Tsarist bureaucrats, White Guards, priests, landowners, nobility, and industrialists.

Kremlin Originally a fortification within a medieval town, containing palaces, churches, and government buildings. The most famous is the one in Moscow, which is the seat of the Soviet government.

Kritika i samokritika (criticism and self-criticism) Pointing out errors and faults of one's peers and confessing publicly one's own mistakes, a prescribed duty of Party members. This technique provides a safety valve for disgruntled Communists who are encouraged to criticize people and implementation of policy, but never policy itself and never the Central Committee. Self-criticism, although practiced sincerely by some, has become formalized for many and may mean little.

Krokodil A weekly humor magazine issued by the *Pravda* publishing house. Much of its humor is directed against capitalist societies, but some of its double-meaning jokes and cartoons quite daringly castigate the Soviet establishment.

Kronstadt Rebellion A rebellion by the sailors in the Kronstadt naval base at St. Petersburg who had provided key support to the Bolsheviks in the 1917 uprising. Thus, their rebellion in 1921 against the excesses of the new regime was a serious blow to Lenin and his colleagues.

Kto kavo A Russian phrase meaning "Who would destroy whom?" regarding the final reckoning between the "Imperialists" and the Communists. Brumberg says: "The truth of the matter, however, is that this phrase summarized not only the attitude of the Party toward its external enemies, but toward its perennial internal enemies as well." *Russia Under Khrushchev*, Abraham Brumberg, (ed.) (New York: Frederick A. Praeger, 1962), p. 69.

Kulaks (tight fists) Well-to-do farmers, many of them products of the 1917–1918 Peasant Revolution expediently sanctioned by the Bolsheviks. During the period of the NEP, they were depended upon to provide the surplus for urban consumption. Force was often used to procure the kulaks' stores of produce. They were eliminated as a class shortly after a campaign was initiated against them by the Party, in 1929.

Kunayev, Dinmukhamed Aphmedovich (1912–   ) A graduate of the Institute of Nonferrous Metals, he has long been a leader of the Party in Kazakhstan. He first joined the Party in 1939 and became a candidate member of the Politburo in 1966.

Labor camps Corrective camps established in 1930 to isolate "socially dangerous" persons and to reform them through labor. The severity of these camps under Stalin has been highly publicized; presumably, they are now less severe and less populated. Much of the USSR was built by using such labor.

Labor Day See **Trudoden.**

Lenin, Vladimir Il'ich (1870–1924) The revolutionary name taken (from the Lena River) by V. I. Ul'yanov. Lenin successfully led the Bolshevik split from the Social Democrats and guided the Bolshevik *coup d'état*, in 1917. As the first head of the Soviet state, his abilities as a theoretician and an effective administrator have resulted in his being revered by the world Marists as the "George Washington" of the Soviet Union and the leadership model for all successful Communist state systems.

Leninism The Western term to describe Lenin's view of Marxism. Although Lenin and his followers argued that he was completely consistent with Marx's views, Western observers point to his views of organizing a party and a state and his ideas on imperialism as fundamental changes in Marxism.

Liberman proposals Suggestions made in 1962 by a Soviet economics professor which emphasize the profit motive, and hence produce a shift toward a market economy, reducing the importance of central planning and control of the Party, and allowing limited freedom for individual enterprises. Some of these proposals have been adopted by the Soviet economy.

Liquidationism Term applied by Lenin to the Menshevik move to abandon the underground Party and to concentrate on legal work in the trade unions and the Duma, thereby making the Party a broad and open one.

Little Octobrists A youth organization for children between the ages of seven and ten. The slogan, "Only those who love labor can be called Octobrist," reflects the goal of the Party leaders to instill in the children a respect for Communist ideology.

Lysenko, Trofim Denisovich (1898–   ) A Ukrainian agronomist and biologist who rejected the chromosome theory of heredity. He gained Stalin's favor since his stress on environmental influence fit Marxian theory. As a result, he dominated the biological sciences for many years, thereby making Soviet genetics the laughing stock of the scientific world. He was criticized in 1953 by Khrushchev and then temporarily reinstated to be finally discredited by Khrushchev's successors.

Machine Tractor stations See **MTS.**

Manifesto See **Communist Manifesto** and **October Manifesto**

Marx, Karl (1818–1883) A German-Jewish economic and social philosopher who migrated to England where, in collaboration with Friedrich Engels, he carried out research and wrote on "scientific socialism." He is considered to be the "Father of Communism." His most important works are *Capital* and *The Communist Manifesto.*

Marxism The name given to the doctrine evolved by Marx and Engels. Although Marx and his followers would argue that the doctrine is a "science of society" based upon economic determinism (especially "dialectical materialism"), many Western critics assert that this work was primarily sociological, resting on questionable assumptions—especially the belief that in the state of nature, man is communal in his relationships with other men.

Masherov, Petr Mironovich (1918–   ) Trained as a physicist and a mathematician, he was for a long time a teacher in secondary schools. His Party work has dealt much with komsomol ("Communist youth organization") affairs. He first joined the Party in 1943 and became a candidate member of the Politburo in 1966.

Masses, the The working people who, according to Marxism–Leninism, play a decisive role in the development of their society. The leaders are merely the people's agents who can function only with the support of the masses. The masses through their labor power are the key to production.

Materialism A term often used to refer to Marx's philosophy, usually expanded to "dialectical materialism" or "historical materialism." Marxism is materialistic in that it assumes that the basis of all nature, including thought and consciousness, is matter.

Mazurov, Kirill Trefimovich (1914–   ) Trained as a specialist in transportation, he has been active in Party work since 1940 and a member of the Politburo since 1965.

Means of production The resources (land, minerals, etc.) and the tools (factories, machines, etc.) necessary to produce goods.

Mensheviks Political party active from 1917 to 1922. This more liberal group opted for a large Democratic party and opposed Lenin and the Bolshevik stand for a tight, disciplined Party organization. It was suppressed in the USSR after 1921.

Mestnichestvo (localism) A negative term applied to various activities by regional economic councils who put the needs of their own area above the strict needs of the current production plan; i.e., diverting capital funds from high priority projects to local projects, creating self-contained regional empires, placing demands of their own plants above deliveries to "foreign" regions.

MGB Ministry of State Security. Security police apparatus replacing the NKGB in 1946, and inheriting the secret-police function of the NKVD.

Michurin, Ivan Vladimirovich (1855–1935) Plant breeder who developed fruit-tree varieties that grow well in central USSR. His belief in inheritance of acquired characteristics provided the groundwork for Lysenko's defiance of modern genetic theory. (See Lysenko)

Militarization of labor An idea propounded by Trotsky that labor should be organized and run like a strict military operation. Labor armies, formerly detachments of the Red Army, were employed in 1920 on heavy work of all kinds.

Mir The village commune idealized by pre-Marxian Russian revolutionaries as an embodiment of cooperative fellowship. The *mir* was considered a stabilizing order for the countryside. This system was overthrown by the Stolypin Agrarian Reforms of 1906 under the Third Duma. The term also means "peace" and "world."

Molotov, Vyacheslav Mikhailovich (1890–   ) One of the "Old Guard," long-time Foreign Minister, and faithful supporter of Stalin. A member of the 'anti-Party group in 1957, he was expelled from the Central Committee and the Presidium and demoted from his post of First Deputy Prime Minister. He is famous for his stubbornness as a diplomat.

MTS Machine Tractor Stations. A state agency, created in 1927 and abolished in 1958, designed to serve the needs of a group of neighboring collective farms, intended to make maximum use of equipment. More important, they served as agencies of procurement and spearheads of Party control in the countryside, fulfilling the Marxist–Leninist dictum that he who has control over the means of production is the master of political power. They exemplified the use of the inspectorate principle. Generally, one MTS was responsible for 12–20 collectives.

MVD Ministry of Internal Affairs. Internal police apparatus replacing the NKVD in 1946. In 1953, it absorbed the MGB and its security police.

Mzhavandze, Vasiley Pavlovich (1902–   ) A lieutenant general in the army and active in Georgian affairs, he was trained in the Lenin Military Political Academy at Leningrad. He first joined the Party in 1927 and has been a candidate member of the Politburo since 1956.

Narodnaya Volya (People's Will) A Populist revolutionary group committed to assassinating leading government figures. Lenin's older brother, who was hanged for an attempt on Alexander III's life, was a member.

Narodniks (Populists) Pre-Marxist agrarian Socialists who advocated salvation for Russia under a strong peasantry. Some of these people (especially Tkachev) wanted to seize power in a "preventive revolution" to insure an agrarian path of development rather than development under the bourgeoisie.

Nationalism Emotional identification with one's nation. Nationalism, rejected by the Bolsheviks as a fragmenting influence in their plea, "Workers of the World, Unite," was revitalized in the 1930s by Stalin to solidify opposition to the Nazi threat.

Nationalities problem The difficulty (which the Soviets say no longer exists) of absorbing the national republics and their various cultures and languages into the union.

Naturoplata Payment in kind (e.g., farm produce).

NEP The New Economic Policy. Begun by Lenin in 1922, the NEP tried to improve relations with the peasantry (abandoning forced requisitions in favor of a tax in kind), attempted to increase flow of consumer goods by concentrating on small industries and industrial cooperatives, and sought to attract foreign capital by offering concessions to capitalist entrepreneurs.

Nepmen Private traders who were active during the NEP.

New Soviet man The man to be produced by the Communist system, marked by a Marxist–Leninist social consciousness.

NKGB People's Commissariat of State Security. Security police unit split off from the NKVD, in 1943.

NKVD People's Commissariat of Internal Affairs. Police apparatus replacing the OGPU in 1934 and uniting all police activities under its jurisdiction. In 1943, it was split into two: the NKVD for internal policing and the NKGB for security matters.

Nomenklatura (Jurisdiction) Lists made by the Party, of people to be appointed to various key posts.

Nonparty active Although they are not Party members themselves, these are eager citizens marked by being at the forefront of championing Party programs and interests.

Obispolkom The regional (oblast) executive committee of a soviet (council).

Obkom (Regional Party Committee) A regional committee elected by a Party conference in the region every two years. In practice, the obkom's first secretary has important powers and independent authority for dealing with special regional problems. (This is especially true in areas remote from Moscow.)

Oblast A regional administrative unit that is subordinate to the republic Party committees. In general, the focal point for power in the countryside, often superseding the authority of the raykom (subdivision of the *oblast*), especially where the vital interests in Party control of kolkhozy ("collective farms") and sovkhozy ("state farms") are at stake, as in the selection of the kolkhoz chairman. After the Party decision of November 1952, there were separate oblasty for both agriculture and industry within a region. This organizational principle was rejected by Khrushchev's successors.

October Manifesto Tsar Nicholas' reply to the 1905 uprising, promising freedom of speech and assembly and voting rights as well as a representative legislature.

Octobrists The pre-Revolutionary party of liberals, slightly to the left of center, who took their name from the 1905 *October Manifesto* and demanded the establishment of a constitutional system. See also **Little Octobrists**.

OGPU (Organization of State Political Administration) The secret police organization in the early 1930s, becoming the NKVD in 1934. See **NKVD**.

Okhrana This was the Tsarist secret police.

On the conveyor This was a secret-police technique commonplace during the Stalinist years whereby the accused was deprived of sleep, interrogated constantly by rotating teams of examiners with the objective of exacting a confession of the accused's guilt.

ORGBURO Abbreviation for Organization Bureau. Worked with the Politburo as a junior partner. Abolished by Stalin in 1952.

Otrezki The land that was cut off from peasant allotments by the landlords at the time of the emancipation. Lenin issued a call for a return of the otrezki to the peasantry in a rather weak plank in the 1903 Party Congress. He was soon to learn that the peasants wanted more than just the otrezki—they wanted all the land.

Otryady A detachment. See **Zveno** ("link").

Partiinost Party consciousness and Party spirit; in practice, it means total dedication to the commands of the leadership of the Party.

Partorg A Party organizer employed mostly at the primary level of the Party. His goals are to stimulate the growth of Party organization and to strengthen the loyalty of Party members to the regime. In contrast to the *partorg* of larger organizations, he usually devotes all his time to Party work.

Party commission An apparatus of the Central Committee which enforces Party discipline and examines appeals from members of local Party units who have been expelled or otherwise penalized.

Payment in kind Payment to a collective-farm peasant in the form of a portion of the farm's produce.

Peaceful coexistence A policy toward capitalism which is characterized by all-out economic, social, ideological competition, even "just wars of national liberation or local wars" which preclude a direct nuclear confrontation between West and East. See **Coexistence.**

Pelshe, Arvid Yanovich (1899–   ) Chairman of the Committee for Party Control, he has made his career in the Party which he first joined in 1915, and he has been a member of the Politburo since 1966.

People's Courts Informal courts at the rayon (subdivision of the oblast) level consisting of a judge (serves a five-year term) and two assessors selected from a group of citizens elected for that purpose. These people are elected for two-year terms, but each serves no more than ten days per year.

Permanent Revolution, Doctrine of The concept that holds that the bourgeoisie are too weak, so the proletariat through its vanguard must take power and keep the revolution going until socialism is established in Russia and abroad, especially in the advanced industrial states of Western Europe which could aid Russia.

Personality cult See **Cult of personality.**

Planning A vital part of the Soviet economic system. Theoretically, the plan for each enterprise is made up by the workers and is then sent up for approval within the framework of the entire economy. Actually however, the plans are drawn up by the central planning organ of the state, and then sent down to the enterprises for worker discussion and approval.

Plekhonov, Georgiy Valentinovich (1856–1918) Sometimes called the "Father of Russian Marxism." He was a key person in the founding of the Social Democratic party that later split into the Menshevik and Bolshevik wings.

Podgorny, Nikolay Victorovich (1903–) A graduate of the Kievian Polytechnical Institute of Food Industry, he has combined a career of working with food problems with activity in the Party. He first joined the Party in 1930 and became a full member of the Politburo in 1960.

Politburo Abbreviation for Political Bureau. The chief policy-making body of the Central Committee. First created in 1917 and consisting of the seven top leaders, it remains the center of power in the USSR. Stalin changed the name of this ruling Executive Committee of the Central Committee to the Party Presidium in 1952. Subsequently, however, the old name, Politburo, has been readopted.

Politruk The political company leader to curb independent thought among the military until 1955 when the office as such was abolished.

Polyansky, Dmitrij Stepanovich (1917–) His has been a combined Party and government career. He is a graduate of the Kharkov Agricultural Institute. He first joined the Party in 1939 and has been a member of the Politburo since 1960.

Pood A measure of weight equal to 36,113 pounds.

Populists See Narodniks.

Pravda The Russian word for "truth" and the name of the Soviet Communist party's leading daily newspaper. *Izvestia* means "news" in Russian, and there is a Soviet joke that quips that there is no truth in *Izvestia* and no news in *Pravda*. See Izvestia.

Presidium of the Supreme Soviet Elected by the Supreme Soviet (council) and serving as the chief legislative body between sessions of the Supreme Soviet. The chairman of this body is the president of the USSR. For a few years the name of the Politburo was changed to that of Party Presidium.

Primary party organ (PPO) The cell, the basic unit of CPSU organization; it can exist anywhere where three or more Party members can meet.

Procurator The public prosecutor. Although he has much more power than his United States counterpart the procurator of the USSR is somewhat similar to the United States attorney general.

Procurement price In agriculture, the price paid by the government of the USSR to collectives for the legally required delivery of food and raw materials to the state. Prior to 1958, collective farms had to deliver a prescribed quota to the state at a very low price, often covering only a fraction of the cost of production. Higher purchase prices were paid for additional deliveries. This form of "tax" on collectives, this multiple-price system, was abolished on July 1, 1958, although in the late 1960s, a new double-price system appeared.

Proletariat   The exploited workers' class in capitalist society.

Propaganda   Selected information and admonishments directed at the masses to train them in Marxist theory and to direct them toward current goals. In the USSR, it is an integral part of the communications media and the educational system. See **Agitprop.**

Provisional government   Transitional government set up in February of 1917 upon the abdication of Nicholas II. First headed by Prince L'vov and later by Kerensky, it was overthrown by the Bolsheviks in late October of that year.

Public-norm setting   The government's statement of the amount of productivity each factory is to maintain.

Purge   (*Chistka*)   Cleansing the Party, or the administration, or various social strata of unreliable members, or those who are suspected of being unreliable. To Westerners this implies a wave of terror. See **Shatky prosecutions** and **Yezhovshchina.**

Quintal   The translation of the Russian word *centner*. A measure of weight. As used in the USSR, it is the equivalent of 100 kilograms (220.46 pounds).

Rab-Fak   The workers' faculty which provides elementary schooling for adult workers. Khrushchev was once enrolled in one in 1918 while he was working his way toward the Party's "inner circle."

Rabsel'kor   The use and encouragement of peasant and worker comment and criticism (usually in the form of letters) by the Soviet press. This process serves to link the masses with Party goals and to give the people a sense of participation.

Raiispolkom   The Executive Committee of a district soviet ("council"), also the District Executive Committee which controls the key personnel on a collective farm.

Rashidov, Sharif Rashidovich (1917–   )   Graduate of a pedagogical institute, he has served as a teacher and a newspaper editor. Active in Uzbek and foreign affairs, particularly in relations with Arab countries, he first joined the Party in 1939 and became a candidate member of the Politburo in 1961.

Raykom   The Party District Committee. In the November 1962 Party reorganization, all rural raykoms were abolished, and authority was invested in agricultural-production, administration Party committees; the jurisdiction of the new units was three times greater than the former.

Rayon The urban and rural subdivision of the oblast (regional administrative unit).

Rayvoenkomat The district military office that performs such functions as reviewing the recruits' political records.

Raznochintsy "The men of different class" who, during the latter half of the nineteenth century, infused new blood into the Russian intelligentsia. These men were not, as the earlier intelligentsia had been, of noble blood or of the landed gentry; they were of a plebian character, i.e., sons of doctors, clergymen, lawyers, journalists, and teachers.

Recoupment period The period of time necessary to recoup a given investment. If it takes 100,000 hours of labor-time to produce a certain machine and if by using this machine the factory can save 25,000 hours of labor-time per year without a diminution of output, the recoupment period would be four years. Recently, some Soviet economists have proposed the use of the concept of the recoupment period to decide among various investment alternatives, although, for practical reasons, monetary savings rather than savings in hours of labor-time are usually used to compute the recoupment period.

Red guard Armed factory workers (mostly) who as a unit participated in the 1917 Bolshevik *coup d'état*.

Reformism Improving society by change through the existing political structure, not by changing the structure itself.

Revision (or auditing) commission The commission on a collective farm that serves as a watchdog over financial activities. Personnel on this body differ from those in other key positions.

RSFSR Russian Soviet Federalist Socialist Republic. The largest republic of the USSR, comprising the major portion of European Russia.

RTS Repair and Technical Service Stations; succeeded the MTS in 1958, but they did not control the equipment as the MTS did. They were more a repair service, a parts distributor, a supply depot for new agricultural equipment. Abolished in 1961 in favor of the All-Union Farm Machinery Association.

Ruble The unit of Russian and Soviet money, currently the official rate of exchange equals $1.10 in US currency. The ruble may be subdivided into the smaller unit—kopeck—of which 100 equal 1 ruble.

Russification The imposition of the Russian language and culture on non-Russian peoples, a policy of tsardom now officially frowned upon but still practiced subtly in the USSR.

Samokritika (self-criticism) see **Kritika i samokritika.**

Scissors crisis The crisis which developed during the NEP in the 1920s because consumer goods were scarce and high priced and the peasants were hoarding their grain rather than selling it on the market. Industrial development demanded the sale of this grain at low prices in order to feed the cities, pay for imports, and produce goods for which the peasants would spend money. The dilemma produced a stalemate resolved only by Stalin's "emergency measures" of 1929 against the peasants and especially the *kulaks* (well-to-do farmers). The description was originated by Trotsky who observed that on a chart the reversal that had occurred in the "terms of trade" between the products of the town and those of the country was similar to the opening blades of a pair of scissors.

Seksot An informer who reports the activities of his comrades to the secret police.

Self-criticism See **Kritika i samokritika.**

Selkhoztekhnika An agency responsible for agricultural supplies.

Serf A peasant under obligation and therefore a virtual slave to his landlord. In fact, distinction was made between serf and slave after the reign of Catherine II. Serfs could be bought and sold, punished, or exiled, and their goods could be confiscated by the landlord. The latter's obligations were merely to feed his serfs during a famine and to furnish seed in event of a crop failure. Serfdom was abolished in 1861.

Seven-Year Plan, the First Grandiose plan adopted by the Twenty-First Congress in 1959. Its ambitious goals included catching up with and surpassing the US in food production. The results fell far short of the plan.

Shakhty prosecutions A trial held in the city of Shakhty in 1928 for a number of engineers accused of deliberately "wrecking" production. This was the beginning of a wave of terror directed against the technical intelligentsia. See **Purge.**

Shcherbitsky, Vladimir Vasilovich (1918–   ) Trained as a chemical technologist, he has been active in Party work in the Ukraine. He first joined the Party in 1941 and was made a candidate member of the Politburo in 1966.

Shelepin, Alexainder Nikolaevich (1918–   ) A graduate of the Moscow Institute of History, Philosophy, and Literature, he first joined the Party in 1940 and has been a member of the Politburo since 1966.

Shelest, Peter Yefimovich (1908–   ) Long active in Ukrainian Party work, he first joined the Party in 1928 and has been a member of the Politburo since 1966.

Siberia A rather vague term usually referring to the vast central and eastern area of the USSR west of the Ural Mountains.

Slavophiles Those who opposed Westernizing Russia, who revered the "Slavic" culture and historic tradition. See **Westernizers.**

SNK Soviet Narodnykh Komissarov (Sovnarkom) The Council of People's Commissars. Former official designation of what is now called the Council of Ministers.

Social science Social studies which prove the superiority of Communist society over others or which produces information that will be useful in molding society into the prescribed pattern. The Party campaign, started in the 1960s for the development of Soviet social sciences, could result in a turn toward greater objectivity.

Socialism According to Marxian theory, the transitional period between capitalism and communism during which the workers would be building their ideal society. Near the end of his reign, Khrushchev announced that the state was withering away, and the USSR was entering the first stage of true communism.

Socialism in one country This is the official Stalinist dogma (with strong nationalistic overtones). The USSR, in theory, would remain a beacon for the oppressed of the world, a self-sufficient citadel that could then be used to expand Communist power into the rest of the world. This nationalistic theory of communism was developed by Stalin after Lenin's death. Essentially, it stated that communism was possible in a predominantly agricultural and underdeveloped country.

Socialist competition Organized production contests among similar economic enterprises or among similar units within a given plant or farm. This is a method designed by the Party to increase production.

Socialist construction A concept resulting from the view that the revolution envisioned by Marx and Engels has now assumed a worldwide character. Every Communist state will have to be made fit for the machine age after its emergence on the world scene even though it will require sacrifice and some alienation.

Socialist discipline Discipline that encourages the integration of the individual in his level of society and aligns his purposes with the goals of the state.

Socialist legality Since the legal systems of bourgeois societies are adjudged incapable of dispensing justice, the Communist states have felt the need to distinguish between their "new" legal system and the one evolved in "capitalist" states.

Socialist realism A vague term meaning "realism" as seen by the Central Committee. This expression is applied to the various art forms, and artists are admonished to reject "formalism" (modern Western trends) and create art forms expressing "socialist realism" which assumes that nineteenth-century art methods are superior to any modern approach and which insists that everything Communist be portrayed as good. See **Formalism.**

Soviet   The Russian word for "council."

Soviet of Nationalities   See Supreme Soviet.

Soviet of the Union   See Supreme Soviet.

Sovkhoz   A state farm. The ideal of the Party leadership for agricultural production. These farms reflect the Soviet penchant for gigantomania and were originally envisioned as great grain factories, fully mechanized. Farm workers on Soviet state farms are paid a living income and are entitled to many of the benefits (such as paid vacations) that industrial workers enjoy.

Sovnarkhozy   National Economic Councils, excluding agriculture. These are the relatively decentralized administrative units, resulting from the 1957 economic reorganization, which were subsequently abolished.

Soznatelnost   Consciousness or state of mind.

Stakhanovites   Taken from a coal miner by the name of A. Stakhanov, this term was applied to outstanding workers of the industrialization era who, under ideal conditions, had produced well above fixed norms. They were awarded bonuses, honors, and special privileges and were held up as examples to the other workers who resented them very much.

Stalin, Joseph Vissarionovich (1879–1953)   Stalin ("steel" in Russian), the revolutionary name of J. V. Dzhugashvili, the successor to Lenin, who ruled Russia from 1928 until his death in 1953. Lenin had included Stalin in the inner circle after being impressed with his work on the nationality question. During most of his rule, Stalin was removed from the people in a way that many came to revere (or fear) him as a demigod.

Stalinism   The term used to describe "the Soviet atmosphere under Stalin"—emphasizing terror, total planning, forced collectivization of agriculture, and extreme hostility to the West.

State farm   See Sovkhoz.

Stilyagi   Individuals, primarily youths, who "fall prey to bourgeois propaganda" in protesting the drabness of Soviet life by imitating Western dress and music. Also a group of youthful malcontents in the USSR who share indifference and discrete skepticism about the Soviet system.

Stolypin reforms   The program begun under Prime Minister

Stolypin (1905–1911) in 1906 which encouraged individually owned farms and tried to eliminate the causes of peasant discontent.

Sukhovey Desiccating winds.

Supreme Soviet The national legislature of the USSR, made up of two equal houses, the Soviet of the Union and the Soviet of Nationalities. Members are elected for four-year terms. Representation to the Soviet of the Union is by population—one deputy per every 300,000 people; the Soviet of Nationalities is composed of delegates from each of the republics, provinces, and districts. The body normally meets twice a year for ten days, and thus serves largely as a rubber stamp for Party policy.

Surplus Value, Doctrine of The Marxian doctrine explains that the source of wealth and control in a capitalist society is the value created by the exploitation of workers.

Suslov, Mikhail Andreevich (1902–   ) A graduate and postgraduate in economics, he is regarded as a leading Party theorist. He has had a combined government and Party career including teaching for a time at Moscow University. He first joined the Party in 1921 and has been a member of the Politburo since 1947.

Technikum A secondary school for students from ages 15–19. Vocational skills are taught in these schools. They were built after the 1917 Revolution to wipe out illiteracy and to build an industrial working force.

Tolkachi (Expediters) Supply agents whose job it is to use any and all means to obtain the supplies needed in factories (see **Blat**). Plant managers hire these men to circumvent the problems of bottlenecks and restrictive controls in raw-material supplies. The state in recognition of the vital role which the tolkachi play in the functioning of the economy have not initiated any sustained campaign in order to remove or destroy them, although clearly they do not fit in Communist ideology.

Toz The least collectivized and most informal system of organizing agriculture between 1917–1930; a loose cooperative in which some pastures were held and marketing was done in common.

TPA Territorial Production Administrations. Local administrative subdivisions created on the "territorial production principle." Each of the 1,500 TPA were responsible for forty kolkhozy ("collective farms") and sovkhozy ("state farms"). Descriptions of the TPA imply that these agencies (and the farms under them) are dominated by the TPA Party secretary. These were one of Khrushchev's administrative reforms that later were abandoned.

Trotsky, Lev Davidovich (1879–1940)   The "revolutionary" name of L. D. Bronshteyn. This brilliant theoretician was second only to Lenin in power and prestige in the Party at the time of the revolution. However, in the struggle for Lenin's mantle, Trotsky lost out to the superior organizational talents of Stalin. He was exiled from the Soviet Union in 1929 and murdered (probably by Soviet agents) in Mexico City in 1940.

Trotskyism   A term of derision especially popular during Stalin's ruling years to describe those who deviated from his interpretation of Leninism.

Trotskyites   Communists who have broken off from Leninism and claim the ideas of Trotsky as their guiding viewpoint.

Trudoden   (Work-day units)   A measurement used to determine the value of each job on a collective farm (not on the *sovkhozy*, state farms). Every task has its approved norms of daily output, and the performance of that task entitles the worker to a given number of work-day units. Each member participates in the "profits" of the collective according to the proportion of his work-day units to the total work-day units of all members. Nationally there are nine basic categories of work in agriculture, but on some farms there may be as many as several thousand subcategories. Thus, the value of participants' jobs will vary from place to place and from year to year, depending on the circumstances of production.

This system represents a repudiation of earlier utopian approach when it was believed that with collectives, wages and produce could be distributed "according to need."

Udarnik   A shock worker in industry who broke records and was given honors and social benefits, such as food, housing, consumer goods —the giving of which represented a break with the egalitarianism theretofore espoused. Featured as new heroes of the Socialist society, they were sent by the thousands to participate in collectivization of agriculture, to help liquidate the kulaks ("well-to-do farmers") and to establish kolkhozy ("collective farms") and staff MTS.

Ukase   Decree by the Presidium of the Supreme Soviet of the Republic Supreme Soviets.

USSR   Union of the Soviet Socialist Republics.

Ustinov, Dmitry Fedorovich (1908–   )   A mechanical engineer who has been active in his field as well as in Party affairs. He first joined the Party in 1927 and became a candidate member of the Politburo in 1965.

Vanguard, Doctrine of the   A doctrine developed by Lenin which stated that the proletariat needed the guidanceship, or guardianship, of an elite group (Bolshevik or Communist party) to teach them the ways of socialism. Synonymous with the Party which is considered the sole depository of truth and leadership and the keeper of the political conscience.

Vil'yams system of rotation   A system of crop rotation proposed by Vasily R. Vil'yams which presumably could be applied universally regardless of the local soil and climate conditions.

Virgin Lands program   The program introduced by Khrushchev to open up and cultivate the so-called Virgin Lands of Kazakhstan, Siberia, and the northern Caucasus. These areas were seeded with spring wheat and were organized under the state farm system.

Voronov, Gennadiy Ivanovich (1910–   )   Active in agricultural affairs, his education included training both as a technocrat and in Marxist–Leninism. He first joined the Party in 1931 and has been a member of the Politburo since 1961.

Vozhd   The Russian word for "leader" (e.g., Stalin and Lenin).

War Communism   The name given the 1918–1921 social and economic policy which nationalized industry and instituted compulsory food deliveries to feed the Bolshevik army and the factory workers during the Civil War.

Westernizers   Socialists who, in the late 1800s, tried to Westernize Russia by introducing a parliamentary system and instituting civil rights. Their opponents were the conservative Slavophiles. See **Slavophiles**.

White Russians   All anti-Communist Russians.

Williams' system of rotation   See Vil'yams, and so forth.

Withering away of the State, Doctrine of the   The thesis that after communism has been realized and secured from foreign interference, the state, which existed only to protect the interests of the proletariat, will wither away, and a pure Communist society will remain in which the state's old repressive functions and protective functions will be replaced by decentralized administration of things.

Workday   See **Trudoden**.

Yezhov, Nikolay Ivanovich (1895–1939)   Beria's predecessor, during the great purge of the late 1930s, as head of the secret police, i.e., the NKVD as commissariat for internal affairs. He was probably executed in 1939.

Yezhovshchina   (Yezhov's plucking)   The Great Purge of 1936–1938, conducted under Yezhov, a period of universal terror during which millions of ordinary and extraordinary people were executed, imprisoned, or exiled. Their numbers included Party leaders and commissariats, industrial managers, intellectuals, and nearly all of the Old

Guard—Lenin's supporters—leaving Stalin the undisputed head of the Party.

Young pioneers   The junior affiliate of Komsomol which undertakes to harness the energy of youth for the Party. A youth organization composed of those from ten to sixteen years of age and meant to serve as an "example to all children." Members receive intensive indoctrination, and activities involve manual labor. Leaders are usually members of the Komsomol.

Zagotzerno   A grain-collection point.

Zampolity   Assistant commanders for political affairs who replaced the political commissars in the military; their sphere of action is limited largely to political propaganda and education.

Zemstvo   The local popular assembly, established in 1864 as an organ of local government.

Zis   The name of a Soviet car; also, contacts and associations which are useful to the tolkachi ("expediters").

Zubatovism   A plan designed by Zubatov and put into effect between 1900 and 1904 which attempted to organize labor through the use of secret police as organizers, and in this way to keep it under control and avoid trade unionism.

Zveno   (link)   A detachment (otryady). A small team of a dozen or so (sometimes 6–8) agricultural workers who concentrate on working a small plot from the sowing through the harvest. Originally used in connection with technical crops such as cotton and sugar beets, for which much hand labor was used. During World War II and early postwar years, this system was lauded as the most efficient method of organizing kolkhoz ("collective farm") labor. In 1950, the system was repudiated in favor of larger brigades of about 100, but in the 1960s they reappeared.

Index

Decision making, xvii, xx–xxi, xxiv,
  33, 66, 80–82, 84, 96–98, 102,
  104, 111–121, 130
Democracy, 12, 17, 39, 46, 52, 53, 57,
  66–67, 90–91, 96, 98, 106, 243
Democratic centralism, 65–69, 74, 96–
  98, 117, 243
Denisov, A. I., 155
De Tocqueville, Alexis, 156
Deutscher, Isaac, 71
De Witt, Nicholas, 173
Dialectical materialism, 37–40, 46,
  48–49, 59, 243, 250
Dictatorship, 27, 52, 106
  of the proletariat, 85
Discipline:
  Party, 52, 68, 125
  socialist, 151, 259
Dissent, 68–69, 79, 91, 96, 98, 154,
  175, 190, 192, 193, 212
Distributive quota, 152, 159, 160
Djilas, Milovan, 100
Donskoy, Dmitri, 12
Dostoevski, S. M., 157
Druzhina (*see* Voluntary people's
  militia)
Dudintsev, Vladimir, xix, 181
Duma, 15, 18, 21, 24, 26, 53, 244
Dvor, 19–21

E

EASTMAN, Max, 38, 45, 47
Education, 23, 42, 164–165, 170–178
  control of, 107
  under Marxism, 45
  of Party members, 102–104
  reform, xviii, 99, 112
Ehrenberg, Ilya, 188, 192
Elections, 158–160, 244
Emancipation, 13, 15–17, 244
Engels, Friedrich, 25, 33, 36, 44–45,
  61, 150, 244

Exploitation:
  Marxist views, 36, 38, 56, 58
  new class, 100

F

FACTIONALISM, 27, 244
Fainsod, Merle, 109
Family plot, 19
  (*See also* Private plots)
Federalism, 118
Feudalism, 25, 36, 39, 41, 65
Foreign policy, xxiii, 7, 67
Freedom, 85, 180, 202, 210, 244
  of assembly, 98
Freud, S., 172

G

GAPON, father, 18
General Secretary of the Party, 71, 74,
  126
Gigantomania, 75, 82, 84, 245
Gilison, Jerome, 159, 160
Glavlit, 189, 241
Godunov, Boris, 13
Gosplan, 131–132, 135, 245
Grant, Nigel, 171

H

HEGEL, G. W. F., 23, 37
Hertzen, Alexander, 17, 24
  (See also *Narodniki*)
Hubbard, Leonard E., 141
Hunger, 7, 49

I

ILLITERACY, xxii, 14, 22
Imperialism, 45, 55–64, 246
Individualism, 21, 34–35, 151, 156,
  177
Indoctrination, 175, 179–183, 194
Industrial growth, 8, 48
  all priority, 82